Humberto Esteve
11/22/66 Quito.

Policies and Methods
for Industrial Development

MURRAY D. BRYCE

Policies and Methods
for Industrial Development

New York
London
Sydney
Toronto

McGRAW-HILL BOOK COMPANY, INC.

Preface

Like its predecessor, *Industrial Development,* this is a practical book intended as a training and operating tool for people who work on industrial development in or for underdeveloped countries or regions.

Industrial Development was primarily a manual on the preparation and evaluation of industrial projects. It was based mainly on my experience in this field at the World Bank and in Burma, where I was a member of a team of economic advisers. *Policies and Methods for Industrial Development* is not a sequel, but a supplement. It deals with the important policy questions in designing and setting up a comprehensive industrial development program and with the operating methods which may make such a program successful.

This book, like my earlier one, is not a theoretical work. It is a down-to-earth exposition of what an industrial development program may contain, what policy alternatives there are on important questions, and what approaches appear to work best in practice. It is based mainly on my experience during the past five years with the Arthur D. Little consulting firm in industrial development advisory work in Cuba (1959), Peru (1960), Argentina (1961), Nigeria (1961–1963), Barbados (1963), India (1963), and Chile (1964).

In my consulting work I have observed that few developing countries put together an industrial development program which contains all or even most of the elements which have been tried and found successful elsewhere. Usually their industrial programs are incomplete and contradictory. Furthermore, they are often administered in a half-hearted manner, as if industrialization were not a matter of life and death. In this book I have tried to describe most of the "standard" approaches which have proved their value in accelerating industrial development. I have taken pleasure in attempting to "debunk" some of the popular measures, such as overprotection, which I believe to be harmful to sound industrial development and also some of the beliefs of "debunkers," such as those

v

who seek to discredit such proved industrial incentives as tax exemption.

As the manuscript goes to the publisher, I leave the industrial development consulting field to organize a new venture-capital company for investing in joint ventures in developing countries. This will be an opportunity to practice what I preach and to test its validity in the real world of industrial investment and management.

To illustrate various points, I have borrowed liberally from reports of Arthur D. Little, Inc., which were prepared for governments of developing countries. These reports can be quoted since they have been released to the public, although copies of some of them are not available for public distribution. My appreciation is due to Arthur D. Little, Inc., for granting me permission to quote from these reports and also for freeing me from other duties to write substantial portions of this book. My thanks are also due to my daughter Karen for typing most of the manuscript.

Murray D. Bryce

Contents

PART 1

Industrial Development Fundamentals

1

Industrializing in Today's World

This is a good time in history for a country to start industrializing. There are many advantages and opportunities today which were not available to nations even ten or twenty years ago. Offsetting some of the new favorable factors are a variety of negative elements. Both the advantages and the disadvantages need to be understood and evaluated by a country in planning its industrial development strategy. Trying to build industry in the international economic environment of the latter part of the twentieth century is a vastly different business from what it was when the countries which are now industrialized started on the long and difficult path of creating an industrial society.

In the days when colonialism was in style, it was generally accepted that the colonial areas of the world, and independent countries having a similar economic relationship to the industrial nations, would continue indefinitely as producers and exporters of raw material and as importers of manufactured goods. Sometimes factories were built to process agricultural or mineral raw materials, and occasionally industries were started to make consumer goods. But generally, it was considered unthinkable that a country outside the "advanced club" would or could develop industry to the point where most manufactured goods required could be made locally or where manufactured products could be exported successfully to world markets.

All this "colonial" thinking has suddenly given way to recognition in the industrialized nations that most of the underdeveloped countries are in the process of industrial development. While it is obvious that some of the larger developing countries like Brazil or India can go much further in industrial growth than smaller nations which lack the markets and resources for large-scale development, it is equally clear that even the smallest and least endowed country will industrialize to the extent that its capabilities permit. There is therefore a world-wide acceptance of the idea of industrial development as a legitimate objective for every country and a willingness on the part of the industrialized nations to assist such progress in many ways which will be of benefit to all concerned.

The willingness to help takes many forms which developing countries need to know about and take advantage of. In doing so, they should realize that the developed countries are helping, for the most part, not just out of the goodness of their hearts, but because it is in their own interest to do so. That giving assistance to a developing country also serves the needs of a developed country does not imply that the assistance is contrary to the best interests of the receiving country. As in most business deals in which both buyer and seller benefit from a transaction, usually both industrialized and industrializing countries benefit from the newly developed forms of international industrial development assistance which I shall describe.

Advantages in Industrializing at This Time in History

The availability of capital for sound projects in underdeveloped countries is one of the greatest advantages now offered to developing countries. Capital is obtainable today from several international agencies and from dozens of private banking sources, as well as from hundreds of manufacturing companies interested in operating in foreign countries. The common complaint of those with funds to lend or invest in developing countries is that there are not nearly enough sound and well-prepared projects. As capability grows in the developing countries to prepare projects which meet the high standards of international investors, there is every prospect that the flow of available capital will increase. It is therefore fair to say that today, for the first time in history, a country which seeks to develop can obtain, with reasonable promotion efforts, much of the capital it needs. A large part of it can be had on terms which are more attractive than those which ordinarily exist within a capital-scarce country.

Additional capital alone would have limited value to countries lacking people knowledgeable in technology and industrial management. Fortunately the availability of capital goes a long way toward solving the lack of experience problem, for in cases of private foreign investment the know-how comes along with the capital. In other financing circumstances, the technical and management assistance needed can be obtained through management contracts or consulting agreements with private firms or through bilateral arrangements or international agency programs. Those participating in providing the capital, in fact, generally require that needed assistance be obtained as a condition of financing a project. One of the greatest benefits of the new world development consciousness is the ready availability of every conceivable kind of technical and management assistance.

The development of human resources within an industrializing country to meet the needs of industrial growth has also entered a new phase. The growth of educational facilities in most countries is rapidly increasing both the number of people given basic education for business and industry and the amount of education received by significant numbers of people who now can progress into higher technical and management positions. Opportunities for advanced study abroad, both in universities and in industry, are also growing, offering bright graduates of local educational systems the means to gain the high professional qualifications needed by modern industry.

While the explosion of industrial technology in the postwar years has brought some trends which run counter to the industrial needs of the developing countries, there have been advances which are highly beneficial. As a result of technological advancement, much more is known about industrial processes and the uses of various materials. Many materials common to underdeveloped countries, for instance, bagasse, have achieved value as manufacturing inputs. While the minimum economic scale of some processes has increased, in others it has decreased through new developments. Once it was necessary to build a steel plant of several hundred thousand tons annual capacity using the blast furnace process. Now it is possible to use a direct reduction process for which 50 thousand tons capacity is economic. Plants are now being designed for various industries to conform with the needs of countries in which plants of the usual size would not be justified. The availability of "package plants" on a "turnkey basis" enables responsibility for the supply of all parts to be assigned to one company, which will construct, test, and guarantee the performance of the plant contracted for. When coupled to a management contract for the operation of the plant and the training of local staff, these arrangements enable a project to be established properly even though local knowledge of the industry may be entirely lacking.

Vast investments in the infrastructure in most developing countries during the past fifteen years have laid the foundation for industrial development. Reliable electric power is now widely available, sometimes at low cost. Internal transportation facilities have improved immeasurably in most countries in this period. Communication is no longer the obstacle it once was in many countries. The progress of services of transport and communication between countries has also shown spectacular advances. Air transport of people and goods is now possible within twenty-four hours between most places in the world, at rates which encourage movement. International telephone, telegraph and telex communications exist and are improving most places in the world.

Within most of the developing countries the climate for industrialization has also changed dramatically in terms of the attitude of government toward new industry. It is now normal for governments to establish industrial parks providing new industries with facilities they need at low cost, to offer tax exemption to new industries, to provide partial financing at attractive rates to industries, and to offer a variety of other forms of support for new industry. Growing interest in industry in many countries is bringing forth capital from private investors who until recently would not have considered industrial investment, and the improved prospects of industry are attracting more talented people to industrial management positions than hitherto. Attitudes of governments toward private industrial development and toward foreign investment in industry have become more favorable in many countries as the problems and limitations of state industries have become more apparent. There is an increasing recognition of the advantages as well as the inevitability of the mixed economy and of the complementary nature of the private development of industry to the public development of the infrastructure facilities of the economy.

The changing attitude to industry in the underdeveloped countries is matched by increasing interest in the newly developing nations by established industrial and financial companies throughout the world. They are realizing that the newly industrializing countries are establishing a workable industrial sector and that they cannot afford to ignore the advantages of becoming associated, in one way or another, with the new industrial communities. That companies with long experience in their fields of industry, with world-wide market connections, and with outstanding research operations are taking strong interest in participation in the developing countries is a potential resource of the first magnitude.

Industrial growth in any country must depend in the last analysis upon the existence of an actual or potential market for the goods to be produced. Market growth for most products at this point in history is favorable for the expansion of production. Market growth is taking place in most developing countries as modernization, education, urbanization, and rising living standards work together to create effective demands for products unsaleable in earlier years. This process is supported by the growth of advertising and publicity, which help create demand for new products, and by the increasing availability of consumer credit to finance some kinds of purchases. Who would have thought even twenty years ago that there could now be mass markets for television receivers and transistor radios among the comparatively poor people of many underprivileged nations? The growth of markets for potential products of developing countries is world-wide. The affluent countries provide an ever-better market for the "exotic" products of many underdeveloped countries—tropical woods and wood products, unusual textiles, handicrafts, and furniture. They also provide vast and growing markets for the lower-cost mass products, such as garments, which can be made more cheaply in the less developed countries because of lower labor costs. Within regions, such as Central America, and in Latin America, common markets are developing which dramatically enlarge the market opportunities for some products, making their production warranted where previously it would have been uneconomic. All these forces are creating industrial opportunities to make a wide range of products in many developing countries.

Increasing Difficulty in Creating Industry Which Is Economic

Countries industrializing at this moment in history, despite the many favorable factors, also face serious adverse trends which must be recognized if their negative influence is to be minimized. This happens to be a time in history when great advantages accrue to the nations that were early in the race to industrialize. They have the capital, the financial institutions, the technical experience, the business know-how and connections, the reservoir of research knowledge and facilities, the abundance of highly qualified technical and managerial talent, and the skilled workers at every level. While more of this accumulated heritage of industrial background may reach the underdeveloped world than ever before, the part that does is not and is never likely to be more than a small fraction of the industrial assets of the nations which industrialized first. In fact, it is not likely in any year to be more than a small fraction of the annual addition to the industrial assets of the advanced nations. It is only realistic to conclude that the industrial progress of the industrialized nations is bound to continue to outstrip that of the developing countries if measured by any terms more significant than that of the industrial growth percentage rate. This is not an argument against the exertion of maximum efforts on the part of the developing countries. It is a plea for recognition of the reality of a situation which exists, not because of anyone's scheming or ill will, but simply because in industrialization, as in most things in life, certain advantages accrue to those who are first.

Any one country seeking to develop industry must recognize that although more capital is available now than ever before for industry in the underdeveloped parts of the world, the competition for it is also much stronger than ever before. The capital that is available will not be distributed in accordance with any system of allocation by fair shares, not even by international financing institutions, let alone by private investors. The capital will be attracted mostly by those countries which create the best political and economic climate, which develop and present their projects well, and which promote aggressively to attract capital. In this competition for capital, some countries will get far more than their fair share, if measured by any test of needs or even opportunities; others will get far less. More and more the precious capital for industry will flow to the few countries which show by their deeds as well as their words that they really want it and that they will treat it well.

While it is true that more capital is available to the underdeveloped world than ever before and that much more of it can be attracted to industry than previously, the situation is not quite as favorable as might appear at first glance. The growing interest of private companies in investing in manufacturing activities outside their own countries should not conceal the fact that even today a very small minority of companies in America and Europe—probably considerably fewer than 5 per cent of the large and medium-sized companies—are ready to risk their own capital in ventures in the really underdeveloped countries. It must also be recognized that much of the financing available from international agencies will go for infrastructure projects and not for industry and that much of the so-called "international financing" which is offered represents little more than short-term credits for the sale of machinery.

Some of the most important technological trends of our times are working against the developing countries. The economies of scale in most industries are dictating larger and larger plants, making the industries unsuitable and uneconomic in any location that does not provide access to a large market. As plants have to be bigger and bigger in order to be competitive in world terms, they may have to be ruled out in countries where the market for the product is too small, unless the country has a favorable relationship to a larger market which will give duty-free or low-duty entry. As the minimum economic size increases in various industries, plants become more expensive and usually more complex. They become more and more capital-intensive and thus less suitable for countries short on capital and long on labor. The large-scale plants also tend to be monopolistic if placed in a developing country, as the market will rarely support two of a kind.

The march of science and technology is also increasing the technical complexity of many industries at a rapid rate. This makes the establishment and operation of industries more difficult in a nonindustrialized country. More highly trained technicians are needed as well as more laboratory facilities. Continual access to complex research facilities must be had if the industry is to keep up-to-date. The role of research in industry has developed in the industrialized countries at a fantastic rate since World War II. With research daily growing in importance in industry, and the cost of research increasing correspondingly, it is becoming more and more difficult for industries affected to operate in locations remote from their research base. When most industrial processes were still fairly simple, it was easier to establish plants in a nonindustrial environment. Now the transfer becomes more difficult, more costly, and more risky.

The process of world communication of ideas, goods, and people has made the world one market for many products. Coca-Cola, Singer Sewing Machines, and Volkswagen, for example, have become international household names. Desirable as this internationalization may be in spreading modernization, stimulating consumer demands, and creating worldwide quality standards, it is a barrier to starting new industries in the developing countries, unless the new factories produce products bearing the familiar brand names. Introducing a new brand name, even on a good-quality product, may be a nearly impossible task in a country where the public is firmly attached to the product of an established manufacturer. Even if a new brand can be sold, the public, whether in the mountains of South America or the jungles of Africa, will expect the quality which they know from the world-famous branded products. Gone is the day when consumers even in areas remote from world manufacturing centers will be happy with the inferior-quality goods which often are the output of new industries lacking the equipment and experience of their international competitors. To say that the wanted foreign product can be excluded in favor of the local infant industry product is merely to say that the consumers can be forced to accept something they do not want in order to support industrial development. They may be forced to accept the unwanted product, but they cannot be made to like it, a point which should be of importance in any democratic country.

Within most countries, developed or otherwise, existing market channels may be a serious barrier to the introduction of the products of new local industry. Not only do the consumers tend to seek the product they know and like, but also the distributors, with their established trade connections, prefer to maintain their existing profitable relationships rather than take on new and competitive products. Natural though this situation may be, it can prevent a new industry from breaking into a monopolistic market and competing successfully with established imported or locally made products.

Because of the combination of the great and growing strength of established companies, the entrenchment of their brand names and distribution channels, and the increasing complexity and cost of establishing a new industry, it is becoming more and more difficult for people who are new and inexperienced to break into an industry successfully. This is true in the industrialized countries, but in some lines it is even truer in the developing countries. This suggests that in many places entry into some industries should be attempted only through joining with the established firms in some arrangement which enables the newcomer to share in the strength of an established partner.

In projects designed to cater to the "unlimited" world markets the countries which are developing at this moment in history find themselves faced with severe competitive problems. While there are many sharp competitors in almost any line that can be thought of, the problem can be stated in its ultimate extreme by simply mentioning the one major competitor in a very wide range of products: Japan. There are few products that anyone can make which the Japanese cannot make as well, and cheaper. While nobody in the development business can have anything but the utmost admiration for the one non-Western nation which has so far industrialized, the fact remains that it is a competitor which can render unfeasible many otherwise sound export industry projects in the underdeveloped world. To enter world markets despite the competition is not impossible in today's world, but it is increasingly difficult.

The rapid growth of industrial capacity throughout the world since the war has led to excess capacity in many industries. Overcapacity makes it more difficult if not impossible for new plants in the developing countries to enter the world markets, and it also leads to dumping situations. Dumping of a product is something that is hard to define. Sometimes the term is used to refer to any export sales of a product for less than the total cost of production—that is, the unit cost of the product obtained by dividing the total cost by the total number of units. However, this is an unreasonably harsh definition, since a company may logically want to export excess production once its overheads are covered, provided the export sales cover the additional or "out-of-pocket" costs. From the viewpoint of a developing country, importing dumped products may save foreign exchange. On the other hand, it will discourage the setting up of local plants as the consumers will prefer to economize by buying the imported product. Here again, the country may go ahead and establish a local plant, but only by forcing the public to act against what it considers to be its best interests.

The trend toward lowering trade barriers in many parts of the world may do much to stimulate development within those areas, but it may also serve to close markets which would otherwise be open to new industries in developing countries. If the European Economic Community grows in membership, for example, more opportunities will be created for industries within the Common Market, but new barriers will be erected against some developing countries which now have preferential access to one or more of the countries in the Market. The same may be true in other parts of the world.

Within many of the underdeveloped countries themselves, trends are noticeable which are bound to have a negative influence on industrial development. There is a growing tendency in some nations for government to become steadily more involved in manufacturing industry and, consequently, for decisions to be made on political rather than on economic grounds. The resulting loss in efficiency is inevitable, as is the discouragement of initiative on the part of both local and foreign businessmen. These private investors might otherwise contribute more to the industrialization process than is added by the government's participation, which is usually less than wholehearted because of limitations of capital and personnel. An equally serious negative trend found sometimes is the tendency of politicians to sponsor unsound projects at the urging of unscrupulous salesmen whose only interest is to sell machinery, in most cases at inflated prices. Government involvement in manufacturing industry in an economy primarily dependent on private investment, whether in sound projects on an honest basis or ridiculous projects on a corrupt basis, is usually a negative influence on private industrial investment and thus is likely to reduce the total amount of industrial growth.

Some Basic Barriers to Industrial Development

Within each developing country there are a host of barriers which stand in the way of economic industrial growth. Some of these, which will be described shortly, are at least partially removable; but others are inherent in most countries seeking industry, and they must be lived with while progress is made slowly to change them.

Most of the underdeveloped nations of the world are small markets compared with the industrialized countries. The smallness is due more to low income levels and the fragmenting of natural economic units into many small political units rather than to small populations or land areas, although these are part of the problem in some tiny countries. Whatever the causes, the smaller the market, the fewer the industrial opportunities, for most industries require medium- or large-sized markets to be economic. While market size may grow if income levels rise, this cannot be counted on because the combination of negative factors may prevent the growth process from ever gaining momentum. The solution to the barrier of market smallness depends upon integration moves through which common markets are developed by adding together several markets which are each too small to be of economic size. This could be done by a process of political mergers, but it is more likely to come about through economic associations. The Central American Common Market, which has made an economic unit for industrial purposes of five national markets which were so small as to severely limit industrialization possibilities, is an example of the type of amalgamation which could widen the industrial prospects of many other areas if development could replace narrow nationalism as the favorite political motive.

A natural barrier to industrial development in most underdeveloped countries is the uncertainty which surrounds the economy. Nobody can predict with much assurance of being right the economic prospects of a country even for a period of ten years, which is about the minimum time span a potential investor needs to feel confident about. This is the greatest obstacle to a major flow of capital and industrial know-how into many countries, for most of the potential investors are accustomed to operating in countries where it is possible to predict the economic future with much greater certainty. The economic prospects of some countries with varied exports whose future is promising may be better than most investors realize, but most developing countries are not in a good position. They may have only one or two major exports, which may be subject to catastrophic fluctuations and may face long-term downward trends due to stable or declining demand coupled with increasing world supply. The creation of a long-range economic picture which is good enough to give investors some confidence that the risks of industrial investment are not excessive will be difficult for most countries, but without some progress in this direction, the prospects of industrialization may not exist.

How can a country improve its long-range economic stability prospects? One of the best ways is to seek expansion and diversification of its exports of raw and semiprocessed materials. This may be easier than one would think, for many countries have major resources which could be developed into important exports but whose exploitation has been bypassed in favor of more glamorous kinds of development. The teak lumber industry in Burma and the tropical fruit possibility in Nigeria are examples. Tourism could be made into a far more important foreign-exchange earner for many countries. South America, with the exception of Colombia, has made little effort to develop tourism, while South America's share of world tourism expenditures has declined in recent decades. Strengthening the economy by sawing logs, or growing pineapples, or attracting tourists may seem far removed from the industrialization of building steel mills, but it may be the most practical way to get a country into shape to be able to expand industry on a sound basis.

Lack of capital is said to be a major barrier to industrial development in most countries, but this oversimplification is far from the truth. As mentioned, capital availability exceeds project readiness in regard to the underdeveloped world. This is also a valid assertion in regard to local capital in most countries. If a country has real opportunities for industry, based on its markets and comparative costs, and if it creates a reasonably attractive climate for industry, it can obtain capital for good projects. Obtaining the capital is not always easy; it may require a long process of interrelated actions by the government. But it can be obtained in most situations.

The lack of human resources that are developed to the state of readiness for industry is a much greater barrier to the industrialization of most countries. The most vital force, entrepreneurship—the combination of initiative, drive, ambition, and organizing talent—is the weakest link in the chain in most underdeveloped countries and perhaps the hardest to do anything about quickly. Without this spark, industry would not have developed in Europe and America, and without it, industry will not flower in Africa or Asia. Can it be developed where it does not exist? This may be the key question on which industrial development depends. While there is not a simple answer to the question, it is apparent that ambition, ingenuity, intelligence, materialism, acquisitiveness, and even greed—some of the elements of entrepreneurship—exist quite widely among human beings in most parts of the world. In most societies, entrepreneurs have arisen and provided a push to progress. From the example of countries which have grown a healthy breed of entrepreneurs, we can learn some of the conditions which are conducive to encouraging entrepreneurship. One essential element is that at the time when a country is breeding its entrepreneurs there needs to be a risk-taking atmosphere. People need to grow up wanting, not secure and permanent positions as lowly paid government clerks, but freedom to take major risks in the hope of becoming rich and famous. There must be enough emphasis on adventuring as contrasted to security to draw some of the brightest boys into starting new and hazardous businesses. There must be an attitude in society which gives as much prestige and glamor to a man who is successful in business, industry, and engineering as to one who makes his name in law or politics or the military.

In most countries where the social attitudes are not right to foster the needed entrepreneurs, what specifically can be done to start changing the situation? One practical step is to see that the tax system has room to give a strong financial incentive. This means that it must allow a successful entrepreneur to keep a substantial part of whatever he may make from a risky industrial enterprise in which he has invested. A low rate of taxation of capital gains compared with other forms of income may be what is needed. The ready availability of loans on attractive terms or partial share capital financing, through development banks or other institutions, may do much to encourage a man with an idea to take the step of starting an industry. Support of promising though risky projects through such devices as tariff protection, assurance of government purchase orders, and provision of free or subsidized plant sites are other means by which a potential entrepreneur can be turned into an operating industrialist.

A partial and temporary substitute for local entrepreneurs lies in the attraction and use of foreign entrepreneurs—a subject I shall return to many times in this book. Enterprising foreign investors do exist, even though they are not lined up at the border, as leaders of some under-developed countries imagine. It is not a matter of "letting the pirates in"; it is a question of whether the country is ready politically and mentally to create conditions which will make it possible to use the foreigners without being abused by them. If a country can attract the right kind of outside enterprisers, it will have a means to break its present stale-mate—no industries started because of no entrepreneurs and no entre-preneurs because of discouraging environment. It can create a new situa-tion in which conditions are more appropriate to develop local leaders for business and industry.

Equally serious as obstacles to industrialization are a whole series of barriers which have their roots in the colonial history and the social sys-tems of the underdeveloped world. They are explainable only on the basis of the inexperience of new leaders with the real world of today. The obstacles are like "psychological blocks" which prevent an under-standing of how a country has to create conditions favorable for its eco-nomic, and especially its industrial, growth. Like other psychological barriers, their removal cannot be quick or easy. It requires first that old learning be erased and then that new bases be developed for thinking about the world and about economic facts.

Certain common misconceptions illustrate the blockages we are con-sidering. There is the widespread belief that the world is conspiring to prevent the industrial development of the nonindustrialized nations. This is the idea that the metropolitan areas of the world, despite their pro-fessions of giving technical assistance, really want to keep the under-developed regions as markets for manufactured goods and thus want to prevent them from developing their own industries. This is the belief that a "neocolonialism" has arisen to perpetuate the old relationships be-tween the raw material producers and the manufactured goods pro-ducers. The idea of conspiracy to thwart the reasonable ambitions of those who have been exploited by the old colonialism is an attractive one to any nationalistic leader who seeks a means of holding popular support despite a failure to produce satisfactory results. One cannot say that there is not an element of truth in this as in most misconceptions. There is still one colonial power trying to maintain a colonial system. There are elements of colonialism in attempts to preserve the old chan-nels in the relations between some of the European powers and their former colonies. Sometimes however the channels thus preserved repre-sent an economic lifeline in the form of markets for underdeveloped areas which may keep their economies operating while a more independent economy is developed. In other cases the links that are maintained be-tween a European country and its ex-colonies are private ones—two-way trade channels such as those maintained by some of the large trading companies in what was formerly British West Africa.

For an independent nation, these links of trade and investment between their economies and those of the former imperial powers need represent nothing more than economic relations for mutual benefit. Any time the newly independent nation concludes that the arrangements are not to its benefit, it may terminate them. What is dangerous is not the continuation of channels of business which may resemble those of colonial days; rather, it is the feeling that to have any dealings of trade or investment with the former colonial powers is to accept a relationship which is bound to be detrimental to the developing country. What many new countries have not yet learned is that they now have within their power the capacity to refuse to enter any situation which is not to their advantage and to bring to an end quickly any relationship which proves to be harmful. With this power in local hands, the alternative to cutting off trade and investment through a process of isolationism is to be selective enough to accept relationships which are economically beneficial and to reject those which are not.

An almost universal misconception in the underdeveloped world is that industrialization is a quick, easy, and certain route to wealth. There is a belief in industrial development as a form of magic which is frightening. It stands as a barrier to policies and methods which are essential in obtaining the maximum amount of the kind of industrial growth which can benefit a developing country. It cannot be said too often that industrial development is a slow, difficult, and risky process and that unless it is done right, the losses may easily outweigh the gains. The idea that starting an industry is a quick way to get rich is the common view of the have-nots in the industrialized nations, just as the idea that colonialism was the easy way to get rich was the general view of the colonialized countries. But the belief persists. Those assisting countries to develop must emphasize day in and day out that industrialization has its economic limits, which may be quite narrow for countries with small markets and scarce resources, and that the range in possible value of industrial projects is extremely wide between those which can add much to the national income and those which will require perpetual subsidization on a large scale. Gains from investment in industry may be smaller and less sure than returns from investment in agricultural modernization.

Another problem related to the belief that industry means sudden wealth lies in the tendency of people in underdeveloped countries to try to extract gains from industry prematurely. In the highly industrialized countries the practice of taking too much out of a company is called "milking" it. The practice is much more common in newly industrializing countries where capitalists and workers alike frequently weaken or destroy new industries by extracting excessive dividends or uneconomic wages which the business cannot support if it is to grow to healthy maturity. New industries, especially in the doubtful soil of nonindustrialized societies, need to grow and build their strength slowly like young trees establishing their root systems. They must have fairly high earnings, which means their costs including wages must be held down. Most of the earnings should be retained in the firm to serve as insurance against periods of adversity and to provide the means to grow so the enterprise may make its maximum contribution to the economy. When either worker or capitalist, through greed or impatience, will not wait for the enterprise to mature before taking his reward, he is jeopardizing the project's chances of ever benefiting either individuals or the country as it should. The tendency to take from industry quickly instead of to allow industry to withhold part of its earnings for growth is evident also in the eagerness with which many governments reduce the earnings of new industry by premature and excessive taxation, by exorbitant power rates, and unreasonable land charges. Governments need to realize that preinvestment incentives for new industry are not enough. Governments must also help new industry gather strength through its early years, even if this means foregoing revenue temporarily so that the industry will survive and grow to make its maximum contribution to the national economy.

Prevailing motivation for industrial development is often at the root of unsound industrial policies and decisions. All too often, industry is wanted primarily for nationalistic reasons—to show that a country is "modern" and that it need not depend on others for the goods it needs. This thinking leads to unsound prestige projects, for instance, steel mills, which bleed a country of the strength of money and personnel it needs to finance and manage sound developments. Nationalistic justification for industrial ventures coupled with the "easy riches through industry" belief provides many politicians with a ready audience for wild schemes which soon turn out to be quick ways to waste vast sums of scarce capital in ill-considered industrial projects.

National pride, frequently with its roots in memories of colonial exploitation, tends to erect emotional and legal barriers to the entry of foreign capital and industrial personnel, even when it may be obvious on purely economic grounds that the foreigner has a necessary role to play. That this obstacle is understandable does not make it any less harmful to a country's industrial development.

An unwillingness to pay the price for industrial know-how is another characteristic of many developing countries. It flows naturally from the view that industrialization is a simple and easy road to riches and that it is made to appear difficult only by those who have ulterior motives. What is not recognized is that much of the industrial heritage of the developed world—its technology, its "secret processes," its training and management methods, its production techniques—is as much for sale as the equipment that is a part of the total industrial system. These are market commodities which are subject to the usual laws of supply and demand, and underdeveloped countries can have access to the world of industrial know-how simply by paying the price. That developing countries often will not purchase the help they need, even when they cannot afford to be without it, indicates mainly a lack of appreciation of the necessity and value of industrial know-how.

Even deeper in the roots of the culture and society of many underdeveloped countries lie customs and attitudes which impede industrial development and which are susceptible to change only slowly and, in some places, perhaps not at all. There is the widespread unpreparedness of many nonindustrial people to work as hard or as steadily as industrial workers in the developed countries. Often this is due to the simple fact that, having never seen the pace of a modern factory, workers new to industry have no way of knowing what is expected of them. Naturally they do not feel obliged to work at factory speed. The truth of this is shown by the fact that individual workers from underdeveloped countries who go to Europe or America usually have no difficulty in working at the speed of the factory in which they are employed. In some countries piece-work systems bring about remarkable improvements in the speed of industrial operations; in others they do not. The reason is sometimes that social customs in a country, such as the practice of additional relatives moving in with the employed worker's family, effectively cancel out any incentive offered by ensuring that the worker will not gain by greater exertion. Willingness to work as employees in modern industry must work if the industry is to compete in a competitive world varies, of course, from one part of the world to another. To some extent attitudes toward work and receptivity to incentives vary with peoples of different social and religious backgrounds. We know that in some places modernization may come quickly, in others slowly, and perhaps in some, not at all. The changeability of these underlying attitudes and customs may, more than anything else, determine which countries or parts of the world can industrialize.

Within a country which has industrial opportunities and where the social attitudes and customs do not constitute too serious a barrier, manmade obstacles may exist which prevent development from proceeding on as sound a basis as possible. In countries which have had a moderate amount of industrial development in the past, and in which industry is already a sector of some importance, there is a great danger that the progress of the past may become a barrier to potentially much greater progress in the future. This is because of the likelihood that the old industrialists, who have been spoiled by indiscriminate and excessive protection, will attempt to obstruct policies which could lead to the expansion of the industrial sector through taking advantage of new opportunities, such as the manufacture of goods for export. The old guard has often grown rich and isolationist through the successful development of local market industries which, despite cheap labor, have been so inefficient that they could not compete against imports in their own country, much less against efficient manufacturers in distant free markets. When the entrenched industrial oligarchy consists mostly of family businesses, the problem is further aggravated since the drive for expansion has usually been dulled by the lack of the families' need for further wealth and by the conservativism which comes with age and the absence of inflow of modern ideas. Faced with a small industrial class determined to prevent competition either from foreign manufacturers or from new local industries, a country is in much the same position as it is in regard to land reform. Progress will demand changes in laws, attitudes, and methods which are not acceptable to those who have held control. Development will depend on creating a new environment for industry, just as land reform does for agriculture. While ways can be found to make a transition period to a new system more acceptable to those who prefer the established way of life, the change to a more competitive and dynamic economy must take place if a country is to start making real progress toward its new goals of economic and industrial development.

2

Industrial Development Strategy

When a country decides to adopt industrial development as a major national objective, it has made a historic choice. Presumably the choice has not been lightly made. The costs, as well as the benefits, of building industry should have been understood: the period of industrial development will mean using scarce foreign exchange for industrial equipment instead of for consumer goods; it will mean restricting the public's freedom of choice in their purchases as the market is increasingly reserved for domestic industry; and it will mean heavier taxes in order to pay for subsidies for the new industries. The early years of industrial growth are necessarily years of investment by the people in anticipation of the production of a larger national income in future years.

The choice of industrialization as a national goal may have been made because the country had no alternative to support a growing population. In these circumstances industrial development means not the butter on the bread, but the bread itself; not a means to get luxuries, but a way to survive. In this situation, which is today's reality for many countries, industrial development can be likened to the mobilization of a country which takes place when it must prepare for war to defend its very existence. Like mobilization for war, the drive for industrial development must have broad support from all sections of the population; it must have highest priority in the decisions and actions of the government; and, to have any prospect of victory, it must be based on a sound and thoroughly prepared strategy. The strategy for industrial development must be based on an understanding of some of the fundamental principles of the industrialization process. Without an identification of these principles and a widespread appreciation of what they mean, it would be impossible to get acceptance of the policies needed or popular support for their implementation.

Industrialization Is a Transfer Process

The most important of these principles is that industrialization is a transfer process. Modern industry is a new thing in terms of the time span of world history, dating back only 200 years if we take the invention of the steam engine and the start of the industrial revolution in England as an arbitrary starting point. Within this period great investments have been made in inventing, designing, and building generation after generation of more complicated and more efficient machinery. New processes and products have been devised only to be replaced over and over by better ones. Increasingly successful techniques of industrial management, training, accounting, and distribution have been developed. The evolution of industry from its primitive beginnings to its present state of complexity has required not only the investment of physical resources beyond calculation but also the development of generation after generation of technicians, scientists, managers, and workers, each more educated and skilled than the one before. The process has been a long one, and in recent years the pace has speeded up dramatically as new wonders of electronics, computers, and automation have introduced infinitely greater complexity into industry.

It is on this heritage of the world's long march to industrialization that the underdeveloped countries can now build their industrial development. The essential principle is that the process of industrialization is a transfer process. It is a transfer of industrial knowledge, experience, and equipment from those places in the world where these elements exist to those places where they do not exist. Obvious though this principle may seem to be with a minimum of reflection, the surprising fact is that the policies of many countries seeking development are based on the exclusion of this idea from official thinking. There is an apparent desire to attempt development while limiting or minimizing the transfer of industrial know-how from the outside world. Nor is this blindness to the essential nature of the industrializing process confined to nationalistic politicians. In some countries, technical assistance advisers have been known to place program emphasis on attempts to build industry through internal methods, such as the development of primitive small industry, rather than on approaches which would inject the needed massive input of foreign industrial know-how.

The alternative to industrializing by getting the greatest possible transfer from the industrial world is to attempt to build industry by internal self-help methods with a minimum of importation. It can be done, if time is not a matter of urgency. After all, when Europe industrialized, the process had to be an internal one, at least within the region. Being first, Europe had no place from which to import industrial know-how. America industrialized with a moderate importation of know-how from Europe, but much of the process was internal. The Soviet Union industrialized with surprisingly little importation of industrial know-how from more industrialized countries, although some transfer did take place and the industrial economy was built upon the foundation of industry which had grown over previous years. Now China is in the process of industrial growth in virtual isolation from the rest of the world.

These examples show that industrial development does not have to be primarily a transfer process. But let us look more closely at these examples. Europe and America industrialized by the self-help route because there was no alternative, and the process took over a hundred years. The Soviet Union industrialized mostly on its own over a shorter period, but it still took several decades. Furthermore, the forcible diversion of human and material resources to high-priority industrial objectives was to a degree which would not be tolerated in a democratic country. China is now following the same road. The characteristic shared by nineteenth-century industrialization in Europe and America and twentieth-century industrialization under communism is that industry was built by imposing sacrifices on the workers which would be totally unacceptable in most developing countries today, when governments must win popular support to stay in office, and trade unions are ever-militant to protect their members. Nor would the time sequence of "do-it-all-by-yourself" industrialization meet the needs of the developing countries. The people of these countries are not prepared to wait twenty or fifty years to enjoy the fruits of an industrial society. Long before an internal type of industrial development program could produce noticeable benefits, the governments responsible for the slow-motion process would have been swept from office, probably by those who would promise rapid development without foreign help, but who would produce either economic chaos or regimented development without freedom.

What does industrial development by importation involve? It involves importing foreign industrial equipment and foreign industrial personnel on a large scale over a fairly long period of time—probably for twenty years or more. Since the goal is rapid industrial growth, the importation needs to be on as massive a basis as possible; but there are practical limitations. There is no point importing equipment and personnel for industries which will fail for lack of a market for their products or at a rate which cannot be absorbed in terms of training workers or developing distribution for their output. Even with the best of policies and an ideal program of development assistance, new industries can only be built and brought to successful operation at a moderate rate, especially in the early stages of industrial growth. For many countries the limitation on how fast industry can be built by importation may also be determined by a limitation on how rapidly the capital can be attracted, for under this transfer process, the funds must be largely foreign at the beginning.

Industrialization by importation of industry implies that the process will be of mutual benefit to those in industrialized countries who export the capital, the equipment, and the technical know-how and personnel, and those in the developing countries who import these essentials. If conditions are not created which make the transfer mutually attractive, it will not take place. This means that the arrangements must be profitable, highly profitable in fact, for those who export the elements which are wanted. That the arrangements must be financially attractive to the foreign participants does not suggest that they need be unattractive to the countries which pay the price. For them, sound arrangements to import industrial know-how and capital for feasible projects represent the quickest and cheapest way to move into an industrial society.

Transferring industry includes various essential elements. Most of the equipment for new industry in an underdeveloped country must come from abroad as it cannot be made in the developing country. Most of the spare parts to keep it operating will also have to come from foreign sources for many years. The designing of the plant and its processes must be done abroad or by specialists who come from abroad and who have access to the technology and research upon which the engineering of complicated modern plants depends. The new industry must have access to skilled foreign experts and technicians who can service the new factories and keep them in operation, at least for the first years until local technicians can be trained. To keep abreast of developments in the industry in order to remain competitive, the new industry must have continuing access to foreign research facilities, or it will soon become outdated. To test and start the complex factory, to train the workers, and to secure production and quality products, the new industry will need foreign production and training personnel for some years, though their number can be gradually reduced. After three to five years most plants established by the transfer process will be able to operate with a much smaller staff of foreign technicians and management personnel than they needed at the start. In most countries, however, the new industry will still need to preserve its ties with foreign collaborators to obtain at least some of the spare parts needed and to have access to research services and technical assistance in adapting to improved machinery, processes, and products.

Perhaps the most important element in the transfer process is the transfer of industrial know-how through the training provided by the temporary industrial specialists from abroad. They may be of many kinds, ranging all the way from instructors and supervisors in machine operation and maintenance to accountants, quality-control specialists, and sales-force organizers. While they will initially do an actual operating job, their real function must be as teachers. Some countries mistakenly regard foreign industrial technicians as being a new kind of immigrant, coming for permanent or at least long-term residence in the country and thus holding tenaciously to well-paid positions which could be occupied by local nationals. Ordinarily the foreign technician has no intention of staying a long time; in fact, the process is best served if he comes as a temporary transferee from a plant of his industry in an industrialized country. He will then be more up-to-date on the latest technology and operating methods than if he had lived and worked for a long time overseas. A supplement to training by imported foreign technicians is the sending of nationals to foreign countries for practical on-the-job training in similar industrial plants. This is an expensive method involving the risk of the trainee's not returning or of his being satisfied upon his return only if made general manager of the entire operation.

Developing industry in association with foreign companies may include an additional important advantage—the ready-made acceptance of the product in the markets of the developing country where the new plant is located. More and more consumers even in the most remote parts of the world expect the products they buy to meet the same standards of quality, appearance, and packaging as the world-famous products of internationally known manufacturers which they have been buying for years. To get the consumers to switch to an unknown brand, even of the same quality, may be difficult and costly in the absence of compulsion. A simple way around the problem is for the local industry to be established in some form of collaboration with the international firm whose product has already gained market acceptance. The new local industry will then make the same product the customers want, even to the last detail of trademark and packaging. Thus the whole difficult problem of winning acceptance may be avoided.

What Prevents the Transfer of Industrialization?

If the spread of industrialization by a process of transferring it from the industrialized countries to those seeking industry is such an obvious solution to a difficult problem, what stands in the way of a more general and open recognition of this process as the way to develop industry? In some cases the reason for the lack of transfer is simply that the country which wants to industrialize lacks the opportunities for industry. If a country has extremely small markets, is not a part of a common market system, and does not have some special advantage which would make it a good location for export industry, such as preferential access to a major market, then in truth it may not have industrial possibilities;

and foreign investors who pass it by have good reason for doing so. Not every country has much scope for industrial development, despite an obvious need for economic betterment and the promises of politicians to bring to the people the advantages of industrialization.

Most countries, however, are not completely lacking in industrial development possibilities, and many have very substantial opportunities for industrial development which are not taken up by the process of transferring capital and know-how. A common reason is that the industrial climate is not good enough to make the country acceptable to the foreigners who have the capital, experience, and personnel needed to start new industries. The country may suffer from a succession of weak and unstable governments given to erratic and irresponsible behavior toward private businesses, especially those that are foreign-owned. There may be a low standard of honesty among government officials which discourages the entry of foreign firms unwilling to be a party to bribery in order to do business. There may be prospects of nationalization of foreign businesses and discriminatory legislation or administration of laws in regard to taxes, tariffs, and entry of foreign technicians. There may be such poor administration of the nation's economy that inflation and chronic foreign-exchange shortages make it hazardous to operate a business. Even more serious, there may be a generally negative attitude on the part of the government and the people toward foreign firms and foreign participation in the economy. This will make a prospective foreign investor hesitate about committing resources or personnel to ventures which must depend for their success on long-term cooperation in the host country. The industrial transfer process will work only if the foreigner and his capital and participation are genuinely wanted and respected and only if a spirit of mutual cooperation and benefit prevails.

There are countries which have plenty of opportunities for industry and which have a basically attractive investment climate in which foreign interests can work harmoniously and safely. They may fail to develop a large-scale transfer of industry into the country through lack of positive incentives and measures of support and assistance. They may feel that since they have a good investment climate and an open economy with worthwhile possibilities ready to develop, nothing more is needed. They may even explain the situation by references to the laissez-faire climate which was commonly thought to exist in Europe and America in their early periods of great industrial development. Whatever the degree of nonintervention practiced in the economy elsewhere a hundred years ago, the comparison has little relevance to the real world of today in which the developing countries have to operate. They must face the fact that there is now intense international competition for capital and that other countries are selling hard and offering lavish incentives and other attractions to get the industrial capital they need. In this competition a country which does less to attract the capital it wants is not likely to develop rapidly. Moreover, the competition is not confined to other underdeveloped countries. Within the highly industrialized countries, states and regions are offering tempting incentives and subsidies to attract industry, and the prospective investor has plenty of alternatives where his capital and know-how will be more than welcome. In later chapters I shall describe in detail how a country can develop incentives and supporting services which have proved their value in attracting foreign-backed industry.

A final reason why the transfer process often fails to work as it should lies in the information gap between the potential opportunity in the underdeveloped country on the one hand and the availability of foreign industrial capital and know-how on the other. With more than a hundred countries in the world it should not be surprising that an industrialist who is starting to think of the possibility of foreign operations may not think of any one country, much less take the time and go to the expense of analyzing each one as a possible place for business. Even if he makes some enquiries about a particular country, he may not hear of a specific project possibility which might be the very opportunity he is seeking. To close the information gap requires an active development program with action at many points along the line: identifying specific industrial opportunities, making feasibility studies of various kinds, locating industrialists in various countries who have reason to be interested in a certain project, and presenting economic and technical information to prospective investors. These will be fully discussed in other chapters of this book.

Advantages Which Can Guide Industrial Development Strategy

When asked what a country should do to get development under way, Teodoro Moscoso, the former head of the Puerto Rican Development Administration, once said, "Find out what special advantages the country has, then make the most of them." This is the starting point of planning strategy for industrial development. There is hardly a country in the world which does not have some natural or artificially created advantage in producing something for some market. The secret of avoiding wasted time and resources is to identify the advantages quickly and build a program around them. Later much can be done to improve on the advantages—even to add new ones—and to minimize the disadvantages. The important thing is not to become so fascinated with the negative factors that it is impossible to appreciate the worth of the positive elements which exist in every country and which constitute the strategic foundation for successful development. The main industrial development advantages which a developing country may have can be classified as follows:

1. *Low-cost labor.* As labor costs make up a large part of the cost of producing some products in the industrialized countries, the large difference in wage rates between the developed and underdeveloped countries creates the possibility of sufficient savings in labor costs to bring total manufacturing costs to a competitive level. It must follow, of course, that the labor is sufficiently productive so that the apparent advantage of low wage rates will be reflected in true low labor costs per unit of output. The availability of labor which is reasonably productive or which can be trained to high productivity is often the greatest advantage a country has. When asked in Haiti what the country's greatest asset might be for development, I replied, "the country's poverty." With wage rates less than 10 per cent of North American levels, the possibility that the workers could be sufficiently productive in some industries to make goods for export with less than one-quarter of mainland unit labor costs created a real opportunity for export manufacturing despite the tariff barriers the goods would face. It should be recognized that low-cost but productive labor was the major asset which enabled such places as Japan, Hong Kong, and Puerto Rico to industrialize. Since wages in those locations have gone up and will continue to rise, the opportunity passes to other places, such as Taiwan, India, Southeast Asia, and various Caribbean islands, which can now capitalize on their low-cost labor to provide a starting point for industrial growth. Eventually they may also be able to graduate into levels and types of industrialization which will not have to depend mainly on low-wage advantages.

2. *Labor skills.* The existence in a country of special labor skills may constitute a special advantage. In Puerto Rico, for example, the traditional skills of the women in sewing and embroidery and other types of fine needlework contributed to the success of the garment industry, which became the most important element in the industrial program. In other countries special skills exist which have not been used as they should in the industrialization process—woodworking skills in Haiti and Indonesia and metalworking capabilities in India and the Middle East, for example. However, it should be noted that handicraft skills do not have full transferability into modern industry. It often happens that new industries prefer to train young workers with little or no developed skill than to employ older people who have a demonstrated handicraft skill. Nevertheless, young people who have grown up with a familiarity with traditional handicraft production are better trainees for a modern factory than those who have not had such a background. Even when there is no transference of skills, it is certainly true that children of skilled workers are likely to enter industry with a more responsible and constructive attitude toward manufacturing work than those without such a family tradition.

3. *Entrepreneurial and management skills.* Perhaps the most vital spark needed in the industrializing process is that provided by the entrepreneur who has the initiative and the ambition to take risks and exert skills in starting or developing a new industry. It may also be the hardest thing to develop or provide substitutes for. A country which has a tradition of entrepreneurship, which has probably grown up over centuries of trading, always has a great advantage for industrial development if it chooses to encourage it. Lebanon, for example, has a greater proportion of such enterprising people than most small countries. The existence of a substantial number of enterprising businessmen is also one of India's greatest development assets. Admittedly, the typical entrepreneur in most developing countries is a trader, not a manufacturer. But the important thing is that he is a man of business experience, accustomed to exercising ingenuity in taking risks in the hope of gain. If conditions are made attractive, he will increasingly be drawn into industrial ventures, often providing both capital and management. The skill of the experienced manager of the salaried variety, as distinct from the individual who risks his own funds in ventures, is another element important for industrial growth. Some countries have a good body of such men, usually developed as employees of foreign-run companies. If new industries can draw on this reservoir for engineers, foremen, accountants, and other managerial personnel, one of the worst problems in starting industry in an underdeveloped country can be solved.

4. *Power, fuel, and minerals.* Underdeveloped countries are often rich in unused natural resources—oil, gas, minerals, and hydroelectric potential. Any one of these may constitute a country's special asset for industrial development. In other than oil-rich countries, where this one resource is the cornerstone of the economy, gas, oil, or coal in smaller quantities may provide either the fuel or the industrial raw material for a variety of projects. Electric power, if very cheap, can be the sole justification for some major projects, though these possibilities are few. Electric power at more ordinary costs is unlikely to attract industry, but it is essential to a generally favorable industrial climate. The importance of power as an element in industrial location will be discussed more fully in a later chapter.

5. *Raw materials.* Most underdeveloped countries produce or could produce low-cost raw materials for industry. Often their main economic base already is the production of such products for export to the industrialized countries. The availability of these materials is a major asset for developing industries which require these inputs. Some of these materials could be upgraded by complete or partial processing prior to shipment to world markets. Sometimes there will be a distinct advantage in

locally based processing industries because of low-cost labor and savings in shipping costs. In other cases local processing will be found to be uneconomic due to climate, lack of skills, difficulty in breaking established trade channels, or peculiarities in shipping rates. The cataloguing and analysis of a country's present raw material production and future production potentialities are an essential part of a study of industrial development possibilities. The industrial opportunities which may be uncovered can include new products based on more valuable uses for materials as well as the upgrading of materials into traditional products.

6. Location. A country's location is sometimes an important asset for some kinds of industry. The islands of Curaçao and Aruba near Venezuela, for example, have major oil refineries because of their location. Italy's island of Sicily has a successful ship-repair industry because of its position astride important shipping routes. Some Caribbean islands are logical locations for industries processing Central and South American hardwoods into lumber. Location of industry may be influenced by sources of raw materials, shipping routes, transportation rates, and changing patterns of world markets and sources of supply. Thorough examination of these factors may reveal industrial advantages which did not previously exist.

7. Developed markets. Most developing countries are at a great disadvantage as far as industry for local market is concerned because their markets are small, due to low income levels and sometimes due to small population. An underdeveloped country which already has large developed markets has a great advantage which can be the basis for a major growth of domestic industry to serve established demand. This advantage is the key to development in countries with large-sized markets such as India and Brazil; it is a moderately good advantage in countries with medium-sized markets such as Mexico, Colombia, and Egypt.

8. Climate. Most of the underdeveloped countries are in the tropics or the semitropics, and their climate is generally regarded as a negative factor in their development prospects. The wider use of air conditioning has made some areas more suitable for industry, for example, the southern states of the United States, but artificial climate for a factory is not to be had without considerable cost. The main areas where climate may be a development advantage are those which, because of location or other factors, can make themselves into tourist attractions. The trend in world tourism is sharply toward the sunny vacationlands, and strangely enough a climate regarded as unattractive for economic development generally may be the most important asset for creating a major source of income through tourism. As air travel becomes more economical and as more people in the affluent countries travel more widely, no country in the world need feel itself too remote to attract tourists if its climate and other features are right.

9. *Industrial sites.* A country which has an ample supply of well-located and developed sites for new industry has an advantage in attracting new industry. Partly this is a matter of the land-use pattern which has developed, leaving either good or poor sites for industry; but partly it is a matter which can be consciously developed. A country which has had the foresight to plan its land use to reserve attractive areas for industry and which, through industrial estates or other means, has provided the sites with transportation facilities, power, water, and other essentials, has created an advantage of real importance for developing new industries.

10. *Infrastructure.* Much of the emphasis on development financing by the World Bank and other agencies during the past fifteen years has been on creating the infrastructure of power, transport, and communication facilities which are needed before industrial and agricultural development can proceed as it should. A country which has developed these facilities to the point where the necessary services are available on a reliable basis and at reasonable cost has established an important precondition for industrial development and has a distinct advantage over places which have not done so.

11. *Market access.* Industrial location is increasingly being determined by the advantages of one place over another in terms of access to the market the industry is being built to serve. Plants are being built in European countries because they are members of, or associates of, the European Common Market. Others are being built in Central American countries because they are a part of the Central American Common Market. Most of the plants built in Puerto Rico and Jamaica have been established to serve the United States market. For export industries, the location chosen is likely to be the one which can provide duty-free entry for the products. Entry to the United States market without tariff barriers was a major reason for Puerto Rico's success in attracting industry. Developing areas such as the former French African colonies and the islands of the Netherlands Antilles have a great industrial development asset in their duty-free entry into the European Common Market. British Commonwealth locations have an advantage in preferential rates when their products enter Commonwealth markets. If a country has a right of free or preferential entry into any important market, or if such a right can be negotiated, it may constitute a major advantage in establishing industry.

12. *Incentives.* A country which has established a broad range of attractive industrial incentives and subsidies has already created for itself an advantage in industrial development. The various incentives, which will be discussed in detail in later chapters, include some which a country needs to give in order to be competitive in the race to get new industry, as well as others which a country may give to establish for itself a specially attractive position in regard to some kinds of industry.

13. Local capital. While some underdeveloped countries are so lacking in capital that it is impossible to obtain even partial local financing for new industry, they are exceptions. Those countries which, through oil royalties or other special situations, have substantial amounts of local capital have a unique advantage. They will have to plan their development carefully to avoid losing their capital, which may not be replaceable if it comes from a depleting asset; but the existence of the financing in itself is half the battle.

Elements of Industrial Development Strategy

Some countries may become industrialized without devising a strategy for industrial development or doing much to encourage or promote industrial growth. This book is not for them. It is for countries for whom success will not come without organized planning and aggressive effort. These are the great majority of the world's underdeveloped nations. For them, development of all kinds must be recognized as a process which can be accelerated by the right kind of action by government or slowed down or stopped by the wrong kind of action or by inaction. A basic thesis of this book is that almost any country can achieve more industrial development, and achieve it more quickly, if it organizes a comprehensive industrial development program built around elements of strategy which have been tried and proved successful by other countries.

When a country decides to embark on an industrial development program, it is deciding to take the active as contrasted to the passive approach to industrialization. It is resolving not to wait for industrial growth to take place on its own, but to seek and promote it. It is deciding not to sit idly by until investors discover the country and knock on the door, but to go out and look for them. When a country adopts the aggressive approach to getting industry, the change involves more than simply accepting a plan and setting up an office. If the active approach is to mean anything, it has to signify a change of attitude on the part of the government and the people in the country who are influential in determining its policies. The passive approach was rooted in an attitude of acquiescence—"let development come, we will accept it." The active approach is founded on an attitude of creation—"we must industrialize, and we will industrialize."

The new attitude toward industrial development which must be the basis for a dynamic program cannot be limited to a few top officials of the government. The idea of industrial development, of creating conditions which will attract industry and make it successful and of supporting the industrial development program financially, must be widely held in a country or there will not be an atmosphere conducive to bringing about the necessary changes. For best results, industrial development must be made into a national crusade, a cause which will evoke an enthusiastic response from the man in the street. For industrial development to appear in this light, the public must be sold on what it can do for them and their children in terms of job opportunities, higher incomes, and better living. At the same time, they must not be oversold and led to believe that the riches of an industrial society can be theirs without investing in the acquisition of better skills, working harder than was customary in nonindustrial days, helping subsidize new industry by paying higher prices for locally made goods during the early stages of industrialization, and paying the costs of the industrial development program through the use of public funds for this purpose rather than for immediate welfare benefits. For those who are first convinced that a dynamic approach must be taken to industrial development, usually top political or business leaders, the first step in strategy is to build a broad base of support for the program. The concept must be "sold" in such a way that it will also be "bought." This requires generation of interest in the approach in an analytic, documented way at top levels in the community and in a popularized manner at the level of the general public. The goal must be acceptance of industrial development as a national objective and of the aggressive approach to industrial development as a method of "saving our country and creating a great future for our people."

For this strategy to work, acceptance of the objectives and methods of an industrial development program must not be limited to a narrow group or class in the country. It needs to be a national movement, transcending political, social, and economic lines. It needs to be bipartisan or multipartisan, with support from as many and as diversified political groups as possible. If the program were to become tagged with one political label, it might be doomed because of the opposition generated from other political groups. While starting a country successfully on the road to industrial development is about as great a political achievement as any party can aim for, the realization of it requires a fine element of willingness to embrace other political interests so that narrow partisanship or at least the appearance of it is avoided. The industrial development cause needs support at the same time from diverse and even opposing economic groups—businessmen on the one side and organized labor on the other. It cannot afford to be labeled as a device of the "capitalists" to divert the workingman's attention from his immediate demands. Nor can it become regarded as a campaign to attract foreign investors while ignoring the local businessman. Does this mean that industrial development and the program to bring it about must be "all things to all men"? In a way it does, for a successful industrial program will benefit every special interest in the country as well as the general interest of all in terms of higher national income, more jobs, higher wages, and more profitable investment opportunities.

Another essential element of industrial development strategy is that it needs to be frankly experimental. It cannot afford to be rigidly constrained in terms of ideology or methodology. There should be an open and declared willingness to try any approach or device which seems promising and to drop any policy or method which proves impractical or unrewarding. Most developing countries go through a phase in which industrial development is a goal to be attained by one narrowly defined approach. Usually the predetermined method is the establishment of state-owned industries. The worthy and perhaps realizable objective of development is thus subordinated to a notion as to method which has been enshrined as a dogma. It is as much as to say, "We must have industrial development, but if it can't be brought about the way we say it must come about, then we don't want it." Most countries which try a narrow and doctrinaire approach to industrial development see the error of their ways and move into broader and more productive channels. But others stick to their "principles" to the point that industrial development is strangled, leaving the politicians no option but to find other, and usually irrelevant, explanations for their failure.

When we say that industrial development strategy needs to be experimental, what does this imply? It means that there should be readiness to leave completely open the question of whether there should be government involvement in industrial projects and if so, how much and what kind. It means willingness to decide such questions on a case-by-case basis as projects and problems arise. Sometimes it may mean that the government should take the initiative in starting a project, even with majority government financing. Other times it may mean that important projects should be left entirely to private investors, with considerable support from government but no interference or control of any kind. It may mean that foreign control of some projects is welcomed, while local investors are preferred in other instances. Flexibility means that there should be no rigid adherence to preferences to favor one kind of industry over another, such as heavy industry over light industry or small industry over large industry. What is needed is a readiness to consider any project and any idea on its merits. It means that there should be willingness to adopt any kind of industrial development organization which seems most promising—a division of a ministry, a government corporation, a joint venture, or a private but officially endorsed activity. In short, there needs to be a desire to experiment and learn. The basis for the desire must rest ultimately in the existence of a spirit of tolerance and enquiry, as free as possible from prejudices held over from colonial days which might otherwise distort the program into serving special interests and preconceived notions.

While it is important that the program be flexible rather than doctrinaire in its approach to both policies and methods, there is one element of strategy which is basic: the recognition that in any dynamic type of industrial development program the government must take the initiative. This does not mean that the government must be a major financier of industrial projects; more often the financing should be largely or entirely private. The initiative which must come from the government is one of leadership, organization, financing of the industrial promotion activities as distinct from the projects, and general support through measures to improve the industrial investment climate. This kind of initiative is properly that of government, for only the government in a country reflects the over-all needs and views of the country. Moreover, it is only right that government should pay all or most of the cost of a development program which will be as broadly valuable to the whole country as a successful industrialization drive. Participation and support by private groups such as businessmen or labor unions is essential, especially to build up the spirit for development which is needed throughout the country. But in the last analysis, national development is the responsibility of government, and in this day and age few would suggest that it can or should be delegated to a private group, no matter how competent or altruistic.

As will be discussed in detail in this book, the role which the government must play is a broad and active one. It has to go far beyond legislation to improve the investment climate, for the essence of an active program is that the government's industrial development agency should take the initiative in finding industrial opportunities, studying and developing projects, identifying potential investors (both local and foreign), promoting the appropriate projects to them, and assisting the investors to put their projects together and build their factories. The ramifications of each of these elements in the program are great, as will be seen. Assisting investors, for example, may involve aid in making factory sites available and even erecting buildings to lease to the new industrialists. It may involve running recruiting and training programs so that the new factory can obtain at least partly trained workers when needed. In all these activities it is the government's industrial development agency that is the initiator, the salesman, the promoter, the troubleshooter, the consultant, and the adviser. In regard to each project it must take the initiative from the beginning and never let go until the investor has made his commitment and the new industry is operating successfully.

The strategy of rapid industrial development through private investment must rest on a recognition that conditions must be created and maintained which will enable industrial investment in the country to be highly profitable from the start. Only if this environment of profitability exists will the country have any hope of a continuing inflow of outside capital and industrial know-how or a steady diversion of local capital from other uses. There must be plenty of incentives. No country ever failed to develop because of too-generous incentives, but many have stagnated for lack of incentives which were attractive enough. The fact that some subsidization of industry is necessary, at least at the start, to get a country moving into industrialization must be accepted. For local market industries this may mean protection, which one hopes will be only temporary. For export industries it may mean generous tax exemptions and indirect subsidies of one kind or another. Unless a country's industrial development program is founded on a recognition that generous incentives of one kind or another have to be offered, there is no point in embarking on industrial development activities.

With regard to foreign capital, there should be a genuine and widespread acceptance in the country of the idea that foreign participation is necessary, desirable, and beneficial. Unless this view is widely held, there is no sound or even honest basis for a program which must count heavily on attracting foreign investment. If a common understanding of these points is lacking in a country, as well as a general readiness to go along with the policies they require, the time is not ripe to start a real industrial development effort. It would be much better to lay a foundation first by an educational campaign to outline the basic principles of industrial development economics.

In accepting what may be a bitter pill to swallow, that industrial development must be made highly profitable to private investors and even worse, to foreign private investors, countries should not lose sight of the need to appraise incentives and subsidies in terms of what they cost the economy and of what the new industries will be worth to the economy. Too often the costs of industrial subsidies are not counted. The revenue "lost" through tax exemptions may become a major issue on the mistaken assumption that without the exemption the new industries would exist and could be taxed. The real subsidy, and the one that is usually largest is that which occurs through tariff protection. It forces the public to subsidize the local industry through paying higher prices for the locally made products than for imported items. Methods of evaluating the value of industrial projects to the economy have been described in detail elsewhere and will be summarized later in this book. Calculations as to the cost of any kind of subsidy or assistance offered a project also need to be made. The results may indicate that in one case the country will gain much by paying the subsidy and getting the project and that in another case the costs of the subsidy may far outweigh the potential benefits. People in developing countries sometimes ask, "Is it worthwhile to pay foreign investors the high profits they demand?" The answer is that sometimes it is, sometimes it is not. The strategy behind the idea of subsidizing new industry must always be that subsidies will be readily available, but only within the limits set by the costs and benefits to the economy.

At the core of industrial development strategy there must be recognition, and plenty of evidence of it, that the underdeveloped country needs foreign capital much more than the foreign capital needs the particular country. For the country which wants to develop industrially, the capital and the know-how which goes with it are a necessity without which there will be no real development. For the foreign company, there is no necessity in the proposition whatsoever. The company, if it is a good prospect for new operations in a developing country, has already been highly successful in an industrialized country. It probably has important and profitable industrial works in a variety of countries. But chances are that within the company there are high officials who do not favor the risky and difficult entry into underdeveloped areas, especially at a time when the company has immediate and lucrative opportunities in America and Europe which would make good use of its available capital and personnel. Until the politicians and government officials of the developing countries realize that foreign capital is less than eager to invest in their countries, they will not take steps to create the conditions which will bring in the urgently needed capital and industrial technology.

The development of the right environment to attract capital to industry depends both on attitudes and on specific legislation. Individual measures such as tax incentives, grants and other subsidies, and tariff protection are an essential part of the package. They will be examined in detail later in this book. Underlying attitudes are even more important. An appreciation of the attitudes which are needed to provide a foundation for specific measures is necessary in developing industrial development strategy. Nationalistic attitudes, for example, can be beneficial or harmful. If the stress is on building up the nation through education and development, nationalistic fervor can be a driving force behind a constructive program. But if the nationalistic attitude is of the kind which is antiforeign, it can isolate the country from the international resources it needs so desperately. The nationalistic type of industrial growth—development with a minimum of outside help and contact—may be observed in many countries. Burma is a sad example of a potentially rich country which has not done well, in part because it has directed its strategy toward discrimination against foreigners and foreign capital to the point where it has isolated itself from world forces which could have done much to develop the country's industrial and other economic opportunities. The strategy of development in a country should be to create the atmosphere of international association in which the country may draw in capital and technicians on a large scale to participate in legitimate and productive nation-building enterprises.

The stress on the need for an open-door policy in regard to foreign financing and industrial specialists is not intended to suggest that this strategy should be carried beyond reasonable limits or that it should be pursued without discrimination. The airports of the underdeveloped world are busy these days with hordes of machinery salesmen who refer to themselves as "investors." They have been aptly called "the new imperialists," for their purpose, all too often, is the exploitation of the less developed countries for the profit of interests in the industrialized countries. The protection of underdeveloped countries from those who seek to sell unsound projects under the guise of investment is a primary responsibility of development-minded statesmen and their advisers. It is a subject I shall return to later in this book.

When one advocates that developing countries should base their industrial strategy on a maximum importation of industrial capital and skills, doubts are often raised by sincere nationalists as to the potential dangers of the country's economy, or at least of the new industrial sector, falling into the hands of foreign interests who may lack genuine identification with the legitimate needs of the country. Canada is often cited as an example, for Canada is one of the world's wealthiest countries not only in terms of per capita income, but also in terms of resources. Canada is nevertheless an underdeveloped country if its present level of development is compared with its potential, and it is a country which needs vast amounts of capital for development. It has been the most successful country in the world in attracting outside capital for its industrial development. A huge capital inflow permitted the country to maintain its dollar at or above par with the United States dollar for many years in spite of a large excess of imports over exports. The great capital inflow created impressive economic and industrial growth, especially as American capital frequently went into ventures which could not obtain financing from the more conservative Canadian investors. Nevertheless the country's success in attracting foreign capital was so great that a large part of the nation's industry came to be owned by foreign capital. Examples came up of management decisions and policies of American-owned companies which were regarded as being contrary to Canadian interests. The problem of foreign control of industry became a political issue capable of making or breaking governments. Even though the country continued to need the inflow of foreign capital, measures were taken to discourage it and to loosen the outside control on industry.

Does Canada's experience have any relevance for an underdeveloped country seeking a basis for its industrial development strategy? Not much. Many people in the developing countries have the illusion that an almost unlimited number of foreign investors are eagerly waiting to invest in their country, provided they are given generous concessions. Except in a few industries of an extractive nature—oil and minerals particularly—the view of ready and impatient investors is a sadly distorted one. For many reasons it is unlikely in our time that any of the underdeveloped countries of Asia, Africa, or Latin America will be embarrassed by the amount of investment which is offered for manufacturing industries. The problem will be to get enough outside capital and know-how for industry so that a moderate amount of growth can take place. The difference between the position of underdeveloped countries and that of Canada merits emphasis. Canada, for all practical purposes, has been regarded by American investors as being virtually part of the United States. Political stability and safety for investments have been looked upon as being better than could be found elsewhere in a country having such vast resources ready for development. And all this with no capital gains tax! No amount of effective investment promotion by most developing countries is likely to bring about such a flow of foreign investment in industry that it will parallel Canada's situation. It will be time to start closing the door when the traffic of legitimate investors gets too heavy.

The strategy in regard to foreign industrial investment should be to create conditions which are so attractive that the country acquires a world-wide reputation as being a "good place to do business in." While a country can gain much by treating capital well, this does not mean that it has to treat it too well. For example, a country does not need to allow a foreign company to get involved in political activities, or to evade taxes, or to follow antilabor practices. A foreign-controlled company must be required to act like a good citizen, as most of them in their own self-interest would prefer to do anyway. As will be discussed later, incentives need to be generous, especially at the beginning; but they do not need to go beyond certain limits, and most of them do not need to be permanent.

Another important element of industrial development strategy is that while government must be prepared to do much for new industry, it must at all costs avoid getting too involved in industry in bureaucratic ways which will discourage development. It is one thing, for example, to make feasibility studies and offer incentives. It is quite another to have licensing systems or other controls under which government approvals are needed for various management decisions. There usually are reasons for government controls, though often the reasons disappear while the controls survive; but the delays and uncertainties they create often outweigh the benefits the country gets from insisting on a say in decisions which, in free countries, should be left entirely to business.

In dealing with industry and potential industrialists, the aim should be to do only what is needed in order to get the industrialist, local or foreign, to develop the industry and make a success of it. Then the officials of the government development agency can move on to the next industrial possibility. The tendency to try to retain control or at least an influence over a project once it has been launched should be avoided. It can soon poison the industrial development atmosphere and divert the development personnel from their primary task of finding new opportunities and locating investors to perform the entrepreneurial functions.

A constructive approach to dealing with private investors lies in making the incentives as automatic as possible. Delays which can drive investment away and corrupt practices which can offend reputable investors thrive in a situation where substantial concessions are offered as incentives only to projects which are approved by government officials. Sometimes approvals have to be based on value judgments which must be made by government officials, but more often incentives can be granted on the basis of published regulations. Obviously all incentives cannot be made completely automatic or the doors would be wide open for abuse. Nevertheless, the aim of strategy should be to set up systems which minimize the opportunities for delays and malpractices. This aspect of industrial development administration will be enlarged upon in a later chapter.

Policies aimed at development of human resources for industry are as basic as anything to strategy for industrial growth; for in the last analysis, it is the people who will make industry a success or a failure. Investment in people for industry is even more basic than investment in machinery. Unless a country's people are ready for industry—as managers, technicians, and workers at all levels—acquisition of factories will only mean the start of a long period in which industrial inefficiency will lead to disillusionment about industry as a potential asset to the country. Preparing the people means much more than investing in technical education at all levels, important though this is. It also means raising the prestige of industrial management and employment by measures which make it sufficiently more attractive both financially and otherwise to attract the best talent the country has to offer. Starting graduate-level colleges of business and industrial management is one way in which the prestige of industrial careers can be raised. Taxation may also be used as a tool to create financial conditions for salaried personnel in industry which will be more attractive than for those in other occupations which are of lower priority for national development. Expansion of industrial management and technical scholarships for study abroad can do much to attract outstanding people to industry, but care must be taken to ensure that local conditions and opportunities will be good enough so they will return home after their studies abroad.

Perhaps the mistake which is most commonly made today is to give industrial development such great emphasis that it is pushed too far at the expense of other development opportunities which offer greater advantages. Industry tends to be too glamorous compared with some other activities which may do more for a country at certain stages of development. The need to avoid overemphasis on industrial development and the need to avoid neglect of agricultural development which may offer greater opportunities for economic gain are included in the idea of "balanced growth," which recognizes the complementary nature of development in various sectors of the economy. The relationship between industrial and other sectors of development naturally varies from one country to another. Every sector has some advantages as well as disadvantages for development. To invest too much in the wrong thing, or even in the right thing at the wrong time, is bound to bring poor results. The goal in development planning is to achieve the right emphasis on the over-all strategy of investment so that the gain in terms of increase in the national income will be maximized. Viewed in this light, industrial growth may not deserve as much preferential emphasis as it receives when considered alone from the point of view which automatically accords highest priority to industrial development because of its apparent modernity.

Summary of Elements of Industrial Development Strategy

The elements of strategy which have been found to be most effective in mounting a successful national effort for sound industrial development have been mentioned briefly above and will be expanded upon throughout this book. They may be restated as follows:

1. Industrial development must be approached actively and aggressively, not passively.

2. Industrial development must be made into a national crusade, supported broadly by all groups in the country.

3. The approach must be frankly experimental and as free as possible from preconceived prejudices as to policies and methods.

4. The government must take the lead and supply the initiative and drive to industrial development. It must do much to assist new industries.

5. An industrial environment must be created which will offer incentives sufficient to make industrial investment highly profitable.

6. There should be frank recognition of the fact that in most underdeveloped countries most new industries must be given protection or some other kind of subsidy.

7. There needs to be acceptance of the importance of getting foreign capital and of the necessity for seeking it out and treating it well.

8. The industrial development approach must be based on the principles of industrial internationalism, not nationalism.

9. Government should avoid getting in the way of private industry through bureaucratic requirements which create delays, uncertainties, or situations inviting corrupt practices.

10. Considerable emphasis should be given to the training and development of managerial and technical personnel for industry.

11. Industrial development should be placed in proper perspective in relation to other sectors of the economy whose development may be equally or more promising and whose growth may be an essential basis for industrial expansion.

3

Approaches to Industrial
Development Policy

What Part Should Government Play?

The viewpoint was expressed early in this book that if a country is to embark on a comprehensive industrial development program likely to achieve worthwhile results, the government must take the initiative and play a key role in the development drive, even though it is wise in the majority of cases to leave the management of manufacturing industry to private businessmen. The role I envisage for government in the industrial development process needs enlarging upon for it is central to all the elements of a dynamic industrial development program. Rather than discuss the alternative approaches in the abstract, I shall quote excerpts from the chapter on industrial development strategy in the study prepared in 1960 by a team from the Arthur D. Little Company for the Government of Peru: [1]

> A limited amount of industrial development will take place regardless of what the Government does, even if the Government is indifferent to the needs of business, and even if the Government does nothing to encourage or to assist private industrial development. We believe, however, that a rapid acceleration of private industrial development will take place only if the Government assumes leadership and does many things to assist and promote industrial development on the scale needed to meet the targets of the program. The Government, both directly and

[1] Arthur D. Little, Inc., *A Program for the Industrial and Regional Development of Peru*, Cambridge, Mass., 1960, pp. 7–8.

through the proposed Development Corporation, and such related organizations as the Industrial Bank, can do much to create the investment climate which will give investors confidence in Peruvian industry. . . . We have observed a strange misconception in Peru with regard to the role which Government planning should play in a country which has a tradition and a policy of private investment in industry. Some people appear to feel, we believe mistakenly, that there is a contradiction in Government research and planning and activity in the field of industrial development in a country which accepts the principle of private investment and initiative in manufacturing industries. Those who hold this viewpoint believe that the Government should do little in regard to industrial development, other than granting tariff protection and perhaps tax concessions. They feel that if projects are to be discovered they should be found by the private investor and developed by him. . . . They believe it is contrary to sound principles of private industrial development for the Government to do anything in the industrial finance field other than provide low-cost loans through organizations such as the Industrial Bank. . . . This extreme viewpoint of laissez-faire stems apparently from a fear that if the Government intervenes actively in the field of research and planning, Peru may be on its way toward a controlled economy in which the state assumes the role of entrepreneur, owning and managing industries. We believe that this dispute over the role of economic planning and Government activity to promote industrial development is pointless and can be extremely harmful to the development of the country. While we agree with those who believe that the Government of Peru should avoid state ownership and management of industries, if for no other reason than because of the operating problems involved, we believe that an active program of research, planning, and promotion sponsored and paid for by the Government is essential to increase the amount of private investment in Peru, from both local and foreign investors. . . . For a country such as Peru, which has invested practically nothing in economic research, development, resource exploration, and investment promotion, the amount of Government activity in this field will seem large and expensive. The experience of other places, such as Puerto Rico, has proved that Government activity and expenditure of this kind can bring forth a vast increase in private activity and investment. The country therefore stands to gain and will find that the private sector, far from diminishing under such a program, will be considerably increased in scope and strength. . . . There is also a mistaken idea that Government activity in this field will lead to more controls and regulations and thus to a less free and open economy. This fear is equally groundless, as one of the objectives of Government activity for industrial development is to make the economy more open in order to improve the climate for private industrial investment.

The role we are suggesting for the Government of Peru in the industrial development field is that of a catalyst. The objective should be to secure as much private industrial investment as possible for every million soles spent by the Government in one way or another on research, exploration, development, and promotion. As in a chemical process, where a small amount of essential catalyst is needed to bring about the desired reaction, so it is in the field of industrial development. What the Government must supply is the missing ingredient to start the chain reaction which will create a new industrial development project. The missing element may vary greatly from one case to another. In one instance the Government through its development organization, may need to supply the original element of discovery of the existence of a potentially attractive investment opportunity. In another case it may be necessary to make a detailed technical-economic feasibility study of a project, or conduct market research to prove to an investor that a market exists. In another case the Government may have to assist by locating and providing, perhaps at low cost, a suitable site for a factory. In other cases it may be necessary to set up training schools to train the technicians needed for a new industry. It may be necessary to complete the financing by a loan through the Industrial Bank. It may be necessary to grant a temporary development tariff for a limited number of years . . . or it may be necessary to grant an additional tax exemption. . . . It may be necessary to find a foreign partner who can provide capital, management, know-how and marketing connections for a project sponsored by a Peruvian investor. Or it may be necessary to find a local partner who will provide part of the capital and local connections for a foreign investment in Peru.

In these as in hundreds of other ways, the Government, through its development organizations, must provide the missing elements so that projects which are otherwise sound may be carried through to make their contribution to employment and the national income. The amount of catalyst which will be needed to get a large scale industrialization drive going will be larger at first than later.

The role suggested for government in the proposed industrial development program for Peru stands in contrast on the one hand with the laissez-faire attitude which prevailed in that country at the time of the report and on the other hand with the "government-do-everything" approach which has been the order of the day in many other countries. It represents a practical attempt to find a way to make the best of both worlds—to use private enterprise in what it can do best and to use government initiative in those areas in which private initiative is lacking or ineffective. The environment in Peru at the time the study was made was that of an open economy with free currency convertibility, low taxes, and only a moderate level of protective tariffs. Industrial development was limited by the higher returns available to capital in agricultural plantations, urban real estate, and trading. The inflow from abroad of foreign capital to industry was small, as nothing was being done to promote investment. Some parts of existing industry, such as textiles, were high-cost producers in need of modernization, a situation caused partly by overprotection. Much of industry was in the hands of family firms who lacked the resources or drive to seek export markets, preferring a small but protected area of operations in a market where competition was limited. One purpose of the report was to give a jolt to prevailing viewpoints on the role of government in the industrial development process. The same sort of jolt is needed in most developing countries, for few have arrived at a workable way to combine the strengths of government-initiated action and private investment for speeding up the industrial development process.

Government or Private Industries?

The debate on the respective merits of state and privately owned industries in the developing countries is an old one which still goes on. It is central to determining a practical approach to industrial development. Some of the arguments on both sides were given in my first book, *Industrial Development*. I pointed out that there are persuasive reasons why governments often start industrial projects: some of these involve the unwillingness of private investors to start sound and high-priority industries and the unreadiness of local investors to invest in industry; others have to do with the country's unwillingness to depend solely on foreign capital and with fears of monopoly and excessive profit taking. Despite these reasons, which are understandable and often sound, it must be recognized that in most countries where industry is primarily in the private sector, most government industrial projects have not been successful. It is not too much to say that the underdeveloped world is full of state-owned industrial white-elephant projects, and it is not too difficult to list a variety of reasons why they have failed to live up to expectations despite the apparent advantages to be had in being officially sponsored. The advantages of private ownership and management of industrial enterprises—the pressure for reducing costs, the drive for expanding the markets—are more widely recognized now than in the past. There has been a noticeable swing toward an increased role for private industry in some countries, such as India, which look to state enterprises for an important part of the country's industrial development.

One of the strongest of the ideological arguments in favor of state industries is that this form of ownership enables the profits of the investment to accrue to the people of the developing country through the medium of the government agency which operates the ventures. This is contrasted to the flow of profits to wealthy individuals or small groups in the community in the case of private investment by local investors or to interests outside of the country in the case of private foreign investments. One weakness of this argument is that a country and its people may get a higher return on their investments if capital which is channeled through government investments is placed in investments in education, health services, highways, power, and similar sectors where private capital may not be a practical alternative, as it is not in most countries. Another weakness of the argument is that the prospect of a significant return on investment in state-owned industries is likely to be an illusion, for experience in many countries has demonstrated that more often government manufacturing industries lose money and have to be subsidized from the public purse.

Nevertheless, the concept of the people as a whole sharing in the risks and the profits of industry is an appealing one which should not be dismissed too early or too easily. What is needed are ways to get the benefits through means more likely to bring about the desirable results than government operation of industries. One way is to rely on private investment and operation of industry and obtain the public "dividend" through income taxes. If, as in the United States, the income tax rate on the profits of corporations is about 50 per cent, it is only realistic to regard the taxes as a means by which the public through the government shares on a rather generous basis in the profits of the industry. At the same time, industry remains under private control, which enhances the prospect that it will be efficiently managed and thereby earn a return on the investment. Another way, which will be discussed more fully in this chapter, is through joint ventures in which the government makes an investment in the equity capital of private industrial projects and thus shares in the return as a shareholder, as well as a tax collector. If, for example, the government holds one-quarter of the shares in a company, and the corporation tax rate is 50 per cent, the public through their government would end up with about two-thirds of the profits before taxes of an enterprise set up on a joint-venture basis. This would come about through half of the profits accruing to government through the income tax on the total profit, plus one-quarter of the remaining profits accruing to government as owner of one-quarter of the shares. In an enterprise in which the management and three-quarters of the risks are assumed by private investors, this appears to be a reasonable, if not a generous, return to the public.

As the pros and cons of government versus private industrial development were discussed quite fully in my other book, there is no need to go over the same ground again; but it may be useful to examine some elements of the situation which have come into greater prominence in the past few years. Perhaps the most persuasive argument for the starting of a new industry directly by a government has been that if the government fails to go ahead with the project, nobody else will. But the evidence in many parts of the world is now tending to show that if projects are economically and commercially sound, and if a country has created a reasonably good investment climate, private investment can be obtained for most projects if a real desire for it exists. While total capital available for industry in the underdeveloped countries remains limited, mainly because of the greater attractiveness of investment alternatives in the advanced countries, the fact still remains that the number of really good projects in countries which are attractive to investors is small enough that capital can be attracted to them. As will be pointed out in Chapter 8, organized effort may be needed to attract investment to a specific project; but if the project is good and the country situation is right, it can be obtained.

In countries where industry is basically in the private sector state investment in industry tends to be made in situations where the conditions described above do not exist. Sometimes the country, because of economic or political instability or because of nationalistic attitudes, does not offer conditions which a foreign investor would regard as safe and attractive. Sometimes the country may have a good enough investment climate, but the project may be marginal as a commercial proposition or too risky in itself to attract a foreign investor. In such situations a government may be reduced to the alternative of either doing the project itself or of not getting an industry which is economically sound for the country. Faced with this alternative, some countries, perhaps because of ideological inclination, tend to rush into a state industry investment, despite the inherent difficulties involved. Sometimes they do so without adequate consideration of alternatives which might meet the situation more effectively and more safely.

If a government, faced with a multitude of high-priority demands for the funds it has available for development and aware of the difficulties it would have in making a new industry efficient, wants the advantages which can come from private management, it can usually obtain them. One way is to try to set the project up as a joint venture in which a thoroughly experienced foreign firm assumes the management responsibility and perhaps the bulk of the financial investment. The government participation in such an enterprise may reduce the private investment needed to the point where a foreign partner can be attracted. It may also give the needed assurance that the project will have official support. The joint venture may be able to obtain partial financing from a variety of development banks and other financial institutions, thus reducing further the call on the government and on the technical partner and making it easier to bring in the management experience which is needed most of all. The joint-venture method will be discussed further in Chapter 10.

The role just outlined for a government in a joint venture—as a minority participant in the financing—illustrates one of the most important and basic principles in industrial development. This is the point which was mentioned in the Peru report quoted above and which will also be discussed at greater length in Chapter 10: that government has an important role as a catalyst in industrial projects. Like a catalyst in a chemical process which may be small in size but critical in importance, a small amount of government financial participation in an industrial project may cause the entire process of investment to take place. This is a role which gives ample scope for government initiative in sponsoring and pushing projects of high priority for the country and which offers a means to bring in the technical and business management needed to make the project successful. At the same time, the capital committed to the projects is only a small fraction of the financing which would be needed to launch wholly owned government projects. Moreover, the amounts which are invested on this basis are likely to prove to be good investments in sound projects. The earnings on these investments may constitute, over the years, a source of capital for catalyst-type investments in more new industries.

The wisdom of a policy of making catalytic investments in industries in which experienced private companies hold the majority financial interest and exercise management control has been demonstrated in the Western Region of Nigeria. Using profits derived from the sale of major crops through government marketing boards, the Government of the Western Region invested many millions of pounds in industrial and commercial enterprises of various kinds. Some of the investments were made in projects which were wholly owned by the government and which were operated by state agencies. Other investments were made as minority participations in more than a dozen projects which were privately controlled. The results were clear confirmation of the soundness of the principle of government investment in private projects: these projects were almost all successful, while the state-owned and operated projects were mostly quite unsuccessful.

If a country fails to attract private investment for a project which has been thoroughly studied and found to be sound and of high priority, it may be possible that the project can be changed in such a way as to make it more attractive to a prospective investor. In the investment field this is known as "sweetening up." It may be justified for the government to offer additional incentives to the project—greater tax exemption, more complete relief from import duties on materials, or long-term assurances of government purchases of the product. It may be worthwhile to provide a higher level of tariff protection. It may even be justifiable to give special guarantees of one kind or another. It may even be necessary to give a direct subsidy—a free piece of land, or free roads, or utility connections, or even a grant to cover part of the cost of the equipment or its transportation to the country. As will be discussed more fully in later chapters of this book, the range of possible incentives is wide. Some are expensive, yet providing them may be less costly to a government than setting up a project without outside financial participation and without experienced management.

To attract private participation to a project a government may only have to give tangible evidence of its support for the project in one of the forms just mentioned—by making a minority financial investment or by giving an incentive which goes beyond the minimum available to all new industries. Sometimes what is needed is to recognize the place which the proposed project should have in the economy. Such recognition may be given by assurances that the special benefits granted will not be given for a specified period to competitive projects.

The decision that a new industry should be in the public rather than the private sector may rest on a legitimate desire for the public as a whole to share in the profits of industry or upon the unwillingness of the private sector to take up an investment opportunity. In many parts of the world it is increasingly evident that the decisions to start government industrial projects are not based on these legitimate justifications as much as upon some other motives which are never mentioned but which may constitute the real reasons for the decisions. An example of this trend is the virtual exclusion of private business from industry in Burma in recent years. While ideological considerations undoubtedly played some part in establishing the official policy and in providing a publicity cover for the policy decisions, a larger part was probably played by a nationalistic desire to prevent industry from being controlled by minority groups which had more capital and business initiative than the Burmese. The exclusion from industrial development of those most able to make a contribution is a matter within the authority of those who control a country, but it is not a step likely to add to the national income or to bring the other benefits which should be expected from the industrial sector.

Another real but illegitimate basis for government industrial projects in some countries is that the purchase of industrial plants or equipment by government provides an opportunity for politicians to extract private considerations which are financed, of course, by inflating the cost of the projects to the government. The projects may be advertised to the public as great steps in industrial development which have been taken to benefit the country as a whole; but the real reason for their existence may be that a minister of industry was sufficiently derelict in his public trust to be susceptible to a machinery salesman's offer of a bribe. The serious cost to a country of such situations may not be the inflated cost of the projects themselves, but the subsidies which must be fed to the white elephants over the coming years. It should not be assumed, however, that every white-elephant project necessarily involves this kind of collusion against the interests of a country. There are many white-elephant industrial projects in the underdeveloped world which are nothing more than monuments to impatient but honest politicians who were so anxious to see some industrial development that they had no time to wait for feasibility studies, competitive bids, or private investors.

Monopolies or Competition?

The problem of monopolies will always exist in most developing countries, for most of them do not have markets large enough to permit competition which is both economic and effective throughout the whole of the industrial sector of the economy. The development of a practical set of policies for industry must deal with the problem of how to avoid, or live with, monopolistic industries. The harmful effects of monopoly in industry need little elaboration, for every country has its own examples. Generally, when an industry has a monopoly position, it produces inefficiently: its costs are high because it can be profitable without really trying. At the same time its goods are usually below quality standards, for the industry generally has protection from the higher-quality foreign merchandise. The high prices charged for the products limit the size and growth of the domestic market for the item, and the high cost and low quality usually eliminate the possibility of developing export markets. The monopolistic industry tends to remain small, inefficient, but profitable. Often such industries are family firms, a restricted form of organization ideally suited to a business with limited growth prospects. Industrialists in this kind of business naturally seek to preserve their small gold mines and usually have enough political influence to do so. They do not bring to a developing country the drive or initiative which private enterprise is supposed to provide and which the country needs if it is to develop rapidly. On the contrary, the proprietors of monopolistic industry in many countries are united in their opposition to granting incentives to new industries which might compete with old industries. They are wary of reciprocal tariff-cutting arrangements which might create export markets for some industries but at the expense of their own established enterprises. If the industrial sector in a country is composed mainly of monopolistic, inward-looking industries, this may well be a major cause of public attitudes which are hostile to industry and to private business generally. This is natural because monopolistic local industries tend to be highly profitable and separate a few wealthy industrial families from the mass of the people who are unable to purchase the high-priced goods.

The harmful effects to an economy and to a country of a tight little sector of industry which is largely monopolistic are easy to see but difficult to avoid. There is no standard solution which can be applied to the problem, but there are a number of approaches which can be used selectively according to the needs of the various situations which may exist:

1. It may be decided that it is better for the economy to import a given product indefinitely than to give a monopoly position to a new industry either by government edict or by incentives which would encourage the establishment of a plant bound to have a monopoly position. It is hard for a government to turn down a new industry for any reason; but unless it is clear that there are ways to control the monopoly, and unless the project is clearly of high value to the economy, this may be the only wise decision.

2. It may be decided that although the industry would have high national economic profitability, it would be difficult or impossible to control or limit the harmful effects of a private monopoly; so the project may be undertaken as a state industrial project. The probability of equally harmful effects due to the inherent problems of managing government industries may be great, but they can be minimized if management is divorced from politics, preferably by making a management contract with an experienced firm in the industry.

3. The project may be organized as a joint venture in which control would be in the hands of technical partners to ensure management efficiency, but with sufficient power retained in the hands of government representatives to lessen the dangers of restrictive pricing policies which would limit the market.

4. The enterprise may be encouraged as a purely private venture, but with a clearly stated policy from the outset that the maintenance of tariff protection or import restriction on competitive goods will depend upon prices to the public not exceeding a specified percentage over the c.i.f. cost of alternative imported goods of the same quality. Failure of the local company to live up to this arrangement would result in admitting sufficient imports to force the monopolist into line.

The best solution to the problem of monopoly, of course, is to have competition whenever it is economically practical. A government which places the interests of the economy and its growth ahead of established interests will not hesitate to foster competition whenever it is justified. This may mean undertaking efforts to promote investment in new plants which will be competitive to some already established, even granting incentives to new industries over the opposition of the existing firms. The government can use its own purchasing power to encourage competition by placing orders with new firms which compete with old ones.

A government which gives highest priority to speeding up development must be ready to expose and take action to break up monopolies by encouraging competition whenever it is possible. Otherwise, the country will pay the price in retarded economic growth.

On the other hand, there is a danger in promoting too much competition. Some countries in a natural desire to encourage local small industry have encouraged the setting up of so many small plants in some industries that extreme fragmentation results in inefficient high-cost production. A few years ago, for example, the Government of India licensed and fostered a proliferation of factories in some of the motor-vehicle ancillary industries. Vehicle costs have been inflated because vehicle manufacturers have had to buy parts from makers having only a small fraction of the output volume needed for low-cost production. It is much better in such a situation to have two or three manufacturers with plants of economic size than to have ten or twenty producers each operating inefficiently. India provides another example of the dangers of developing a too-fragmented industry in the motor vehicle itself. With a total output of vehicles which would represent only the part-time output of one modern vehicle plant of economic size for lowest-cost production, India has six producers of vehicles. Such a situation arose almost by historical accident; but it is a serious cause of economic waste since automobile costs can be as much as 40 per cent lower in a plant of optimum economic size than in a factory of minimum operational size.

No simple approach can be suggested through which a country can shape its industrial policies to avoid both the dangers of monopoly and the hazards of too much competition. Clearly the problems deserve more attention than they get in most developing countries, and the absence of policies is hardly a safe course to follow. While each situation needs to be analyzed on its merits, these should be the guidelines: monopolistic industries should be fostered only if the country is prepared to take the measures necessary to avoid the dangers of monopoly; a country should recognize that it can afford to pay a fairly good price in most situations to get some real competition; and a country should take care not to encourage the uneconomic fragmentation of an industry in the name of competition.

Location—a Basic Factor in Industrialization

When asked to list all the important factors which affected the saleability of residences, an American real estate agent once said that the three most important factors were location, location, and location. The same might also be said about the factors that determine the amount and kind of industry a country may be able to get. Of course there are other elements which are also important, such as the existence of enterprising businessmen, the energy and skill of workers, the availability of materials and fuel, and the stability of the country's economic and political situation. Nevertheless, location is an overriding factor which is basic to what is economic in a country, and it is something which a country has to live with even though its effects are subject to some modification over a period of time. An appreciation of the economics of industrial location should be a basis for determining industrial development policies and for identifying projects which might be promotable.

The problem may be examined first in the context of a country's situation in the world to see how location is the underlying economic factor which will make some kinds of industrialization feasible and other kinds unfeasible. In his book on international trade, Prof. Charles Kindleberger logically opens with a chapter on transport and communication.[2] He points out that

> If transport costs for goods were infinite—and if consumers did not commute internationally—there could be no international trade at all. All production would have to be consumed locally. If, on the other hand, transport costs were zero, practically everything would be exchanged in international trade—at least, all goods whose comparative costs of production differed from one place to another. . . . But transport costs are not infinite. International trade does take place. And transport costs are not zero, so that not all goods are freely traded.

Between the two theoretical extremes just described lies the real situation in which transport costs are an important part of the total cost of most products at any location far removed from their place of manufacture and in which the production costs of most products do vary significantly from one location to another. Both of these factors vary widely depending on the location, the goods, and the infinite number of factors that affect the costs of production and the cost of transportation.

The complexities of locational economics may be simplified by thinking of how a country's location affects the range of products which it can make economically, that is, without subsidy of one kind or another. I am using the word "economic" to mean "of value to the economy" and not to mean "commercially profitable" as some people do. If goods which are heavy and costly to transport in relation to their value, such as bricks, are imported from a distant source, the high transport costs constitute a natural protection and make the local manufacture of the goods economic even if local production costs are high compared with those in more favorable locations. At the other extreme, goods which are light and not expensive to transport in relation to their value, such as radios, will not be economic to manufacture locally unless the location offers some special production-cost advantage. This suggests that the farther a country is from places where an industry is already established,

---

    [2] Charles P. Kindleberger, *Foreign Trade and the National Economy*, Yale University Press, New Haven, 1962, pp. 8–9.

the more likely it is to be able to develop the manufacture of things which are costly to transport and, incidentally, the less tariff protection or other subsidy the industry will need to be commercially attractive as an investment. It also indicates that a country is not likely to get into the manufacture, on a really economic basis, of products which are light and of high value unless it has some distinct advantage in production costs.

The fundamentals of transport costs and comparative production costs determine what is really sensible to make in one place or another. These economic elements are usually concealed by the cloud of artificial factors which have been introduced by governments in a futile attempt to overcome the natural economic factors. Local production is usually encouraged in a country by making local manufacture of a product commercially profitable through tariff protection. This is really just a way to force the consumers to subsidize something which is not basically economic. Justified though tariff protection may be under certain circumstances, there are limits beyond which no country can afford to go in subsidizing what is uneconomic.

The basis for international trade has been described in classical economics as the law of comparative costs, which Professor Kindleberger set forth as follows: [3]

> Trade is based on differences in the costs of production of given articles that are wider than their costs of transport in terms of some absolute measure of real costs. These are not absolute differences in costs, but relative, or comparative. It is not necessary for trade that the United States produce electrical machinery more cheaply than Britain, and that Britain produce textiles more cheaply than the United States. If the United States produces both textiles and machinery more cheaply than Britain but its margin of advantage is wider than in textiles, it will pay to export machinery and import textiles.

For a developing country this suggests the emphasis of industrialization policy: the country should concentrate on developing the industries in which it has the greatest cost advantage compared with other countries or the least disadvantage if it does not have an absolute advantage in anything. This rule is basic to production for both local and export markets. Departures from this rule can be made only with some economic loss. Sometimes there may be reasons for taking a loss through choosing to develop a kind of industry which is not the most economic; but losses are usually a poor substitute for gains and rarely represent a way to progress. A realistic use of the rule just described requires that the relative position of a country in regard to a product should be calculated by combining production costs and transport costs. If we are

[3] *Ibid.*, p. 26.

estimating the comparative cost position on making a product for the local market, we must compare the probable local cost of manufacturing with the delivered cost of the product if imported, before any local tariff or taxes are added; that is, the c.i.f. cost should be used. If we are calculating the comparative costs for a potential export product, we have to add the cost of transport, insurance, and handling to the local costs of making the item to determine whether it can be delivered in an export market at a cost which is competitive on that market. If, in terms of employing people and other resources that would otherwise be idle, it is necessary to develop industry beyond the limits which would be strictly economic on these calculations, a country should choose the kinds of industry which are the least uneconomic and which thus would require the least subsidy. These fundamentals are sufficiently obvious that their reiteration is only justified because of the extent to which many developing countries ignore the realities of what is economic in the field of industrial development.

For many countries much of the industrialization opportunity lies in the field of developing export industries. An understanding of why foreign investors choose one location rather than another is therefore essential if foreign investment is to be attracted for this type of industry. The technical factor that is critical in plant location decisions is the total combined cost of production and distribution in and from one location compared with alternative locations. As many alternative locations for a wide range of industrial export products have few or no local materials to offer, ocean or air-freight costs are incurred on the inputs as well as on the outputs of the factory. Under favorable and unusual circumstances the combined transport costs may be less than those incurred by plants in continental locations, for example, the freight on some products from Puerto Rico to certain places on the United States mainland is less than from some alternative locations on the mainland. This is not common. Usually transport costs at the underdeveloped country locations are higher than at alternative plant locations within the country whose markets are to be served.

The effect of transportation cost is much like that of a tariff. Where it is high in relation to total value, for example, stone and clay products, some refrigerated products, and bulky products, the producer closest to the market in terms of freight cost has the most protection. Conversely, transportation costs are of negligible protection to producers of transistorized electronic equipment, jewelry, and many pharmaceutical products which can be transported around the world for a small fraction of their total value. Just as transport costs provide a natural protection to local market industries in a developing country, so do they also provide similar protection to industries in countries which might be the export-market targets for developing countries. For products which are of low transport cost in relation to value, the distance between a developing country and its potential overseas market is not important. Present transportation methods are in a state of development and change. New and more efficient methods of transport and handling are reducing transport costs for some kinds of products. Identification of export manufacturing product possibilities requires investigation of transport costs toward the developing country for materials and toward the export market for the finished products.

The cost of labor, not in terms of wage rates per hour, but in terms of labor cost in a unit of product, is a second variable which may provide a basis for identifying export possibilities. If because of special skills, labor in the country is more productive at one type of manufacturing than another, or if female labor offers a more favorable comparison with labor costs in other countries than male labor, these facts may indicate the kinds of export manufacturing most likely to succeed.

Many other elements of cost have to be taken into consideration. These include the cost of power, interest rates and exchange charges, living costs for foreign managers or technicians who will have to be given overseas allowances, the cost of training workers, the cost of factory space, and the costs of social welfare charges. They will vary from one location to another and will affect the total calculation made to select the best location to manufacture a specific product for a specified export market.

The total effect of comparative costs for a factory in an underdeveloped country which has to import its materials and export its product and for a factory located in the market country is shown by the following hypothetical calculation adapted from operating experience in Puerto Rico. This experience was that of profitable subsidiary plants of United States companies producing products for entry (duty-free) to the American market. Table 1 has been adapted to show the possible situation of a plant in a developing country which might export to the United States despite a tariff barrier.

This table shows the kind of relationship which may exist between costs at an overseas location and at a location within the country whose market is being served. In this example it is assumed that the export project as a new industry is tax-exempt during the period being examined and that the product would face a 25 per cent tariff barrier to get into the American market. This illustration assumes sufficiently low labor costs that the higher transport and other costs can be more than offset. This gain plus the tax exemption is enough to give the prospect of two and a half times the profitability of the location close to the market at the overseas location. A difference of some such magnitude may be necessary to interest a foreign investor in setting up an overseas branch operation to serve his established market at home.

Although the cost elements which go into the calculation to measure

Table 1

	Possible overseas location	Alternative location in United States
Material at source.....................	$20	$ 20
Transportation costs:		
Materials to factory................	2	1
Product to market.................	5	3
Labor costs.........................	10	44
Other costs.........................	15	12
Total operating costs.............	$52	$ 80
Taxes..............................	(exempt)	10
Operating costs plus taxes.............	$52	$ 90
Profits of factory....................	25	10
Costs plus taxes plus profits...........	$77	$100
Duty on product (25%)..............	19	...
Delivered cost to distributor in United States...............	$96	$100

the economics of alternative locations for an industry to serve an export market always exist, their amounts are subject to change. New and better transport facilities may reduce the cost of transporting goods. An example of this is the reduction of international air-cargo rates following the increasing availability of jet cargo planes. Another illustration is the development of bulk-handling equipment and methods which has lowered sea-transport costs sharply for many commodities. New methods of processing products may also have the same effect through reducing their weight or bulk or through making special handling unnecessary. The development of better and lighter packing materials, such as the solid foam packages now used for cameras and other fragile goods, has reduced transport costs and the damage-in-transit losses which are responsible for high insurance rates.

Many of these developments which lower transport costs and thus change the elements of international comparative cost calculations occur without any action on the part of the governments of developing countries. They are like sea- or air-rate reductions which are brought about by economies realized through handling larger volume. Sometimes transport costs can be brought down by the direct intervention of governments. They may be able to negotiate better sea or air rates, either in general or for specific products of industries which are being promoted. They may be able to reduce rates by encouraging competition or the threat of competition by negotiating for new service with shipping or air-transport lines. They may be able to use their power to give or withhold landing rights as a weapon to get better air service or rates which will reduce transport costs for new export industries. Sometimes a government may reduce transport costs by putting up better facilities for ships or planes, such as better docks to reduce turn-around time for ships, better material-handling equipment, or improved airport facilities.

What a government can do to change the comparative cost picture is not limited to action related to transport costs. The cost of putting a product into a foreign market in competition with goods made in that market country may involve a serious element of import duties. These are subject to negotiation to a degree which is not usually taken advantage of by governments of developing countries in furthering their industrial development programs. Despite the limitations arising out of GATT agreements on discriminatory restrictions on the imports of goods from another country, a country has many ways to apply pressure on other countries to secure more favorable entry for its products. Usually what is needed is an identification of what export products might be feasible so that negotiations of a selective nature may be directed toward opening up the market.

Within the developing country itself, the government can do a great deal to alter the figures which go into the calculations of comparative costs. If, from a national economic viewpoint, a certain industry is highly desirable, the government can do much to "sweeten up" the opportunity for the private investor so that he will conclude that the location is advantageous despite whatever negative features it may have. This may be accomplished by giving tax exemptions or other incentives, which will be described in detail in Chapters 12 to 14.

For many products one of the most important elements in the cost calculation is labor cost. Low wage rates combined with reasonably high productivity give many underdeveloped countries their great advantage in attracting export industries, especially those which depend on materials bought on world markets. Such industries often involve relatively low investment and can move easily, so they are referred to as "footloose industries." Whether a country wants such industries depends on its alternatives. If a country cannot do better, it may have no choice but to sell its labor at rates which are sufficiently low to offset the cost disadvantages which the location has in terms of transport costs and tariffs when the goods enter the export markets. The redeeming feature of "sweatshop industries" is that they may constitute, for some countries, the only way to get industrialization started on an economic basis; they may provide stepping stones for developing skills which will lead to industries which can reward labor better. One of the greatest successes of the Puerto Rican development program has been the upgrading of jobs away from the low-wage home industries of the garment trades and into better-paying work in electronics and metal fabricating. The same trend has taken place in Japan.

The emphasis given to factors affecting the calculation of costs of manufacturing a product in one location compared with another should not conceal the fact that there is another element in locational decision making which looms larger in many cases than transport and other costs. The overriding factor is often the investment climate and especially the economic and political stability of the country being considered as a possible location for either export or local market industry. This is more often of importance if it is negative than if it is positive. Private investors do not invest in industries in uneconomic locations just because they have good investment climates, unless the projects are subsidized enough to make them profitable. However, they will not invest in a country which has a bad investment climate even if the cost calculations are favorable. This is an area of psychological reaction rather than economic analysis, for the decision on whether the investment climate is to be considered a deterrent to investment in a good project is likely to rest more heavily on the feelings and impressions of a potential investor than on any calculable reality.

The Place of Industry in a Developing Economy

Anyone who has had anything to do with international industrial development realizes that industry is wanted by many countries for reasons other than the benefits it might bring by way of adding to the national income and thus raising the living standards of the people. It is wanted for reasons of national prestige and national pride. It is wanted to show the world and the people at home that manufacturing is not something which can be done only by those who have become rich by doing it in the past. Industry is also wanted because it is glamorous compared with other areas of economic development such as agriculture, mining, and fishing. It has come to represent a higher form of economic activity and thus to be regarded as something more worthy of pursuit by those who aspire to make progress. The relation of industrial development to other kinds of development warrants closer examination than it usually receives in determining the priorities and targets in development planning and investment. A more realistic balance between industrial and other areas of development would result in many countries in a greater amount of over-all economic progress and in a sounder industrial sector in the developing economy.

The dependence of industry on the progress of other productive sectors is illustrated by the one factor which is often the most serious limitation to the development of industries to serve the internal market: the small size of the local market. Even in developing countries with tens of millions of population, the level of purchasing power is so low that most products cannot be manufactured at anywhere near world cost levels because of the high cost of low-volume production. Creating large areas of high-cost industry which is maintained only because imports are excluded and the public is forced to subsidize local industry is hardly as sensible an answer to the dilemma as increasing the size of the local market to make local production more economic. The development of other sectors of the economy is the way to create markets for industrial goods.

There are few developing countries in which there are not opportunities to expand the purchasing power of the rural population to a dramatic extent by a proper emphasis on modern ways to improve agricultural production through the use of fertilizers and better seeds. Agricultural development specialists point out that a doubling of production on the farms is usually an attainable target within a few years. Not only is this the shortcut to higher national income and a better foreign exchange position in many countries, but also it is the way to create markets for industry. In some countries it is the development of the extractive industries—mining, forestry, and fishing—which offer the quickest route to economic gains and the creation of growing markets for industrial products. These may not be glamorous areas of development, nor those most in line with the dreams of individuals who see their new countries emerging from centuries in which the only economic activities were those of "the hewers of wood and the drawers of water." However, extractive industries may be the steppingstones to modern economies in which manufacturing industries can survive, not because they are subsidized, but because there are markets for their output.

The support which other areas of economic development can give to industrial growth is not limited to creating markets. The development of agriculture, mining, forestry, fishing, and other nonmanufacturing activities can pay the cost of industrialization, especially through providing the foreign exchange for the import of industry's capital equipment. These other developments can also pay the cost of developing the country's infrastructure—the power systems, the roads and railroads, and the other facilities which are basic to industrial development. Nonmanufacturing activities can do in most developing countries what they did in North America: provide the capital for industry. It should not be forgotten that although an inflow of foreign capital may be crucial for rapid industrialization, the bulk of the capital for industry in most countries will have to come in the long run from the country's own earnings and savings derived from the more traditional forms of economic production. The other productive sectors of the economy have another important role to play in supporting industrial development: the training of entrepreneurs and technicians for industry. To the extent that mining, forestry, fishing, and similar activities are organized on a business basis, they become training schools, and some of their graduates will move into the expanding industrial sector. The growth of the nonmanufacturing activities will also have a beneficial effect in modernizing and commercializing a country and will thus help to prepare the economy and its people for progress on all fronts.

The resource-based activities deserve special mention. A country which has valuable mineral, oil, or forest resources may possess the assets to trade for manufacturing industry, and the development and utilization of the natural resource may be regarded as the steppingstone to industry. This avenue of approach may be much more economic than the commonly followed course of neglecting the development of the resources while subsidizing "hothouse industry." A country such as Canada for example, with vast underdeveloped hydroelectric power potential may well profit handsomely by the export of power, either as power or as power-intensive products such as aluminum.

In what is apparently a different category we have the tourism business, which has great undeveloped potential in many underdeveloped countries. Although sometimes referred to as an industry, it differs greatly from manufacturing: its earnings are largely in foreign exchange, it consumes no natural resources, it is labor-intensive, and it offers a wide range of semiskilled employment opportunities. Not only does it support industrial development by distributing purchasing power, thus creating markets, but also it can perform a valuable service to industrial investment promotion by attracting potential investors to the country. The failure of a large majority of underdeveloped countries to exploit the opportunities of international tourism is one of the most striking of their failures to make the most of what they have. For some countries, such as Mexico, tourism is already the leading foreign-exchange earner. For many others, it could be.

The importance to industrialization of developments in other production sectors is such that a much closer coordination and integration of planning for the various parts of the economy is advisable than occurs in most countries. The objective should be to promote a growth of industry which is balanced in relation to the growth of other sectors. The rate and kind of industrial growth which is needed is that which will maximize the national income by producing more of an increase in the national income than the same investment devoted to the development of other productive sectors. Total investment for development which is properly balanced should at the same time create the kind of a base for industrial expansion which would not occur if investment were overly concentrated on the industrial sector before the rest of the economy was ready to supply the market for it. This observation applies mainly to industry for the home market. Export industry development is in a different category in that it is not dependent for its success on the growth of the domestic market. In this respect it is more similar to the development of the extractive industries, which can spur the growth of local markets to support a later growth of home industry market.

The interrelationships between the development of the various sectors of an economy can be visualized by observing the sequence of development phases which many countries go through. First, they are at the stage of subsistence agriculture with little international trade. Second, they enter the world markets gradually with raw materials or products extracted from their natural resources. This is usually the colonial phase, for the initiative and capital to develop the basic raw-material export trade has normally been supplied by colonial interests. This trade in fact constituted one of the basic reasons for having colonies. Third, the countries start to develop home-market industries which are limited by the low level of purchasing power. Fourth, the internal markets expand as a result of expansion in the raw-material-production sectors of the economy and in such supportive activities as tourism, and also as a result of the first phase of industrialization. In this stage the variety of products manufactured for the local market can increase because a larger market has gradually become available. By this time the economy is operating at considerably higher levels than hitherto; the industrial sector is more economic as it is supplying a market of better size. The industrial sector itself is of sufficient importance that it tends to become more nearly self-supporting through creating its own domestic markets as a result of the purchasing power it distributes.

The lesson to be learned from the growth experience of other countries as described above is that industry cannot do nearly as much to generate its own markets at the beginning of the process as it can later on. At first it must get its domestic markets from growth in other productive sectors of the economy. This is one reason why industry in most instances has to be subsidized in its earlier stages. Only when industry constitutes a major generator of purchasing power in the community can it be expected to stand alone with some independence from the other production sectors which supported and financed it at the beginning.

Infrastructure—Foundation for Industry

Industry depends on a foundation of common facilities which serve many industrial enterprises as well as the rest of the community. Together, these shared facilities are often referred to as the infrastructure of the economy. They include a wide variety of transport goods and services: roads with related bridges, ferries, and parking facilities; railway lines and associated equipment; airports and air navigation facilities; waterways, artificially made or improved, and docks with cargo-handling equipment. Infrastructure also includes electric power systems; water collection, purification, and distribution systems; sewers; and the communication network of postal, telegraph, and telephone systems.

Occasionally one finds an industry which has provided most of its own infrastructure. It may have its own electric power plant, its own radio links with associated operations, its own water supply from wells or other water sources, its own sewage-disposal system. An industry even may operate its own airline to provide access to its operating locations. Industries which go far in providing the infrastructure facilities they need are usually those which are large and which are far away from cities or other developed areas. Industries of this kind are exceptions and can be regarded as being almost outside the community. Most industries must depend on the economy of which they are a part to provide them with most, if not all, of the infrastructure they need. Sometimes, even in an industrial city, an industry may provide its own power supply by means of its own electric generating plant. This may be necessary to ensure continuous service, or it may be advisable to secure lower power costs. Some plants get the water they need from their own wells, even though they may be located in an area which has a public water supply. Some industries take care of their own waste disposal through private sewers discharging into rivers.

These examples of industries supplying some of the infrastructure items they need are exceptions to the general rule that industry must depend on the rest of the economy for most of the supporting facilities which are essential for the technical and business operation of a manufacturing enterprise. The provision of infrastructure is the responsibility of government. True, in some countries some of the services—power, telegraph, and telephone service; rail transport; city transit; bus, shipping, and airline services—are provided by private companies, usually operating under franchise from the government and subject to close supervision by government. In the developing countries privately owned and operated infrastructure facilities are the exception. The responsibility of government to provide the common services in transportation, power, and communications is generally recognized. In fact, the provision of infrastructure is widely regarded as the primary task of government in creating conditions which are conducive to the growth and development of industry and other productive sectors of the economy.

That the responsibility for infrastructure development is so universally placed on the government to the exclusion of private investment is not a matter of ideology. The World Bank, which makes most of its loans for infrastructure development, is a leading exponent of private enterprise; but it recognizes that much of the infrastructure development which must precede private development in industry and other sectors of the economy has to be made by government, or it will not be made at all. The Bank also emphasizes that the development of the infrastructure is an area where government investment and management is likely to be more successful than in the manufacturing field.

There are other practical reasons why the infrastructure should be developed under government auspices. The amount of investment needed to equip an underdeveloped country with the facilities it needs as a starting point for general development is enormous. In Nigeria, for example, planned investment by government in power, transport, and communications amounts to $770 million or 41 per cent of the 1962–1968 development plan.[4] In India, outlays in 1961–1964 (the first three years of the third Five-Year Plan) for these three infrastructure items totaled $3,404 million, or 39 per cent of government development expenditures.[5] These huge investments are slow to make because of the size of many individual projects and the amount of planning and construction involved. They are often even slower to produce noticeable economic results, for a developing economy cannot make full use of large new facilities all at once. They can become an effective part of the economy only gradually as other facilities, such as new factories, grow up to make use of them. Huge initial investments, long construction periods, and slowly developing markets would be enough to discourage private investment from undertaking most infrastructure projects even if government policy were to encourage private investments in this area. In most countries, infrastructure is also regarded as part of the public sector for the good reason that service facilities are generally monopolies by nature, and it would be difficult to prevent exploitation of the public if the enterprises were privately owned. The possibility of monopolistic overpricing is a more serious danger in the infrastructure field than in most parts of the economy because the productive sector depends upon the common services for its existence and development. Thus the growth of the economy could be strangled if the underlying services were overpriced.

Policy in regard to infrastructure development is a vital part of the over-all strategy for fostering economic growth. Most of the facilities have to be planned and built before they are needed. The services have to exist before anyone will be willing to invest in factories, mines, and other productive enterprises. This means that planning of the infra-

[4] Federation of Nigeria, Federal Ministry of Economic Development, *National Development Plan 1962–1968*, Lagos, 1962, p. 41.

[5] Government of India, Planning Commission, *The Third Plan Mid-term Appraisal*, New Delhi, 1963, p. 17.

structure facilities must come first; but it must be realistic, or vast amounts of scarce capital can be wasted in building facilities which are not needed. A country could be ruined for a generation by too much investment in infrastructure or by the wrong kinds of investment just as easily as its development could be frustrated through lack of enough investment of this kind. Fortunately, developing countries can obtain technical assistance in the planning of their highways and power systems and other services, and they can obtain financing of infrastructure projects from international organizations more easily than they can obtain funds for other purposes.

Planning of infrastructure investments to meet needs and yet avoid waste is one of the most difficult tasks faced by developing countries. It is easy to follow past tradition and put most of the investment in the kind of facilities which were popular in the past, even though alternative facilities might warrant a larger share of the investment if decisions were made purely on economic grounds. For example, India in its first three Five-Year Plans has neglected the development of highways and road transport even though road transport has proved its merits increasingly in the more developed countries. In other countries one can see a great waste of infrastructure investment due to a failure to coordinate planning. In Burma investments were made in railway, highway, airline, and river transport facilities all serving the same route, when better planning might have produced more integrated and thus more economical solutions of the transportation problem.

The development of the infrastructure is important to a growing economy for reasons other than the primary one of providing essential service facilities. The investment of huge sums in building highways, railways, dams, and the like, can do much to start a nation on the way to economic expansion. The employment generated by major projects in this area spreads purchasing power and creates new markets for manufactured goods. There is a multiplier effect which is expansionary, although also inflationary if not kept within bounds. Work on infrastructure projects has a widespread training value, for often the workers thus employed are receiving their first introduction to industrial-type employment and are in the process of becoming better entrants into the industrial labor market. The building of major infrastructure projects fits the early needs of a developing economy well in another way: it provides the means to mobilize idle or semi-idle labor and put it to productive use. As the unemployed are not producing, their labor is a resource which costs the economy little or nothing. They are being supported anyway. Their product is thus the creation of new wealth in the form of capital goods—one of the greatest needs of a poor country.

It is sometimes thought that the development of power, transport, and other facilities will in itself attract industry. This is largely an illusion.

While it is true that the lack of service facilities will often prevent industry from being established, it is rarely true that industry will come just because the facilities are available. Industry cannot do without the services and may not be able to provide them on its own. But rarely do the infrastructure items constitute a major part of the production costs of a manufacturing process. The availability of power and transportation and other things, even at unusually low costs, will rarely make the difference between feasibility or unfeasibility for a new industry. There are exceptions, it is true, such as aluminum refining and a few of the electrometallurgical and electrochemical industries, which can be attracted by very low cost power; but they are rare. More often the availability and cost of power, transport, and other facilities may lead an investor to choose one location rather than another. But this represents an attempt to find the most economic place for a project rather than a readiness to set up in business merely because facilities are available. After all, the same facilities exist widely throughout the world, so their availability in a developing country is hardly a novelty to any prospective investor.

4

The Role of Various Kinds
of Industry

Local Market Industries

The majority of countries starting on the road to industrial development place most of their hopes on the encouragement of industries to
produce goods for the domestic market. This is only natural for many
reasons. Above all, the market for the proposed product is known to
exist. The market can be reserved for the new local industry by the
simple expedient of prohibiting imports or by making them subject to a
high tariff. The profitability of the enterprise can be assured by setting
up levels of protection which force consumers, if they are to obtain the
product at all, to subsidize the firm sufficiently to cover any and all
inefficiencies and still leave a profit margin.

Local market industries may use local raw materials as well as labor.
Their local content may thus represent a substantial amount of the value
of the product. Foreign exchange may be saved even if the materials
or parts have to be imported, for they will usually cost less than the
finished product would cost if imported. Like any other industries, they
should provide a considerable amount of industrial training of a practical sort, and this should include management training.

The disadvantages of local market industries as a basis for an industrial development program are numerous. The fact that they can be
insulated from the price and quality competition of imported goods frequently means that they will start as and remain inefficient, high-cost
producers. More often than not the quality of their product will be in-

ferior to world standards; but the consumer, being unable to obtain the imported item, will be faced with a "take-it-or-leave-it" alternative. Without the pressure of effective competition from low-cost producers of high-quality products, the management of local market industries is likely to remain inefficient for lack of any real pressure which would force it to become efficient or go out of business. Only if protection is kept to low levels and imports are permitted will the local manufacturer feel the healthy pressure of international competition. If more than one firm in the country produces the same products, then, of course, there may or may not be effective competition from within the country which might serve to keep the manufacturers on their toes.

In most underdeveloped countries where the market is small because of the small population of the market unit or the low purchasing power, real competition is not likely to exist in most manufacturing lines. Local market industries may therefore tend to be exploitive. They may survive with high profitability to the owners but only because the power of the state has been used to deliver unto them a captive clientele which must subsidize them whether it wishes to or not. This may mean that tens of thousands of people must pay an extra dollar or two for every shirt or pair of shoes they buy in order to provide employment for a hundred workers in the new factory and to enable the owner to profit from his investment. The inequity of this kind of industrial development often contributes to social and political unrest, which is not surprising in a situation where the many are taken advantage of for the benefit of the few. Market growth is the urgent necessity in many lines if there is ever to be enough volume for an economic scale of manufacturing, but this is often retarded by the high prices which are charged for locally made products. In a South American country which prides itself on the large amount of local market industry which has been developed, I noticed that locally made shirts were priced at about double the prices charged in other countries for the same internationally known brand. When I asked a storekeeper about the saleability of shirts at such high prices, he made this interesting observation: "Before we had our own shirt factories, shirts were cheap and everyone bought them. Now we make our own shirts and the prices are so high that only the rich people can buy them."

Even more serious from a development viewpoint is that when a country acquires a moderate amount of high-cost local market industry which has been sheltered from international price and quality competition, the country's very success in developing this kind of industry will be an obstacle to developing more efficient industries. The owners of the sheltered industries will oppose incentives or any action which might attract new industry. New investors might provide competition in existing lines of production; in any event they would tend to push wage levels up. Sheltered industrialists who are profiting well in their limited but

securely protected preserves tend to become pressure groups for policies of economic isolation. They fear that their positions of wealth and
power will be destroyed if their countries enter into such expansionary
economic moves as common markets or investment import arrangements.
These developments could bring to local industries new opportunities
for export markets and capital for modernization and expansion, but to
many local firms such a prospect is frightening because they lack the
confidence to operate outside of their sheltered environment. More often
than not they are not expansionist in viewpoint anyway as they are
usually owned by a family or a small group which has little motivation
to take risks in the hope of increasing earnings. The industrial sector
in an economy should be the most dynamic sector and should lead the
rest of the economy continually to higher levels. This is what happens
in the advanced countries. An industrial sector based on the local market
as it now exists in many underdeveloped countries, especially the smaller
ones, is likely to become as undynamic and fearful of progress as an
agricultural sector based upon ownership of great estates by an aris-
tocracy.

Inward-looking local market industry suffers from another serious
shortcoming as a basis for industrial development: in any except the
larger of the developing countries, the development of industry for the
local market can only go so far and then it falters when it runs out of
markets. A boom of industrial development may occur up to that point,
but the time soon comes when import substitution has been carried
close to its logical conclusion. At that point everything which could be
made for the local market, even with considerable inefficiencies due to
small-scale production, is being made. The boom will then end, unless
industry can be developed for the unlimited export market. Thereafter,
local market industry can expect at best to grow only at about the same
rate as the national income of the country. In this situation, industry cannot lead the economy to new high levels of growth.

With all these actual or potential disadvantages, does it make sense
to give local market industry any place of importance in an industrial
development drive? The answer depends entirely on the size of the
local market. If the country under consideration is as small as Curaçao
or Barbados or Dahomey, the number of worthwhile opportunities to
manufacture for the local market will be very small. If they can be developed as special cases without the spreading illusion that a large number of sheltered industries should be encouraged, something may be
gained. If the country at hand is as large as India or Brazil, obviously
a very wide range of products should be able to be manufactured for
the home market without having to accept high-cost production as inevitable. The medium-sized developing countries such as Peru, Nigeria,
and Malaysia lie somewhere in between. They have many opportunities

for economic manufacturing for the local market. On the other hand, they should avoid placing their development hopes exclusively on local market industries because to do so would create conditions likely to stand in the way of developing a much larger industrial sector in which many industries produce for export.

Like so many questions in the industrial development field, the question of whether to encourage local market industries does not warrant either a "yes" or a "no" answer. In every country, even the smallest, there are some products which should be made locally because they can be made at costs which are not seriously out of line. There may be opportunities based on the economies of bulk transport, industries producing goods or services which are local in nature, industries whose operation on a small scale is not seriously uneconomic, and industries protected against import competition by high transportation costs. The attitude of industrial development people to local market industry should be that such potential opportunities should be studied carefully to determine what products used in the country could be made on the scale required at costs which would be competitive or nearly so when compared with imported products valued on a c.i.f. basis at a realistic rate of exchange. Calculations made on this basis take into account the cost of transportation if the item is to be imported, and it is proper to do so as this is one form of natural protection which is unavoidable and which can provide the economic justification for many local market industries.

How can a country reap the advantages of developing some industries for the local market while avoiding the danger that they will become a barrier to the development of larger-scale industries for export? The first rule is to give tariff protection or other forms of protection from import competition only in respect to those products whose manufacture in the country has been analyzed as to probable production costs and for which costs are considered likely to be close—say within 10 or 15 per cent—of the c.i.f. costs of the products if imported. For products on the list of approved industries for local manufacture, adequate protection should be assured, but not without some conditions. One condition might be that protection or import exclusion would continue only if the locally made product were priced at not exceeding a specified small margin over international levels for c.i.f. delivery in the country. The level of protection itself can also be used to keep local manufacturers in line on pricing. This would be done by limiting protective tariffs to a moderate level which would offer a reasonable incentive to local manufacturers, and take into account any overvaluation in the local currency, while not making the industry so excessively profitable that an injustice would be done to the public. In using tariffs to encourage sound local market industry, the tariff classes used should not be so broad as to encourage the local manufacture of other products which could not be produced at reasonable costs. Protection given on the basis of "infant-industry" needs should be temporary in duration. These and other tariff methods will be described more fully in Chapter 13. The provision of any kind of import restriction in favor of a local market manufacturer should be subject to some type of quality control designed to press him to meet international quality standards. Control might be assured by making protection or other incentives subject to cancellation if quality standards specified in advance are not met and maintained.

Export Market Industries

Export industries, though often more difficult to start because it is not as easy to give them incentives comparable to those given import substitution industries, have very great advantages to an economy and therefore generally deserve highest priority in industrial development programs. The fact that export industries are continually exposed to world competition ensures that if they are to survive, they must be efficient. They must also meet world quality standards. These are difficult conditions, but valuable insurance against the economy's being called on to subsidize uneconomic industries indefinitely. The fact that earnings of export manufacturing industries are in foreign exchange is particularly important, for it creates foreign exchange availabilities needed for the import of other goods which could only be made in the country at excessive cost. Another great virtue of export manufacturing is that the world offers a market of vast size for almost any kind of production that is competitive in price and quality. This creates an opportunity to build industries to their optimum economic size, which is usually much larger than could be justified for the local market alone. The cost savings which are derived in many industries from larger size not only enable the enterprise to be competitive in world markets, but also enable the firm to produce more cheaply for the local market and thus encourage its growth.

The encouragement of export industries is of crucial importance in the strategy of industrial development because only export industries can be accelerators of development. That is, they can grow faster than the rest of the economy and thus can generate purchasing power which will make possible increased production of goods and services for the local market and also increased imports. This economic effect is in direct contrast to what happens if a country depends on import-substituting local market industry. Local market industry may grow rapidly only up to the point where all feasible opportunities to substitute for imports have been developed. From that point onwards, the local market industries can only grow as national income and purchasing power grow. They are then following the development of the economy, not leading it as export industries can.

Export industries are usually based on sound economic advantages, in contrast to local market industries which often are highly uneconomic and which survive because of heavy subsidies, usually in the form of tariff protection or prohibition of the import of competitive products. Export industries generally base their success on the availability of inputs such as labor, materials, or fuel at costs lower than those in competitive countries, on transport savings, on tariff advantages in certain markets, or on superior skills of management or labor.

The absence of raw materials in a country should never be taken as a basis for rejecting the possibility of export industries. Some of the countries which have been most successful as exporters of manufactured goods have always imported much of their raw material: England, Switzerland, and Japan are examples. Puerto Rico has built a thriving export industry with nearly 1,000 plants producing for overseas markets, and it has done so almost entirely on imported material and parts. Sometimes a country which imports parts or materials for manufacturing may be in a better position to develop an export market for the finished products than the country where the material or parts have originated. For instance, a country which is associated with the European Common Market may find that it can buy material and parts from low-cost sources, such as Japan, process the items into finished products, and export them duty-free into a market which has high barriers against finished products from the country used as a source of materials. In other cases, wages may be sufficiently lower in an underdeveloped country so that it can export its products to attractive markets in spite of tariff barriers. Jamaica, for example, has twenty-five factories making products which are successfully exported to the United States, despite tariffs of 25 per cent or more on many of the items.

When a country approaches industrial development by emphasizing export industries, it has taken a psychologically important step: it has decided to make its way as part of the international industrial community. The world can be its markets, both for selling and for buying what it needs with the proceeds of its export earnings. It must meet world standards of quality and price on what it sells, but it gains on a far wider range of goods by buying them at world prices. Within the country, development based on export industries brings about a very different environment from that created by development based on the economic isolationism of protected local market industry. Export manufacturers have much less reason to oppose the development of competitive plants, for the world market is virtually unlimited. Furthermore, export manufacturers are used to competition and know that it should be dealt with by improved efficiency, not by eliminating it through political lobbying.

The development of export industries is of such importance that much of this book deals with means to foster them. Incentives may play an especially important part in the rapid development of export industries for they provide ways to make a country more suitable, in a commercial profitability sense, than it would otherwise be for this kind of manufacturing. In some cases outright subsidization of export industries may be warranted. In many fields a degree of quality supervision may be necessary, as it was for Japan, in setting and maintaining high standards so the products of the country can develop and hold important export markets.

Raw-materials-based Industries

In starting to think about the various kinds of industry which might be suitable for a developing country in order to create an industrial development program which is suited to reality, it is useful to think of industry as belonging to two basic groups—one based on natural raw materials and the other based on the use of processed or semifinished materials. This is not exactly the same as the division of industry into heavy and light industry, though most of the raw-materials-based industries would be classed as heavy industries and most of the next-stage industries, sometimes called the fabricating industries, would be classed as light industries. Another term, basic industries, describes the raw-materials-based industries well, for they are basic in the sense that they are the starting point in the industrial process: they turn a natural material into material ready for making an intermediate or final product.

Manufacturing must start from raw materials which can be classified, in the simplest way, as being of animal, vegetable, or mineral origin. Without manufacturing, the uses of the natural raw materials in their original state are quite few. Apart from some materials of vegetable and animal origin which can be eaten raw or which can be processed in a simple way by cleaning, or peeling, or cooking, most materials have to go through a series of manufacturing stages to be of full use. As an aid to thinking about industrial opportunities industry can be divided according to the stages of manufacture: basic, intermediate, and final. In some industries these stages take place in different plants at separate locations; in others two or even all three stages are integrated in a plant which starts with a natural raw material and ends with the product in a form directly usable by the final consumer. An example of this degree of integration is the sugar industry, which often starts by crushing the sugar cane and ends with refined sugar packaged for the individual customer. Likewise, some dairy-product plants start with raw milk, pasteurize it, and make ice cream or canned milk for sale to the public. A tobacco factory may take the leaf tobacco and manufacture packaged cigarettes. Food-processing plants often start with the the fruit or vegetable or fish and end with the product in cans or packages for retail sale. This degree of integration is common in industries where the processing steps are relatively simple or few. In most industries integration is less advantageous, and the plant which starts with the basic raw material usually produces a semifinished or intermediate product which then goes to another factory to be made into final products. Sometimes several stages exist beyond the basic manufacturing plant. Examples of this kind of nonintegration are found in the metals industry. A basic plant will make steel from iron ore; the steel will then go to a metal fabricating plant, which may make either a final product or parts which go to an assembly industry or some other final product manufacturing plant. Likewise, a sawmill will make lumber from trees, but the lumber may go to a furniture factory to be made into the final product. In Chapter 6 illustrations will be given of how new industrial opportunities can be discovered at the various stages.

Raw-materials-based industries are obviously of great importance in the development of any country which has the materials or which can create them economically. If a country has minerals of any kind, or petroleum, or natural gas, these may be the basis for major industrialization. If a country does not have the materials of animal or vegetable origin, these may be grown, if conditions are right. Usually supplementary materials and/or fuel are needed along with the basic raw material; but if these are not available, it may be economic to import them. Occasionally the existence of low-cost fuel or energy may make it feasible to import the basic raw material. The refining of bauxite, the natural raw material, into alumina and then its manufacture into aluminum at locations far removed from the source of the basic material is economic at some locations simply because of very low-cost power.

Most of the raw-materials-based industries have characteristics which distinguish them from industries in the later stages of manufacturing. They are generally large because they have great economies of scale. Conventional steel plants, cement plants, pulp mills, and oil refineries are in this category. There are some material-based industries, however, which do not have such great economies of scale, for example, food-processing plants and brick and ceramic plants. Those in the large-scale class, the heavy industries, are usually capital-intensive, requiring large investment but giving relatively little employment. This is not to say that their employment benefits are negligible. There are places, in fact, such as Curaçao and Aruba in the Netherlands Antilles, where employment depends mainly on capital-intensive oil refineries. In situations such as these where the local market is extremely small, capital-intensive industries, if feasible, may represent the industry of greatest employment potential. In the heavy type of material-based industries the trend is clearly toward more automatic processes which steadily reduce employment opportunities. Since material-based industries of the heavy kind are large, they require markets larger than those that exist in many developing countries and often must be export-oriented. Some products, such as cement, are heavy enough in relation to value that transportation costs provide a substantial natural protection to a plant serving a medium-sized local market. For products such as bricks and tiles, plant sizes may be smaller; but product weight compared with value is high, so the same kind of protection occurs and makes local market production more promising.

For the local market, raw-materials-based industries are logical if, because of locally available materials or other advantages, costs will be competitive with the c.i.f. cost of imported products, after due allowance for any overvaluation of the local currency. This is a matter for feasibility study calculation. If the material-based industry is feasible, the country can save foreign exchange, use a material which is often otherwise wasted, and gain some employment. Unfortunately, in many of the smaller countries material-based industries of the heavy type are likely to be monopolies because there will not be room for a second one serving the same small market. The disadvantages of creating a monopoly are great enough that they should be given much weight in determining whether protection or any kind of subsidy is to be given to such an enterprise. Sometimes the economic benefits will be so great that they will warrant encouraging a monopoly; though if they are great, the need for protection or subsidy should be less.

The greatest opportunities which the heavy kind of raw-materials-based industries offers for developing countries occur when the country has some natural advantage. This may be a combination of low-cost materials, fuel, labor, and transport costs which makes the place competitive as a location for manufacturing the product for export. Where such a situation exists, the opportunity should be developed to the largest feasible scale as it can be the accelerator for other types of development. Sometimes the addition of special incentives for heavy industries of the export type may make a location commercially feasible and the developing country can gain the benefits of doing the processing instead of it being done overseas.

Whether a country should seek to develop raw-materials-based industries depends entirely on the calculation of feasibility in each case. There should be no preconceived preference for basic industries or heavy industries merely because by definition they are the starting point of more elaborate types of fabrication. The products of the heavy-materials-based industries are international, with well-established standards and markets throughout the world. Anyone can buy the products of this kind of industry and would be foolish not to do so unless it would be more economic to produce them locally. While world industry could not get along without such products, this does not suggest that every country should seek to produce its own, even if it has some of the raw materials. Nor is there any reason to feel that basic industries are more suitable than light industries for a country starting on the road to industrialization. More often than not, the raw-materials-based industries, if they are of the heavy variety, are less suited to a developing country because they are more often capital-intensive with a minimum of employment and training benefits.

Secondary Manufacturing Industries

I am going to refer to industries which start with a processed or semi-finished or intermediate material as secondary manufacturing industries to distinguish them from the industries which have natural raw materials as their inputs. These industries are often called light industries, for they are generally less capital-intensive and usually produce lighter products than the heavy-material-based industries. Some of the secondary manufacturing industries, however, are anything but light in terms of either their capital requirements or the weight of their products. Examples of this type are the industries which manufacture vehicles, trucks, and massive earth-moving equipment. More typical of the secondary group are plants which make shoes from leather produced elsewhere, plants which make furniture from lumber processed in a sawmill, plants which make garments from cloth produced in an integrated mill from basic fibers, and factories which make household electrical appliances from sheet metal and wires purchased from others.

Secondary industries have quite different characteristics from most material-based industries, particularly from those of the heavy type. Most secondary industries are not capital-intensive; in fact, many of them are among the most labor-intensive industries and are thus especially suitable for most developing countries which have surplus labor and little capital. Many light industries make particularly good use of workers with skills in hand operations. For this reason light industries often employ more women than men, which may be a good or a bad thing depending on the labor supply and demand situation in a country. Light industries can be technologically simple or complex, but usually they do not tend to be as automated as heavy industries. Many light industries do not have the great economies of scale which are normal for heavy industries, and thus they may more often be economic when scaled down to the size of the market available in a small country. Many light industries can produce for export markets, for often labor content is high and products are light in relation to value. Light industries often provide a good training school for large numbers of unskilled workers without previous industrial experience. Since light industries generally buy their materials or parts, they are particularly appropriate for a country which does not have basic industrial raw materials. In other words, a light industry which buys its parts or materials on the world market could be located anywhere. The preferred location may be the place which has lowest labor costs per unit of output, which has duty-free entry into a major market, and which offers highly attractive tax and other incentives.

Light industries can be of various kinds: Some involve assembly of parts or components made by others; some are based on mixing various ingredients purchased from others; some merely break down a bulk product and repackage it with little or no processing; some take a material or ingredient and add final stages of processing or fabrication. Assembly industries may purchase all their parts and components from others, but often they are integrated to the extent that they make some of the parts in their own plants. Mixing plants may merely mix, but sometimes they add a stage to the processing, and usually they break bulk items down into smaller units for the retail trade. Repackagers may merely break down bulk shipments, but they may also do something to the material. For example, a pharmaceutical plant may import some drugs in final manufactured form but may also make pills out of powdered drugs which are imported in bulk.

Some of the most successful industrial development programs have been based on secondary industries—the Puerto Rican program is a notable example. The island has virtually no industrial material. The whole program which made the island a manufacturing economy had to be based on the import of material. Most of Hong Kong's rapid industrial growth has also been based on light industries using low-cost labor effectively. The bulk of the industrial opportunities for most underdeveloped countries is to be found in the field of secondary industry because this is the area which has the greatest number of industries and products, it is the kind of industry which meets the employment objectives of most developing countries the best, and does not have to be based on the natural advantage of having the raw materials.

Small Industry

There has probably been more sentimental nonsense written and talked about small industry as a key to industrial development than about any other aspect of the subject. This is not surprising, for the very idea of the poor but enterprising indigenous industrialist rising to success and leading his country to industrialization is warmly appealing to all who look upon economic development as the progress of people to a better life and preferably a more democratic one. To be against such an approach would be akin to being against progress or democracy itself. The very strength of the appeal of the small-industry approach makes it important to appraise what it really means and what part it should have in a country's industrial development efforts. Properly defined and realistically approached, the small-industry field is important and can contribute much to the whole process of industrialization. If confused by sentimentalism and approached emotionally with little regard for the costs and benefits involved, small industry development can easily become a missionary movement which accomplishes little but which diverts scarce resources of development funds and people away from other activities which, in most situations, could produce much more industrial growth.

The term "small industry" is much too broad and must be broken down if it is to have any useful meaning in discussing the place of various kinds of industry in an industrial development program. Small industry in itself indicates only that few workers are employed in each establishment. Even this is misleading: in some countries only industries employing less than ten workers are put in the small category, while in other countries industries with a hundred workers or more are called small industries. Nor is the problem merely one of size; it is also one of kind. There are primitive small industries and modern small industries. There are small manufacturing industries and small service industries. There are small industries distinguished by the high artistic quality of their traditional products, and there are small industries making products having poor style and little quality.

A large part of the existing small industry sector in the less developed countries, such as those in Africa, is of a primitive and subsistence nature serving an underdeveloped and very poor local market. Much that is called small industry is not manufacturing at all but consists of service trades, mostly repairing of shoes, clothes, buildings, and vehicles. This is not to suggest that provision of local services is unimportant. It is highly important, but it is not industrial development. Most of the remainder of the small-industry field in the very underdeveloped countries consists of establishments with few workers, ranging from businesses employing only the owner up to those having a few dozen employees, some of whom are often referred to as apprentices. One survey in Nigeria, for example, revealed that the average number of workers in the establishments classified as small industries was 3.7, and a high proportion of these were learners who received little or no pay.

The small manufacturing industries under conditions as underdeveloped as I am describing generally make low-cost and low-quality articles under primitive conditions for the local markets. Products usually include household utensils (often made from discarded cans), pottery products from local clay, handwoven cloth, furniture, footwear, and garments. These products can be sold in local markets to very poor people provided they are cheaper than mass-produced goods from local or foreign factories. Occasionally small industry under primitive conditions makes handicraft products, sometimes based on traditional patterns, which are distinctive enough in quality or style that they have real artistic merit.

What role does small industry of this kind have in a program for industrializing a country? Usually very little. Small industries producing cheap products for local markets exist only because their overheads are practically nil and because their owners and workers are prepared to work for subsistence wages through lack of any other economic alternative, except possibly subsistence agriculture. This kind of industry, in fact, is really an adjunct to subsistence agriculture, providing minor advantages through division of labor. If, through a technical assistance program, it were possible to modernize industries of this kind by loans for machinery and proper buildings, their costs, with the addition of interest and depreciation, would often become so high that they could not sell their products in competition with factory-made goods. A changeover to modern industrial conditions would thus eliminate the firms because they would be taking on some of the major cost burdens of modern industry without the advantages of scale to pay for them. Another problem is that a great percentage of the owners and workers of the primitive small industries lack both the motivation and the education needed to take advantage of technical assistance efforts which would attempt to bring them the benefits of cost accounting, market surveys, inventory control, and other sophisticated techniques of modern industry.

The unpromising prospects for remaking traditional village small industry into a real part of a country's industrialization effort is particularly tragic when contrasted with the hopes usually associated with industry of this kind. As it gives employment to large numbers, the decline of this kind of industry adds to unemployment problems at the very time when more job opportunities are needed. It is only natural that politicians grasp at small industry development as an answer to social and economic problems and the political difficulties associated with them. To hold out the hope that the fostering of small industries existing under preindustrial development conditions is a promising approach to solving rural and village unemployment, the "school leaver problem," or that it constitutes a good way to provide steppingstones to industrialization may be cruelly misleading.

The difficulty in retraining and developing the owners and workers of village small industries so that they may become modern and efficient and move on to larger industrial efforts is too great, in most instances, to constitute an effective use of industrial development resources. The problem is similar to that experienced in the highly industrialized countries when they attempt to solve the problems of unemployment caused by automation by retraining the workers for other jobs. Occasionally such efforts are successful; more often it has been found that those who need the retraining most are those who are older and who lack the education and the motivation for training for the more sophisticated skills in demand. The difficulty is also exemplified by the fact that few large and modern industries starting in underdeveloped countries want to hire middle-aged or older workers who have worked in handicraft or small industry, even in the same line of work. It has repeatedly been found that a modern industry will get much better results by training young workers who have had no previous manufacturing experience. This is not to say that nothing should be done to help the small industry personnel who may be losing their way of life through being unable to meet the competition of goods from modern factories. In most cases, relief of some kind is needed, but it should be recognized as social welfare help and not regarded as a road to industrial development.

In this generally bleak field of primitive small industries are there any bright spots which could be used to advantage in an industrial development program? The answer is definitely yes. If the small industry sector includes the manufacture of quality handicraft articles which have sufficient artistic value, it is possible that a combination of quality improvement and quality control may result in volume production which could be marketed. Usually the products which have such possibilities are modernized, semi-mass-production versions of traditional handicrafts firmly rooted in the history and culture of the people. In this class one thinks of the lacquer ware of Japan and Taiwan, the wood carvings of Bali, the wooden bowls of Haiti, the brass work of the Middle East, the hand-loomed silks of India and Thailand, the bronze and niello ware of Thailand, and the reed and cane work done in many countries. These are products which can be sold in large quantities to tourists and which can be exported. A country needs to have an objective evaluation made of its handicraft products and skills to determine whether it has the basis for developing quality, design, and volume and for attempting to develop markets. One country which has done an outstanding job in this field is Taiwan, whose Handicraft Center has provided guidance to handicraft shops in improving designs and quality, in standardizing products, and in finding markets. Not only does the country have an attractive display center for sales to visitors, but also it has developed a substantial export business both through trade channels and through published catalogues from which private individuals can purchase by mail. Another country which has made great progress in this field is India, whose Cottage Industry Emporium in New Delhi is one of the world's largest and finest displays of handicraft products. One only needs to observe the pitiful displays in the gift shops of most international airports to realize that the development of attractive local handicrafts and effective handicraft marketing organizations is one of the great unexplored opportunities for many countries.

Apart from the field of artistic handicraft industries, there are developing countries with small-industry sectors quite different from the situations previously described. India is a leading example of a country with a large and growing small-industry sector which offers much potential for further growth. What distinguishes the Indian situation from the Nigerian? India has its primitive village industries too, but they are not what I am talking about when I refer to small industry in India. In India the term refers to industries with from 10 to 100 employees. Many of them are fairly modern factory operations with a sizable amount of mechanical equipment. Above all, in a country like India, they are likely to have entrepreneurs rather than semiskilled production workers in charge. Under such conditions, in India or elsewhere, small industry can be further modernized and assisted to use the techniques of modern industry, such as the tools of financial management and cost controls. For small industry to be developable certain conditions must exist, as they do in India, Taiwan, and Argentina, three places where the situation is drastically different from most African countries. The prerequisites for real development in the small industry sector include (1) the existence of industrial entrepreneurs with ambition and leadership qualities, strong motivation to modernize and grow, and sufficient education and technical skills to make use of technical assistance; (2) the existence of a market which can support prices adequate to cover the costs of factory-type industry and to allow a sufficient margin for profits and wages attractive enough to interest investors, entrepreneurs, and workers of some enterprise and capability; (3) the existence of a market which is sufficiently protected, at least initially, from extremely low-cost imported goods which otherwise come in at prices which perhaps do not cover the total costs of production including overheads. Given these three conditions in any significant part of the small industry sector, we have an entirely different situation from that which exists among primitive village industries, which are often classed together under the misleading omnibus title of small industry.

It is industries of this kind that I am talking about when I speak of the role of modern small industry, and no doubt much can be done to help such industries grow in number and size. They can be given loans for more modern and more productive machinery. They can be given technical assistance ranging all the way from feasibility studies and assistance in factory layout to help in setting up cost-accounting and inventory-control systems. They can be shown market opportunities by making market surveys. They can be assisted to form joint marketing arrangements so that markets may be opened up which require much larger volume of output than any one small industry can provide. Even export markets may be opened up, as they have for Indian shoes and Thai silk, by organizations which buy the products of a large number of small industries who produce to rigid design and quality standards. Many of the development suggestions throughout this book have some application to small, locally owned industries which meet the three conditions mentioned above.

Locally Owned Industries

In a different class from the traditional small industries and the handicraft industries, there are modern, factory-type, locally owned industries of various sizes which also have to be distinguished from the larger industries having foreign collaboration or ownership participation. They may be of a wide range of sizes depending mainly on the country's level of development. In most African countries they are few and tend to be small. In places like India or Taiwan or many of the Latin American countries, the modern local industries are numerous and often of substantial size. They should be considered separately from the local industries which are not modern and which are not likely to become modern and also from those firms whose technical and management strength is mainly of foreign origin and which still have ties to foreign firms which are important to their progress. In calling the industries in this group "modern," I do not mean that they are technically and managerially advanced, but merely that they are sufficiently more modern than the traditional small industries of an underdeveloped country that the difference becomes one of kind. They may have poor equipment, unsatisfactory production methods, no preventive maintenance, weak quality control, inadequate accounting, and unaggressive marketing methods. In spite of all this, to fit this category an industrial enterprise would have a factory-type of production operation as distinct from an artisan operation and would have management with entrepreneurial capabilities and ambitions. In other words, the enterprise would have potentialities for further modernization and expansion.

In the more industrialized developing countries where locally owned and operated industries of this kind exist, these enterprises may form a large part of the country's industry. Such have usually been the creation of an outstanding individual or a small group of such enterprising people. Often the one who started the business was an ambitious individual who combined management talent with technical capacity. He has often been an engineer educated abroad who has maintained foreign technical and business connections. Most firms of this kind are still run by the individual who founded them or by one of his sons. They tend to be family businesses, rarely being big enough for incorporation and public sale of shares.

Locally owned industries which fit this category are often not as progressive and enlightened as one might think in view of their founders' enterprise and ability. In Peru, for example, a survey revealed that within many local industries there were common attitudes which had an adverse effect on the growth of markets and thus on the industry as a whole. There was a preoccupation with the local market and a noticeable lack of thinking about export possibilities. There was the commonly held opinion that the government had an obligation to make almost any local manufacturing enterprise profitable by tariff protection regardless of its efficiency or the quality of its product. Within their protected markets many of the local industries operated, as is customary in most underdeveloped countries, on the low-volume, high-margin principle. Most of the firms commented upon were family-owned; in some cases the owners were content to keep the operations small even though real opportunities were neglected, for growth would carry with it the prospect of loss of control. These characteristics are, of course, worldwide in local industries of medium size.

In Argentina a study of the problems of locally owned industry revealed a similar situation on a much larger scale with large numbers of local industries operating behind some of the highest tariff barriers in the world. The Arthur D. Little report contained comments on the industries examined which are useful in pointing a way to remedial action: [1]

> A serious cause of the inefficiency of much of Argentina's medium and smaller industrial enterprises is the very small size of most of the enterprises. . . . In 1954, 92.5% of all industrial establishments had 25 workers or less. . . . A five, ten, or fifteen man enterprise is less likely to have trained or really competent management than a hundred man establishment. It is generally run by its owner, either alone or with his relatives; rarely have they had any training or even the kind of experience needed to produce high quality management. The very small firms seldom have good accounting systems, let alone cost accounting and financial control systems. Quality is usually of small concern because of lack of interest in it and lack of facilities to make quality control possible. Very few of the small firms have any idea of market analysis or market development. . . . The very small enterprises generally lack financial resources and the possibility of obtaining adequate financing, even when modernization and expansion are desirable. Few of the small firms do anything to train their workers in an organized way, as many of the large firms do; nor is this

[1] Arthur D. Little, Inc., *Industrial Development in Argentina*, Cambridge, Mass., 1961, p. 98.

condition surprising, for usually the heads of the small firms have no training themselves and consequently do not appreciate its importance. . . . Underlying most of the problems of Argentine industry are a whole complex of attitudes that discourage enterprise, distort objectives, limit growth, prevent public approval of private business, reduce the effectiveness of labor, and generally limit the productivity of industry. . . . The old fashioned attitudes on the management side are much more prevalent in the small firms than in the larger ones, in the older firms than in the newer ones, and in the family type of business than in those enterprises which are more widely held. . . . The high-price, low-volume attitude of many industrialists simply excludes the majority of the population from being potential customers. . . . They are less willing [than those in more industrialized countries] to trust either those in their own industry or those with whom their industry must deal. . . . This attitude costs much. . . . It is an obstacle to any organized programs of productivity improvement, which often require free access of both trainers and trainees to many plants in an industry. A large percentage of the medium-sized and small firms are owned by an individual, a family, or a small group of close friends. Frequently it appears they would rather keep their enterprises small and inefficient than share the ownership and control with others in order to obtain the capital needed to enlarge or modernize them.

These problems, which characterize much of the locally owned industry of Argentina and of many other countries at a middle stage of development, are an important warning to countries which are now at a much earlier stage of industrial growth. Locally owned industries established by an enterprising individual or a small group of enterprising associates are, in many ways, the most desirable kind of industries for a country to acquire. Some of the problems and foreign exchange costs of foreign-owned industry are avoided. Full opportunity is given for local nationals to have access to top positions in the companies. Whether locally owned industries will bring with them a minimum or a maximum of problems of the kind described above depends in large part on government policies, which can encourage or eliminate competition on quality and price and which can facilitate or discourage expansion and modernization. The rest will depend on the innate attitudes and character of the businessmen themselves. If they are modern, progressive, and enlightened, they will welcome competition and seek ways to improve efficiency, expand markets, and add to productive capacity. Upon their attitudes will depend not only their individual success, but also in many countries the future prospects for privately owned industry.

Aside from general industrial policies which are conducive to developing a healthy kind of industrial growth, and these are described throughout this book, there is much of a specific nature which can be done to further the modernization and growth of locally owned industries if both their potentialities and hazards are well recognized. One thing is to encourage and help locally owned industries to get foreign technical collaboration if they are industries in which quality control, product design, production techniques, and access to research are especially important. To foster connections with technically outstanding foreign firms, a government might require such arrangements as a prerequisite for granting tax or other incentives, sites or subsidies for new industries, manufacturing licenses, or low-cost financing. Government may give special assistance to new industries which will support or assist other industries by providing parts or intermediate materials or services. The government may also assist locally owned industries in financing sound projects for expansion and modernization, give tariff protection (in moderation, it is hoped, to avoid the development of hothouse attitudes), identify opportunities for diversification, make feasibility studies, and help the firms obtain outside financial or technical participation.

Foreign-owned Industries

In almost all developing countries, industries which are at least partly foreign-owned have an extremely important role to play in leading the way to modern industry. As stressed elsewhere in this book, industrial development is mainly a process of transferring industrial equipment and know-how from industrialized countries to nonindustrialized ones. In this process, the industry which has foreign financial participation and which often originates on the initiative of a foreign company is crucial. It is hoped that most industrial enterprises established in developing countries by internationally minded companies will eventually become part of the local scene both through an increased amount of local ownership as local capital becomes more readily available and through an increased role for nationals in the management as more local people develop the necessary qualifications. This is the pattern of a large percentage of industrial ventures which are established outside the home countries of the sponsoring firms.

Industries which start through the initiative of a major foreign company and retain a close link with it are in an immeasurably stronger position in regard to acquiring the latest and best in technology and management than those with purely local sponsorship. The foreign firm which has invested its money and its reputation in an overseas operation cannot afford not to help the new enterprise until it reaches a high level of efficiency and produces a product of sufficient quality to do credit to the international brand name it carries. This interest is bound to be continued as long as the parent company has a significant financial involvement in the operation and as long as the product carries the firm's brand name. This means continued access to vast research and development facilities which could not be warranted for the use of one small plant alone. It also means that highly specialized experts are available on short notice to come and help the new plant find the solutions to technical and management problems as they arise.

The foreign firm which fathers a new industry in a developing country has also taken on the role of teacher and trainer, for its success depends mainly upon how well it can train and develop local nationals as personnel for the new company, at all levels from semiskilled workers to top-management staff. Sometimes developing countries write elaborate conditions about training local personnel into their approvals for foreign sponsored industries. Generally they are unnecessary. The companies have a strong financial motivation to train local staff as rapidly as possible to fill all or practically all positions, for by so doing they can reduce personnel costs and also protect the quality of their local image. When foreign companies fail to train and develop local staff rapidly, it is often because of short-sighted limitations which the government has placed upon the numbers of foreign technicians who can be brought in. In the field of technical training, few technical schools can equal the training results obtained in a good foreign-owned industrial plant. The training provided by the new foreign-owned industry is usually a major justification for giving tax and other incentive benefits to attract the new industry.

Foreign-sponsored new industries have other notable features which distinguish them from locally owned industries in most countries. They usually offer better pay to their staff at all levels. They need good staff and are willing to pay well to get and keep the most capable people. Often local industries object to the high-pay policies of the foreign firms, for these policies may raise the general level of wages in a community. While this may help local markets to grow, it may reduce the profitability of established firms. The foreign-owned industries often introduce to a country new and modern concepts of labor relations, such as advancement on the basis of performance rather than seniority or personal connection.

The role of the foreign-connected enterprise, which is usually of large size in the country, is frequently important in providing a market for the products and services of smaller, locally owned enterprises. Many large foreign companies prefer to purchase a wide range of parts and other materials outside rather than make them in their own plant. The initial absence of suppliers of many items may be a factor which discourages a big foreign firm from coming in; but once it does, it often shows considerable initiative in developing local sources of supply. This may involve, as it did for the Kaiser automobile company when it went to Argentina, the need to work closely with hundreds of small firms to help them develop the capability to make the needed parts of the quality required. It is not too much to say that one of the best ways to foster locally owned small and medium-sized industry is to bring in a major plant of a kind which buys large numbers of parts. By thus creating a market for the local industries, they are in a position to grow if they have the inherent capability and motivation. Without such a market many potentially successful enterprises will get nowhere.

In contemplating the role of foreign-connected industries, one must give proper weight, but not too much weight, to some features which may be negative. The foreign-owned plant may involve a substantial foreign exchange drain, especially if it is 100 per cent foreign-owned and highly profitable. (If it is too profitable for the country's good, this probably indicates that it has too much tariff protection and that some competition would be a good thing from a national viewpoint.) Apart from the repatriation of profits, there will also be foreign exchange costs due to license or royalty agreements, technical assistance fees, and salaries of foreign personnel who come to work at the new industry. If the management is slow to replace foreign staff with qualified local personnel, political problems may be generated. If the new industry has a monopoly position, it may be tempted to overprice its products, just as any firm in such a position may do if it is allowed by the government to get away with it.

PART 2

Industrial Development
Functions and Methods

5

Improving the Industrial
Investment Climate

Almost every developing country has inherent negative features which limit or discourage industrial development. These may be that the market is limited in size, the workers lack industrial skills, capital is scarce, industrial materials are few, and so on. However, the most serious obstacles to rapid industrial growth in many countries are not the physical shortcomings due to limited natural resources or even human underdevelopment due to past poverty. The major barriers to industrialization are usually environmental conditions which are man-made and which can be readily changed for the better by a government which is able to give top priority to creating favorable conditions for economic progress. The conditions within which an industry must operate in a country are often referred to as its industrial investment climate. Action to improve this climate is a logical starting point for any country which embarks on a comprehensive industrial development program. This approach has several advantages: The investment climate is something that can be improved quickly, assuming that the general situation is not too negative to start with. The investment climate can be improved with little expenditure. And the improvement which is brought about in the investment climate will do much to attract the attention of those whose capital and industrial knowledge are needed if the country is to develop rapidly.

A country's investment climate is the result of a combination of many factors, some of which are negative and some of which are positive. Some of the factors are psychological, such as the attitude of the government toward private investment and toward foreign investors. Others are matters of laws, for instance, involving taxes and tariffs, based on historical development. Others are indications of a country's desire to attract industrial investment, such as the offering of grants or other forms of assistance as incentives for new industry. Taken together, these factors create conditions which either attract foreign industrialists or repel them. Nor is the effect limited to the foreign investor. Local residents with capital are equally affected in their investment decisions by considerations of the investment climate. Like foreign investors, they do not have to invest in industry, nor in their own country. In any country which has potentially attractive industrial opportunities, the industrial investment climate is the governing factor which determines whether investment will come forward to develop the opportunities. If the investment climate is bad, the opportunities for new industries will not be taken up, no matter how much the country needs development. If the climate is good, the chances are excellent that sound opportunities can be financed and that new industries will be put into operation. Through improvement of the industrial climate almost any country seeking industrial development can better its prospects and frequently may even surpass other countries which may have richer resources and more opportunities but which neglect to create the right conditions for industrial growth. The industrial climate is so bad in the majority of the underdeveloped countries that any country which makes the necessary effort to establish an excellent climate is putting itself in the forefront to attract a lion's share of the industrial investment and experience which are available internationally.

The prevailing attitudes and feelings in the country in which an industry operates and into which a new industry has to be lured are more important in making a good investment climate than the actual laws and regulations in effect. In some countries there is a prevailing attitude of understanding; in others the general attitude is one of suspicion. In some there is cooperation; in others, hostility, or at least indifference. In some countries the officials are accessible; in others, unapproachable. In some, they are honest; in others, corrupt. In the last analysis the investment climate is a reflection of the people. If they are nationalistic in an unreasonable way, the climate is bound to be bad for foreigners. If they are dogmatically opposed to private business, the climate will not attract private investors. To get foreign industrial investment and know-how, a country has to want it and show that it wants it. In order to attract the kind of industries that every country needs—those that will be "good citizens" of their adopted country—the country must create conditions which will attract constructive investment. To get honest and likable partners in the venture of industrial development, a country must be honest and likable itself. These intangibles of atmosphere are not created by laws, although the laws will reflect the attitudes and feelings which prevail. These matters of attitude become known to the outsider mainly through contact with a small number of government officials and political leaders. It is up to them to show to the potential industrialist that the feeling of the country toward new industry is friendly, open, honest, and cooperative.

The political and economic stability of the country and the prospects of future stability constitute another element of the industrial investment climate, although one not quite as susceptible to short-term improvement as many of the other factors. It can almost be said that as a rule, foreign industrial funds and experience will not enter a country unless there is a reasonable degree of stability and confidence on the part of the potential investors that it will continue for ten years or more. In recent years the list of countries which have lost for some time to come the opportunity to attract new industry simply because of their deteriorating political and economic conditions has grown very long indeed. The challenge to responsible statesmen in many underdeveloped countries today is whether they can convince their people and their political parties that political strife and instability will destroy any country's opportunity to develop and that a choice must be made between political ends and economic development goals. It is no accident of history that industrial expansion in Puerto Rico dates from the creation of a constructive political environment through the original election of the Populares Party in 1944 or that India's considerable achievements in development have their roots in the political stability which the Congress Party provided. If there is one condition one should wish for any underdeveloped country, it is that it should have a good government. With a good government, the climate for development will be created. Without a good government, there is little hope for progress.

Stability as a basis for industrial development should not be taken to mean stagnation, nor the suppression of needed change. When I speak of political stability, I mean freedom from political disorder, from riots or other civil disturbances. I mean continuous maintenance of law and order, justice through the legal system, and the orderly and peaceful succession of one government after another. I mean an environment in which opposition is allowed to express itself through peaceful and constitutional channels and not through subversion or violence. Within the framework of political stability there is room for reforms, even drastic ones at times. Industrial development is a form of change in a society. Along with it must come many other changes, such as land reforms, labor legislation, opportunities for women, and the development of more contacts with foreigners. A society with the right climate for industrial growth will make changes such as these with some speed and without undue disruption of political or social stability.

The creation of a sound climate for industrial growth depends much more on deeds than on words, whether they be words of law or words of politicians. A country's reputation in the world, like an individual's, is built slowly over a period of years; but it can be destroyed in an instant. It is built through years of political temperance, restraint, adherence to fair and honorable practices, maintenance of law and order, reasonable dealings with private business both local and foreign, and avoidance of erratic behavior. A country's business reputation requires a record of international financial responsibility and the strict honoring of its obligations. A single careless and politically motivated act of arbitrary nationalization without prompt and fair settlement can deprive a country of the prospect of large-scale industrial development for a generation. No amount of reassuring words can erase the international effect of one bad move. In a country's day-to-day relations with industry, deeds also predominate. Many countries have favorable incentives on the law books. But if inefficient or corrupt administration of the incentives laws prevents their benefits from being received by new industries, the word soon gets around, and investors may regard the country in a worse light than if the incentive legislation did not exist. What counts in attracting industry is the reality of the investment climate, not the appearance which is created by laws or speeches.

Some of the most important elements which make up the industrial investment climate are listed in Table 2. They are restricted to those elements which are subject to improvement by any government which is really serious about attracting more industry. The group of factors shown as incentives are of such importance that they will be dealt with in Part 3 of this book. The remainder of this chapter will discuss approaches and policies for improving the industrial climate.

New Attitudes Needed for Industrial Development

The more one works in the field of industrial development, the more obvious it becomes that in most underdeveloped countries the most serious limitations on industrial growth are set by the prevalent attitudes toward industry, especially new industry, and toward private business, particularly foreign private business. Even in countries where legislation and official policy pronouncements show a recognition of the importance of attracting new industry, there are all too often underlying negative attitudes which cancel out the efforts to create a good climate for industrial progress. The harmful attitudes are not limited to any one group —frequently they are held in varying forms by industrialists, by labor, by the general public, and by the politicians who reflect and sometimes stir up the feelings of the general public. Some of these attitudes may best be illustrated by drawing on comments made in two recent surveys

Table 2. Checklist of Some Important Investment Climate Factors

General environment:
  Honesty and efficiency in the government
  Political and economic stability
  Friendly attitude toward local and foreign private investment
  Policy of no nationalization of manufacturing industries
  Constructive attitudes on the part of local industrialists and labor
  Policy of no state industries competing with private industries

Incentives:
  Tax exemption
  Grants or other special assistance
  Tariff protection
  Exemption from import duty of capital goods
  Exemption from import duty on materials and parts
  Training for workers
  Land and/or buildings for factories
  Consulting-type technical assistance
  Tax exemption for temporary foreign staff
  Funds of minority equity participation or low-cost loans

Favorable conditions:
  Moderate level of taxation on companies and individuals
  Protection against dumping
  No restrictions on conversion or remittance abroad of capital or earnings
  Easy entry for temporary foreign technical and management staff
  No price controls on product
  No onerous labor legislation
  Guarantees against adverse changes in taxes or tariffs for specified period

of industrial development problems. The first examples are from Peru, which has a better-than-average industrial investment climate.[1]

Traditional attitudes in Peru in regard to industry present a whole series of problems. We refer to the attitudes of capital, labor, and consumers—which today are barriers to increased investment in industry, which limit the size and growth of markets, which restrict labor mobility and productivity, and which limit public acceptance of locally made goods. The origins of the attitudes are clear, and the reasons for most of them understandable, but taken together they constitute an environment which seriously slows down the rate of industrial development.

The traditional Peruvian attitude of people with capital toward industry is a negative element. . . . Private capital generally avoids industry altogether, preferring investment in commerce, mining, agricultural land, or urban real estate. This is due to unfamiliarity with industry, and a feeling that industrial investment involves greater risks and lower profits. It is also due to tax discrimination against returns on industrial investment as compared to real estate.

When an investment is made in industry it is too often with the inten-

[1] Arthur D. Little, Inc., *A Program for the Industrial and Regional Development of Peru*, Cambridge, Mass., 1960, pp. 10–11.

tion of quickly withdrawing most of the profits instead of plowing them back for expansion, an action which would probably be highly profitable over a longer period.

Peruvian investments which are made in industry are generally made as investments . . . by small, family type groups of friends, relatives or close business associates. . . . The family type of industrial company is of course seriously limited in its ability to attract capital, and frequently in its ability to secure modern management and technology. Sometimes the owners of this kind of company are content to keep the operations small, even though this means neglecting real opportunities to grow, for fear of losing control. Only when the companies go beyond the inherent limitations of the closely held firm are they able, in most industries, to realize their growth potential.

Within local industrial companies we note traditional policies which are typical of industrially underdeveloped countries which have a very adverse effect on the growth of markets and thus industry. There is a preoccupation with the local market as being the important target, and a noticeable lack of thinking about export possibilities. This viewpoint is related to the commonly held opinion that the Government has an obligation to make almost any local manufacturing enterprise profitable by tariff protection regardless of its efficiency or the quality of the product. Often because of lack of capital, management, or technical know-how, a local manufacturer fails to develop the efficiency to make quality products competitive in outside markets, and exists by over-charging the local consumers because of excessive tariff protection. . . .

In pricing policies, another example of detrimental tradition may be seen. . . . Both manufacturing and distribution in Peru operate on the low volume, high-profit margin principle. This is a vicious circle in which prices and profit margins are high because of the low volume of sales, and the volume of sales is low in part because of high prices. It was in breaking through this circle and developing larger markets through lower prices that the industrialized countries established the basis for modern industry and for a more acceptable distribution of its products. We believe that Peru has reached the point where profitable opportunities exist in manufacturing and distribution for enterprising people who are prepared to break through to larger volume operations by cutting unit profit margins enough to open up new and wider levels of markets among people who can and will buy things at lower prices.

The lack of pressure in overprotected industries to produce goods whose quality is equal to that of imports, along with the natural problems of improving the quality of items being produced for the first time in Peru, has resulted in enough poor-quality merchandise to spoil the reputation generally for products bearing the Industria Peruana label. . . . We believe that sooner or later the Government must protect the consumer and also help to improve the reputation of Peruvian products by action to deny tariff protection or tax concessions to producers which fail to meet reasonable quality standards.

The negative attitude to competition which is prevalent in Peru is another disturbing element. . . . In cases where only one local plant is feasible, we believe the public should be protected and efficiency and quality production in the local plant encouraged by permitting, without prohibitive tariffs, the importation of competitive foreign goods. Whenever practical, the Government, through its development organization, should attempt to introduce competition into local industry by attracting additional producers whenever the existing manufacturer cannot meet the demands of the public as to quantity and quality of product. Naturally such a policy will not be popular with local industrialists who wish to maintain a monopoly position, but we believe that the wider objectives of protecting the public, and at the same time promoting rapid industrial development, require the injection of more competition into the economy.

Detrimental attitudes are by no means limited to capital and the consuming public; labor is also involved. In its very understandable efforts to get some employment security in an economy where there are not enough jobs to go around, labor has severely restricted the growth of new employment opportunities by making it so difficult to discharge workers who are not needed that employers have a natural reluctance to hire additional workers when they need them. They have made it almost impossible to improve manufacturing productivity by installing more efficient labor saving machinery. . . .

The pressure of labor to secure "fringe" or supplementary benefits—holidays, vacations, paid sick leave, termination pay, and pension rights—has been carried to the point where the cost of these benefits to the employer is often over 50% of direct cash wage costs. This is one of the most extreme situations of this kind in the world, and one which has a highly adverse effect of reducing the rate of industrial development, because market growth is held back through lack of cash purchasing power in the hands of employed people. Instead of having more cash, which they would spend immediately and thus create larger markets, too much of their earnings are deferred.

The attitudes of capital and labor in Peru which have been described are typical of what one finds in one form or another in most underdeveloped countries. In some countries negative and restrictive attitudes have gone much further and have cast a black cloud over all prospects of development. Such a country is Argentina, once one of the most promising nations in the world for economic development. Some of the attitudes found in Argentina, which may serve as a warning to other countries, have been described in this way: [2]

Underlying most of the problems of Argentine industry are a whole complex of attitudes that discourage enterprise, distort objectives, limit growth, prevent public approval of private business, reduce the effectiveness of labor, and generally limit the productivity of industry. These negative attitudes are mainly held by industrialists, but labor also has

[2] Arthur D. Little, Inc., *Industrial Development in Argentina*, Cambridge, Mass., 1961, pp. 101–104.

negative attitudes that constitute barriers to rationalizing industry. The old-fashioned attitudes on the management side are much more prevalent in the small firms than in the larger ones, in the older firms than in the newer ones, and in the family type of business than in those enterprises which are more widely held. . . .

The high-price, low-volume attitude of many industrialists simply excludes the majority of the population from being potential customers.

An attitude which is common . . . is the belief that any industrialist has the right to high tariff protection regardless of the price of his product, its quality, or the fundamental economics of producing it in the country. This belief has been fostered by Government policies of restricting imports for reasons of foreign exchange shortage and nationalism, but it has now become so imbedded in the thinking of Argentine industrialists that many seem to regard a high level of protection to be a natural right. . . .

Throughout our investigations we were repeatedly told of instances of other aspects of a lack of public consciousness on the part of many industrialists. There is apparently a tendency . . . to adulterate products, to reduce quality, to sell goods of lower quality than advertised, and to generally seek short-term profits by taking advantage of the consumer. That such practices are common indicates anti-social viewpoints on the part of some industrialists; it indicates, too, that there may not be enough competition for the public to have a choice of products of honest quality. . . .

Attitudes of management toward labor also leave much to be desired in many industries. We found few enterprises, especially smaller ones, in which any serious efforts are being made to train or upgrade labor. We heard of few examples of industrial firms sharing their generally high profits with labor, or of giving their workers any part in the increased capitalization which is arising in many companies due to high profit levels (thanks to high protection) and to high retentions of profits in the business.

Most Argentine industrialists appear to be more inclined to secrecy than are their counterparts in most of the more developed countries. They are less willing to trust either those in their own industry or those with whom their industry must deal. There is a common feeling that each firm has its secrets which must be kept from others, even if, in fact, it has no real secrets. This attitude costs much more than any value it may have. It discourages and limits the sharing of know-how about production and marketing which can be usefully interchanged by firms in the same line of manufacturing. It reduces the value of the industrial camaras which, if a free exchange of information existed, could do much to improve the technical and management level of their members. It is an obstacle to any organized programs of productivity improvement, which often require free access of both trainers and trainees to many plants in an industry.

A large percentage of the medium-sized and small firms are owned by an individual, a family, or a small group of close friends. Frequently it appears they would rather keep their enterprises small and inefficient than share the ownership and control with others in order to obtain the capital needed to enlarge or modernize. . . .

The attitudes of many labor people must also be faced as a negative element in the development of industry . . . some Argentine unions reportedly stand in the way of efforts that will modernize plants by the introduction of more efficient labor saving machinery. . . . Unions in Argentina are also credited with having much to do with the narrowing of the difference in wages between the unskilled workers and the skilled. In some industries this has reached a point where there is no incentive to workers for them to upgrade themselves by investing the time and money needed to develop a skill. At a time such as this, when the country is desperately short of skilled workers, any attitude which denies enough incentive to workers for them to upgrade themselves runs strongly counter to the needs of the economy, and thus in the long run, counter to the needs of the workers for increased production.

How to Develop an Action Program to Improve the Industrial Climate

The sad state of the industrial investment climate in many countries is a subject for endless discussion, but the talk will be of no value unless it leads to action to improve the situation. Fortunately the investment climate is something which can be improved rather quickly and economically if the will to do so results in an orderly program of action, supported at the highest levels in government. An action program to improve the industrial investment climate should contain the following elements and should be implemented in about the same order as the points are described:

1. Survey to identify the problems. The negative features of the industrial climate vary from country to country in their degree of seriousness as obstacles to industrialization. What is needed first is a realistic identification of the problems and an evaluation of their relative importance. The survey is not a task for library or statistical research; it must be done by interviews in depth with a wide range of knowledgeable people who have had direct experience with the problems of starting or operating an industry in the country. Usually such people will talk frankly on the subject if they are convinced that a sincere effort is being made to eliminate the problems and to create more favorable conditions for industry. In the survey attempts should be made to learn in detail of the experiences of the majority of industrialists who have started new industries in the past few years. They should be questioned about difficulties they may have had in obtaining the necessary government approvals, incentives, and special concessions, such as tariff protection or import-duty relief, and on their views as to the adequacy of the incentives and assistance available to new industries. They should be asked to identify all the things which could be done to make it easier or less risky for investors to set up new industries. The survey should not be limited to those who have actually succeeded in getting new or expanded industries going. It is even more important to seek the opinions of those who had considered the possibility of starting new industries and for one reason or another gave up their projects. Interviews with actual and once-prospective investors should be supplemented by discussions with government officials, bankers, and others familiar with the problems of both new and old businesses. The survey should also include a thorough examination of the mechanics of applying for concessions and other forms of assistance from the government to determine what delays are involved and how valid the complaints against the system really are.

2. *Preparation of the plan.* The survey will reveal a number of major bottlenecks and other obstacles which are serious barriers to industrial investment either through discouraging potential investors for one reason or another or through not offering sufficient inducements to attract investors to all feasible projects. The next step is to prepare a plan of action to remedy the situation. For each negative feature which is to be attacked, one or more practical courses of remedial action should be developed. Some problems will require legislation, some will need simplification of administrative policies, some will depend on initiating new activities of assistance to new industry, and some will require educational or publicity campaigns. There may be problems which must be attacked on all these fronts, but for the solution of each major problem specific action steps must be developed in detail.

3. *Approval of the plan.* The survey and the plan will not result in any improvement in the investment climate unless the plan has the approval of government at the highest level, for support will be needed for legislation, for budgets for new activities, for directives to government agencies and for appropriate policy statements. The plan may have to be "sold" to the President or the Prime Minister. The success of the entire effort to improve the climate will depend on his being convinced that it is an important key to development and that his personal involvement is warranted to get results in the face of opposition, which is certain to develop from various ministries and their officials as well as from private individuals who feel their position is threatened. Moreover, the chief executive, more than anyone, has the capability to carry the message to the public as it must be done if industrial development is to be made into a national campaign and if the right public attitudes toward industry are to be created.

4. *Legislative and administrative action.* Many of the points of action will require legislation and/or administrative policy changes to alter tax and tariff rates or regulations, to modify immigration restrictions, to reform restrictive labor or social legislation, and to streamline customs practices in regard to imports. Budget allocations will be needed if land or industrial parks are to be made available for new industry, if training programs are to be financed, and if technical assistance of various kinds is to be offered to prospective industrialists. Often those surveying the investment climate cannot merely rest with recommendations that something be done on these matters. It may be desirable for them to draft the necessary legislation and administrative orders so that implementation of the changes can follow quickly upon high-level approval. Legislation may also be needed to give guarantees for the protection of foreign investors. These guarantees might give assurance against nationalization of the new industry for a specified period of time and promise fair compensation in the event of expropriation at a later date; they might assure convertibility of capital or earnings of approved new industries under specified terms; they might provide that necessary technical and management personnel would be granted entry for temporary residence; and they might provide that no changes in tax or tariffs would be made to affect adversely an approved new industry for a specified time. There is considerable difference of opinion as to the value of such investment guarantees. While the passage of such laws does indicate the prevailing attitude of the existing government, there can be no assurance that a future government would necessarily honor the guarantees. There is also some feeling that a government which has to advertise its good intentions may not be as reliable as one which has earned its good reputation by deeds over a period of time.

5. *Education and publicity support.* Changes in the industrial investment climate are basically dependent on changes in beliefs and attitudes toward a variety of questions. Legislation and administrative action can only follow changes of attitude in these matters. An essential part of the investment climate improvement effort is therefore a mobilization of the forces which can educate and influence people to adopt more progressive attitudes toward industry and thus to welcome the changes which need to be made. The range of people who must be influenced is wide—all the way from ministers of the government and opposition political leaders to industrialists, labor union leaders and members, and the general public. The leadership in the educational campaign must come from the highest officials in the government, and they should be supported in this effort by those who lead opinion in business and labor. The creation of an industrial development atmosphere requires wide interest in the promise and the problems of industry. Industrial development must be made a popular subject of discussion by a barrage of speeches and newspaper and magazine articles which generate enthusiasm for the subject. Efforts to popularize industrial development and thus to lay the foundation for acceptance of changes in the investment conditions should not

be limited to one political or economic group in the community. Industrial development should be made a nonpartisan national objective, a crusade to improve the country and the position and the prospects of all its people. Toward this end the support of leaders of all political groups should be sought, as well as of those influential in other fields in the community. The formation of an industrial development advisory committee of leading citizens representing all viewpoints may be a valuable device for publicizing industrial development as a national goal and educating the people to its requirements. The Puerto Rico Plan contained these comments and suggestions on the problem: [3]

> It is not enough that an understanding of industrialization be accomplished among the leaders of the community and Government. It is desirable that this filter far back into the general population. There are two important reasons for this: (a) that the citizens as voters may participate most intelligently in the support of sound industrialization activities, and (b) that the citizens, as workers, may better understand their own individual responsibilities within the industrial community and on the job.
>
> This program should certainly include substantial efforts in the schools and the setting up of local discussions of productivity problems among the service clubs and other local forums. Discussions should be encouraged on such questions as "What creates jobs?", "What factors set limits to the earnings of industrial workers?", "How does the availability of machinery and other capital equipment affect the earnings of workers and the ability of an enterprise to compete?". Industrial firms, plant visits, product exhibits, and other educational tools should be used.

[3] Arthur D. Little, Inc., *Report on Ten-year Industrial Plan for Puerto Rico*, Cambridge, Mass., 1951, reprinted 1961, available from AID, Washington, p. 60.

6

Identifying Industrial Opportunities

It is a well-recognized fact that one of the greatest barriers to industrial development in most underdeveloped countries is the lack of industrial entrepreneurs—men who can see a potential industrial opportunity, who can measure its soundness, who can put together a project in a way which can attract financing, and who can do all the many things necessary to get a new industry into operation. In a highly developed society, private businessmen are continually looking for new industrial opportunities, and rarely is a really good possibility neglected for long. Many companies have highly qualified technical and business experts on their staff who conduct never-ending searches for diversification opportunities which would enable their company to expand into new and profitable manufacturing projects. Many of the leading American companies engage technical and scientific consulting organizations to make diversification studies, which are technical-economic explorations aimed at discovering new manufacturing opportunities for the client company. Out of all this effort, new project ideas keep coming up which warrant more detailed feasibility analysis. Some of the industrial opportunities thus brought to light turn out to be sufficiently promising that the interested companies go ahead and build the production facilities. Soon the economy has a new product being manufactured or expanded capacity to produce something already on the market.

In a very underdeveloped country, this private searching for new industrial opportunities does not take place; or if it does, it is on a very limited scale. As a result, good industrial possibilities may go unnoticed and undeveloped indefinitely. This is not surprising. Not only does an underdeveloped country lack industrial entrepreneurs with the initiative, the motivation, and the capital to discover and develop new industries, but also it lacks people with enough business and technical knowledge of most industries to recognize specific possibilities and test their feasibility. Those who have a knowledge of one industry are often too busy with it to look further afield for opportunities in other industries, and the American custom of engaging consultants to look for diversification opportunities has not yet been introduced. The absence of continual and intensive searching for new industrial projects by established industrial firms is particularly serious, for they should be the innovators in an economy because of their industrial and business experience. The inability of private businessmen in most underdeveloped countries to discover new industrial project opportunities is even more marked among those who have capital and wish to consider entering industry for their first venture.

The failure of anyone to make the explorations needed to find new industrial opportunities is one of the most serious shortcomings of the industrial development situation in many countries, because the first discovery of industrial possibilities is the starting point for the whole chain of technical and economic studies and the subsequent financing and management arrangements which must take place before a new industry can be established successfully. If the first link of the long chain is never forged, the rest will never come into existence, and the potential industry will never be committed and put into operation.

Supplying the missing link of industrial opportunity identification is one of the most important functions which the industrial development organization of any country can undertake. It is also one of the simplest, cheapest, and quickest things which can be done when it has been decided to embark on a comprehensive industrial development program. Moreover, it is an effort which can be undertaken with the prospect of a good deal of cooperation from existing businesses and industries, for in effect what is done in this field is to provide them with free consulting service in finding profitable investment opportunities. Even absence of qualified staff in the industrial development agency able to undertake a systematic search for opportunities need not stand in the way of starting this important work, for this is an area where experienced outside experts can be called upon to apply their knowledge of industry to identify the projects which are worth further examination and promotion.

The identification of industrial opportunities is an endeavor which can benefit from a well-organized and systematic approach more than most activities. Without a clearly defined way of doing the job, the task is not likely to be done well, and important opportunities may be missed. In this chapter I shall describe a systematic way of screening all possibilities which may be worth listing for further investigation. I shall also discuss specific approaches to various types of industry.

Selecting Promising Kinds of Industry

Before attempting to list possible products, some broad strategy analyses should be made in order to focus attention on the kind of industries and the sectors of industry which are worth examining closely. First, it is important to identify the factors (existing or potential) which might give the country an economic advantage in some kind of manufacturing. Some of the most important factors which might exist are the following:

1. Good investment climate
2. Favorable tax and other incentives
3. Good factory sites and/or buildings
4. Sizable local market
5. Low-cost but capable labor
6. Labor and/or management skills
7. Low-cost raw materials
8. Low-cost fuel or power
9. Duty-free or preferential entry to important markets
10. Low transport costs to potential export markets
11. Low transport costs for raw material from nearby sources

No country will rate high on all of these factors; but a country with any development future is likely to rate sufficiently high on a number of points to give strong clues as to what kinds of industry are the most promising to examine. It should be noticed that some of these factors, especially the first three, are things a country can do a good deal about to improve its position. Others are things a country can do less about. If they do not exist, or cannot be created, the government must look to other factors to gain a competitive advantage for industry.

A study of the country's strengths or weaknesses in regard to the factors listed above should eliminate some kinds of industrial development possibilities and should strongly suggest others. For example, if the country has a large internal market, local market industries need to be emphasized. On the other hand, if the country is very small and there is practically no local market, it is clear that attention must be focused on export industry opportunities. If the country has only high-cost power, then heavy power-consuming industries can be disregarded without further study. The availability of low-cost power, either existing or potential, will attract attention to possible opportunities among power-consuming industries. Duty-free or preferential entry to important markets such as the European Common Market, the United States market, or the British Commonwealth market, opens up a significant area of possibilities. Convenient access and low transport costs to major export markets will suggest one kind of opportunity. Long distance and high transport costs will indicate the need to think mainly of high-value, light products to minimize the transport cost disadvantage. Proximity to sources of raw materials in nearby countries may suggest whole groups of possibilities worth looking into.

Another way of focusing attention on groups of industrial possibilities which may warrant special attention is to give thought to types of industry such as these:

1. Expansion of existing industry. If firms are already manufacturing goods, some of the best opportunities for industrial growth may be in modernizing and expanding production of the same items. Cost reductions may make exports possible for what were purely local market products. Sometimes competitors to old firms are desirable.

2. Diversification of existing industry. If a country has various industries already, many opportunities may be found for them to diversify into related products. This offers a minimum of risk because of the demonstrated experience of the existing firms.

3. Manufacturing for the local market. If there is a substantial local market for any product, its manufacture may be economic if there is a favorable combination of material and labor costs.

4. Upgrading of exports. If raw materials are shipped abroad in volume, a whole group of possibilities may exist in processing them to either intermediate or final products.

5. Manufacturing products for export. If a country has low-cost labor, good labor and management skills, good investment climate and incentives, and free or preferential access to a major market, it may have many opportunities to export manufactured goods, even if some or all the materials or parts have to be imported.

6. Adding value to imports. It may be possible to establish industries which will enable the country to gain significant value added by importing parts or semifinished goods for assembly or finishing rather than importing the fully finished products.

Systematic Research for Specific Industrial Opportunities

Having decided after a good deal of analysis and thought which types of industry are likely to be most promising on the basis of the factors which give the country definite advantages in industry, the foundation is laid to build up the system for identifying specific products which might be manufactured. The word "product" must be emphasized. Industrial opportunities should be thought of and dealt with in terms of the individual products which could be made, rather than in terms of broad types of industry. This is part of the process of being specific rather than general in approaching industrial development. For example, one should think of an opportunity to make radios or even portable transistor radios, not an opportunity to create an electrical products industry or even an electronics industry. In practice, an opportunity to make portable transistor radios might well be combined with an opportunity to make television sets and record players in the same electronics factory; but much will be gained in developing useful information if the opportunities are broken down to the final product for purposes of investigation. This is a way to avoid generalizations which have little value in attracting industry. It is also a way to avoid prejudging what opportunities should be combined in a single investment project. One investor might want one combination of products to be made in the same plant, another might prefer a different mixture.

Screening for industrial opportunities is a process of elimination. The starting point is the whole range of products which are manufactured anywhere in the world. Nobody knows how many such products exist, for the number would depend on how finely a product is defined. One could classify radios as a product; or one could define some or all of the following kinds of radios as separate products: transistor radios, tube radios, portable radios, short-wave radios, all-wave radios, frequency-modulation radios, amateur communication radios, professional communication radios, and so on. For our purposes it is usually sufficient to define a product without such detail by using only the general and common name of the article—radios, television receivers, record players, telephones, etc. Even with this degree of product classification, the number of possibilities is enormous. The *United States Standard Industrial Classification*, which does not go into nearly this much detail but classifies all "radio and television receiving sets, except communication types" as one group, has 433 industrial product classifications. The *United Nations Standard Industrial Classification* divides manufacturing into 62 groups; but a large number of products are listed under each group, so the total number of products or distinct manufacturing operations which are recorded is over 4,000. Most of the latter constitute industrial project possibilities one place or another in the world and therefore make up the starting point for the screening process I shall describe.

The process of screening for industrial opportunities may start out with some 4,000 possibilities, gradually reduce the number to several hundred, and eventually end up with 100 product possibilities. To handle not only the product names but also dozens of pieces of information in regard to many of them requires a highly systematic approach, or confusion will result and many of the possibilities may be missed. One method which the Arthur D. Little advisory team developed in Nigeria was to list each product which appeared worthy of any serious investigation on a separate card large enough to hold all the basic information needed for the screening process. Table 3 is a revised and improved version of an industrial possibility card. The purpose of the card was to bring to-

Table 3. Industrial Possibility Card (Condensed)

PRODUCT:_____

_____

MATERIALS:_____

_____

MARKET:

	Year	Imports	Local production	Apparent market
	___	___	___	___
	___	___	___	___
	___	___	___	___
	___	___	___	___

Industry class. no.......

New industry... _____
Expansion..... _____
Additional plant......... _____
Local market.... _____
Export market.. _____
Import substituting.... _____
Export upgrading..... _____
Service or ancillary...... _____

EXISTING AND PROPOSED PLANTS:

Name	Location	Year established	Capacity	Status

PROBABLE LOCATION FOR NEW PLANT:_____

POSSIBLE BASIS OF ECONOMIC JUSTIFICATION:_____

_____

OBSTACLES TO PROJECT:_____

INFORMATION AS TO ECONOMIC SIZE:_____

PREVIOUS REPORTS OR STUDIES:_____

QUESTIONS NEEDING STUDY:_____

Date carded	By whom carded

SOURCE OF PROJECT IDEA:_____

PRELIMINARY CONCLUSIONS:_____

ACTION TAKEN:_____

(More details may be recorded on reverse)

gether in one convenient place the preliminary data needed to decide whether the product should be dropped from the list of active possibilities either because of fairly obvious unfeasibility or because of a previous commitment made by an investor to establish a factory to produce the product and the consequent unjustifiability of a second plant at the time. The cards which remained active after successive reviews by various industrial experts gradually came to represent the group of strong possibilities. They also became the collecting place for information as the work progressed.

It would be possible to start the screening process by making out cards for all 4,000 or more manufactured products which could be extracted from the United Nations classification book. If this part of the work is being done by people with limited experience in industrial economics, this is the way to avoid the possibility of overlooking any products which might be worth consideration. If the screening is being done by experienced industrial development people who have been through such an exercise before, it is possible to save time by a shortcut, with only a moderate risk that something important will be missed. In this case, cards should be made out only for the products which strike the experienced screener as being worth looking into for some reason. Under this approach, it is unlikely that the set of cards will ever total more than a few hundred. In the Nigeria example, the active possibilities listed never amounted to much more than 200, although a more detailed breakdown of some of the products would have taken the total past 300.

If the product possibility cards are to be made up by this second method, many sources should be used to identify products which are worth a mental screening to decide whether they warrant entry on a card for serious consideration. There are many places where ideas may be found, and the duplication between sources will be helpful in casting different light on some of the possibilities. The following steps will lead to some of the best sources of product possibility ideas:

1. *Analyze imports.* This is the way to find most import-substitution possibilities. The information is contained in the country's most detailed listing of products imported; but in order to get individual product data it will often be necessary to break down a customs classification. It may show "cosmetic products"; but to learn local market size we need to know volume and trends for the main individual products such as toothpaste, shaving cream, lotions, shampoos, face powder, hair-coloring products, and many other items. This kind of analysis can be done with sufficient accuracy by analyzing the import documents filed at the customs office for sample months over a period of years. Interviews with importers will also be useful.

2. *Analyze exports.* This is the way to find opportunities for upgrading existing exports by some degree of processing. The information in statistical records should be supplemented by discussions with businessmen who gather, grade, and ship the export products. The product opportunities which may be based on existing raw material exports will need further checking in industry lists.

3. *Analyze materials.* A thorough analysis of the country's known animal, vegetable, and mineral resources and of the country's suitability for developing new animal or vegetable material for industry may suggest many processing possibilities. Again, this may lead into studies as to what products are made outside the country from the existing or potential material inputs.

4. Analyze fuels and energy sources. A review of existing information, or better, a thorough survey of the country's fuel and energy resources may indicate industrial product possibilities. Low-cost power would suggest electrometallurgical and electrochemical products. Natural gas would suggest fertilizer, and so on.

5. Analyze imports of promising foreign markets. Imports of countries with large markets to which the products of the developing country have duty-free or preferential access should be the first to be examined in this approach. Imports of other countries would merit analysis if there were a likelihood that production costs in the developing country would be so low for some kinds of products that tariff barriers could be surmounted.

6. Analyze existing industry for expansion and diversification. What industry already exists? What can it do next by way of expansion or diversification? Are there other products which could share the overheads and make use of labor or management skills? Does successful production of certain products suggest other similar things which could be made in the same or new plants? Has the market grown to the point where the economy would benefit from the establishment of a competitor making the same product as an existing firm? A good way to use this approach is to have industry studies made by specialists in various broad sectors of industry. From their experience they can see the gaps in product lines, the related products which could be made, the skills which could be productive in making new but similar products. This is the process of using what the country has as a steppingstone to new industry.

7. Analyze existing industry as a market. In many lines, industry is its own best customer. Every industry buys a wide range of materials, parts, and supplies. As industry grows, the internal market for such products grows too. Interviews with major industries will suggest products which, though currently imported, might be made locally.

8. Review all pending projects. In most countries many of the industrial opportunities have already been thought of by someone but have not been developed for one reason or another. A thorough search should be made to uncover all such product ideas. Sources for information on old project ideas are: applications for loans or pioneer industry status or for incentives or tariff protection, inquiries for industrial sites, requests for information on industrial registration or company incorporation. Some of these leads may come from searching government files and talking with government officials. Others may come from talks with private bankers and businessmen. This is one of the most promising areas for finding project ideas which may be sound and which can often be brought to life by some development work and by finding a new potential investor. It may even be possible to revive the interest of those who previously looked into the possibility by offering special incentives.

9. Investigate the experience of other countries. An industry which has been established successfully in another country having similar characteristics may suggest the possibility that it could also be an opportunity for the developing country for which new possibilities are being examined. What is needed is up-to-date information on industries, especially new ones, in countries which appear to have relevance for comparison. Visits to other developing countries supplemented by following up industrial information in foreign government publications and in periodicals should bring such news to light. Industrial failures in other countries may also have information value.

10. Review development reports on other countries. The search for industrial opportunities is proceeding in many countries, and results are contained in reports which can usually be obtained. Some of them list specific industrial possibilities for the country being studied, and these are a good source of ideas for other countries. Some of these reports are obtainable from the United States Agency for International Development and some from the consultants who have prepared the reports. The catalog of industrial studies published by AID contains summaries of thousands of feasibility reports.

11. Follow international business periodicals. Many business magazines and newspapers contain information on new industries in various countries, especially if they are large or involve foreign investment. A development agency should keep a card index of new projects going into other countries as a source of product possibility ideas and also as a lead on the firms which have shown their interest in investing in manufacturing outside their own country. Some of the American publications which would be useful are: *Business Week, Business International, The Wall Street Journal, The Journal of Commerce, Noticias, Vision,* and the trade journals of many industries.

12. Review industry checklists. As a source of ideas and as a way to ensure that nothing worthwhile has been ignored, several industrial classification lists should be used in the selective compilation of the product possibility cards, even if all the products listed in them have not been used as a starting point for the screening process under the alternative approach. Two lists of this kind are the *United Nations International Standard Industrial Classification* and the *United States Standard Industrial Classification Manual.*

The screening for industrial possibilities must not be done only as an academic research exercise; otherwise, many good opportunities may be passed over for lack of specific information. To keep this type of work in touch with the realities of business and industry and to gather the additional information which is important input for making decisions as to retaining or dropping products from the active list of possibilities, there must be close contact with industry and business. Interviews with a wide range of businessmen and engineers will be useful in adding to the lists of possibilities; they will be even more valuable in determining the status of pending projects and in pointing out negative factors which might make it advisable to drop possibilities without investing too much research time. The value of talking with knowledgeable people is not limited to the private sector, of course. Government officials in many ministries will have useful ideas on project possibilities and information and opinions on projects which failed to go ahead, resources for industry, and other highly relevant matters.

Identifying Local Market Industrial Opportunities

For the larger developing countries a major portion of the industrial opportunities are those involving manufacturing of products already being consumed in the domestic market. The proved existence of a market whose size and nature can be determined readily shows what can be sold. The cost factors can be studied, and, if necessary, protection can be given to ensure that local manufacture of the product can be a profitable investment. The preliminary identification of specific projects of this kind is mainly a matter of market analysis. The fact that the country imports the product in question is usually enough to suggest the opportunity, and the next step is to determine whether a plant to make the quantity imported would be of economic size. Projections of market growth on the basis of past imports may result in evidence of enough demand to justify local manufacturing. The obstacle often encountered in this approach is that the import statistics are not specific enough. Usually a variety of similar goods is included under one import classification. Determination of the volume of imports will depend in such instances on an analytical breakdown of the imports which are classified together. This may be done by sampling techniques by which import documents are analyzed for several short periods, say of a month each, to arrive at a percentage distribution of each product whose imports are grouped under one category. When the import figures are used in conjunction with statistics on local production of the product, if any, the present market can be determined and trends revealed which can be used for projections as to probable market size at future dates.

At this stage of screening for industrial opportunities, it is not necessary to apply specialized industry knowledge as to what size of plant is of minimum economic size for each product. This analysis can come later, when the cards are reviewed by experts with the required technical knowledge. In preliminary screening every product which is imported in what appears to be sizable quantity should be put on the industrial possibility cards for further examination. If there is doubt as to whether to include a product, it should be included.

Only occasionally should a product be listed as a local market possibility if it is not currently being absorbed by the local market in significant quantities. An exception might exist if someone thinks of a product which might be sold in quantity if available but which has not yet been introduced to the consumers in the country. The basis for including a new product idea might be the knowledge that the product has found wide acceptance in another country with somewhat similar market characteristics.

In small underdeveloped countries—those with populations of less than five million—local market opportunities are obviously going to be seriously limited because of the small population and the low purchasing power of the people. The usual approach of analyzing imports to find out which products are imported in sufficient quantity to warrant even a single manufacturing operation may not uncover many opportunities.

Some local market industrial possibilities may exist in small as well as in larger markets in the following areas:

1. Industries based on the economies of bulk transport. Transportation of commodities in bulk rather than in bags or cartons frequently results in substantial savings; sometimes ocean freight and handling costs combined can be cut to one-third or even one-quarter of previous levels. A country which imports some of its needs from long distances may find various projects which are feasible simply because of bulk transport savings. In this category we might find such industrial opportunities as importing wheat or rice in bulk for local milling and packaging, importing animal or poultry feeds in bulk for blending and bagging, importing fertilizer in bulk for blending and bagging, importing bulk cement for bagging, or importing clinker for grinding into cement and bagging.

2. Industries producing local-type products or services. Some goods and services have to be produced at or near the point of use because the product cannot be easily transported or because the service has to be performed on the spot. Illustrative of such opportunities are manufacture of bread and other bakery products, manufacture of ice, manufacture of soft drinks, tire retreading, and making of custom-designed furniture.

3. Industries protected against import competition by high transport costs. Countries located a long way from the major industrial areas of the world may find opportunities which are justified because of the natural protection of high transport costs for some products, especially those which are heavy in relation to value. In this category may be found such opportunities as brick and tile manufacturing, concrete block making, carbonated beverage production, and the operation of foundries.

4. Industries for which small-scale operation is not seriously uneconomic. Some products can be made almost as efficiently on a small scale as on a larger scale. They may therefore be suitable opportunities for countries with very small markets.

Identifying Material-based Industrial Opportunities

There is a natural tendency in most underdeveloped countries to think of industrialization in terms of making sophisticated products in the chemical, metal, and electronics fields. Yet for most countries seeking to build industry for the first time, there are greater opportunities in establishing industries based on materials which are available or could be produced in the country. There are many reasons why this is so. Often the basic material is available because it has been produced traditionally in the country. The production of the material is within the immediate capabilities of the people without the need for further training. The material often exists because of favorable conditions of climate and soil. The material is ready to use in industry at low cost because it is produced in a low-cost economy and because a minimum of transport expense has been added. In industries in which the cost of materials is a major part of total costs, the advantage of locally available low-cost material may constitute a strong economic justification for an industry.

A logical starting point in searching for material-based opportunities is to identify all presently available materials. These will include agricultural, forest, fishery, and mineral materials now being exported in unprocessed or partly processed form; materials now being used by the public locally, with or without processing, in the home or village; and materials which are available but which are not being used either for export or for local consumption. Information on all materials known to exist in the country should be systematically collected. A good way to proceed is to set up a basic data card on each material, supported by files containing more detailed material such as agricultural, forestry, or mineral survey reports. For each material attempts should be made to determine present uses, costs, quality, quantities available, location, and possibilities for increasing the supply. Table 4 is an example of an industrial material card suitable for collecting basic information about each material which has a potential industrial use.

Developing a fairly complete set of industrial material cards will require a thorough analysis of whatever survey reports are available in regard to agricultural-based materials, either wild or cultivated; fisheries resources; forest resources; and mineral deposits. Research into printed reports should be supplemented by a program of interviews with knowledgeable people in the various fields. Such people will usually include government officials in the ministries responsible for activities in the natural-resource fields, university and research-station personnel conducting work on resource development, foreign technical-assistance personnel making resource studies in the country, local or regional government officials concerned with developing transportation or public works

Table 4. Industrial Material Card (Condensed)

MATERIAL NAME:_____ _____	Vegetable........	
Detailed characteristics:_____	Forest.........	
_____ _____	Fishery........	
_____	Mineral........	

LOCATIONS: 1. _____

           2. _____

           3. _____

PRESENT USE:_____

COST AT LOCATION:_____

QUANTITIES NOW AVAILABLE: _____

OWNERSHIP:_____

INCREASED SUPPLY POSSIBLE?_____

REPORTS AVAILABLE:_____

PROBLEMS:_____

FURTHER INFORMATION NEEDED:_____

ACTION BEING TAKEN:_____

in their parts of the country; and private businessmen interested in purchasing the materials and selling them in local or export markets.

From the collection of information on known existing materials it is an easy step to gather data on materials which might be developed or discovered if some work were done or if it appeared that there would be a market for the item if it were available. A study of agricultural reports and discussions with agricultural specialists should reveal many crops having industrial uses which are known to have possibilities in the country on the basis of experiments or which should be growable because of the similarity of soil and climate to other locations where they are being produced. Also, trees which could be grown on a plantation basis may be identified. Enough may be known about mineral or fish resources to indicate possibilities which might be verified if certain surveys were undertaken.

Sometimes an examination of imports will reveal products being brought into the country in substantial quantity which might be made from materials which are available or which could be developed in the country. Nigeria, for example, has traditionally imported large quantities of sugar; but the climate and soil are suitable for growing sugar cane, and eventually a project was developed to grow the cane and make the sugar. Many countries import paper which could be made from trees either available or growable in the country, although the problem may be insufficient market to justify a paper mill of economic scale.

In most unindustrialized countries the value of materials used locally without processing could be enhanced by processing which would make them more transportable or resistant to spoilage. The processing of food products through drying, canning, or other methods may be the first step in industrializing local materials for a local market. For some products, home or village-type processing is primitive and unsatisfactory and could be replaced by modern industrial methods. The development of facilities for freezing fish and meat so that they may be transported to locations remote from the source of supply illustrates possible opportunities for processing, transport, and distribution.

The upgrading of materials already being exported represents a major area for new industrial opportunities, for most underdeveloped countries are established exporters of raw materials which are processed in the industrialized countries. The search for possible projects should involve a study of each material being exported to determine all the products being made from that material, for each such product is worth examining as a potential opportunity. At a later stage of detailed feasibility analysis it may be found that there are good reasons why processing would not be economic in the country where the material originates. At the preliminary stage, every product being made from the country's materials should be listed as a possibility.

Identifying Ancillary and Service Industry Opportunities

Many opportunities exist in developing countries because an industrial community needs plants which supply parts or intermediate processing services for manufacturers in the area. The lack of such enterprises in nonindustrial areas is one of the obstacles which stand in the way of industrial growth. Experience in advanced countries indicates that manufacturers requiring diverse parts, accessories, processing functions, and many supporting services often prefer to buy these from firms specializing in them rather than produce them on a small scale in their own plants. Examples of these ancillary and service industries (sometimes called core industries) are plants doing plastic molding, machine shop job work, metal casting, rubber goods forming, metal stamping, enameling, electroplating, and container manufacturing. A single plant which specializes in one or more of these operations may serve a whole community of manufacturing plants.

In addition to these general ancillary and service industries, parts and process suppliers have grown up which serve product manufacturers within a single industry. An example is the jewelry findings group, which supplies ear wires to the manufacturers of earrings or standard clips and pins for a wide range of jewelry. Other single-industry-oriented operations would be the manufacture of shoe findings, waste utilization in the textile and leather trades, leather finishing, and freezing plants serving the food-processing industries. Table 5, adapted from the Ten-year Industrial Plan for Puerto Rico prepared by Arthur D. Little, Inc., suggests other possibilities of this kind which should be considered in screening to find specific industrial opportunities.

Table 5. Examples of Ancillary and Service Industries Serving Industry in General

General production type	Specific industry type	General service type
Metalworking and processing group:	*Jewelry findings*	*Die makers*
Casting—especially light metals	*Shoe and leather findings*	*Machine shops*
Enameling	*Waste recovery*	*Gasket makers*
Metal specialties—spinning,	*Textile-finishing Group:*	*Electrical contractors*
stamping, etc.	Bleaching and dyeing	*Office duplicating*
Metal treating—galvanizing,	Silk-screen printing	*Packing, crating, and*
plating, etc.		*shipping*
Sheet-metal work		*Testing laboratories*
Welding and cutting		*Electric-motor rebuilding*
Paper and printing group:		
Bags and envelopes		
Boxes		
Labels		
Lithography		
Printing and embossing		
Plastic products		
Rubber products		

SOURCE: Arthur D. Little, Inc., *Report on Ten-year Industrial Plan for Puerto Rico*, 1951, reprinted 1961, available from AID, Washington, pp. 94–97.

Preliminary Appraisal of Industrial Possibilities

The screening process just described should result in the setting up of a large number of cards, each containing information on one product which may represent a manufacturing opportunity. How large the original set of cards will be depends on whether the work was done simply by listing practically all manufactured products made anywhere or by listing only those products which appeared to be worth preliminary investigation to the experienced eye of the industrial specialist doing the analysis. Under the first approach there may be as many as 4,000 cards; under the second, probably not more than 200 to 300. Any relevant information which has been uncovered will be recorded on each card, at least in abbreviated form. The cards thus serve as a collecting point of much information and as an index to more voluminous material, such as supporting reports, which may be on file. In setting up the cards most of the spaces on most of the cards may be left blank; but as the work proceeds, pieces of information are added as they are acquired.

The process of adding information onto the cards and the process of thinking about the feasibility of each potential opportunity should go on simultaneously. At any point it may be decided to drop a card from the active file because the latest bit of information obtained on the possibility indicates clearly either that the project is unfeasible or that the opportunity has been definitely taken up by an investor who has made a real commitment to go ahead with a project which will fully take care of the opportunity for the time being.

The question of when a project is sufficiently firmly committed so that it should no longer be kept active as a promotional possibility is a difficult one. On the one hand, there is no point in wasting time and money in making a feasibility study or promoting a project which is going to be built anyway. On the other hand, if all projects which someone talks about investing in were removed from the active list, many of the best possibilities would be held in abeyance, while only a few of them would ever go ahead. If all the projects which people announce for many developing countries were built, the countries would be as industrialized as the United States. In reality, people tend to announce their intention to build factories long before they are prepared to risk a penny, and in most cases something comes up to prevent the project from ever being put into operation. Perhaps the best policy for an industrial development agency is to keep all possibilities on the active file up to the point where it is clear that the financing has been arranged and in some cases until the equipment has been ordered. Then the cards should go into an "under construction" file and should be periodically reviewed to pick up any projects which have fallen apart so they can be taken back into the active group.

After all readily available information has been put on the cards, and after many of the cards have been removed in the process as they become either "Committed" or "Unpromising," the time has come for an over-all review of the entire collection by a number of experienced people who may have relevant information to add, but most importantly, who will have worthwhile opinions based on their knowledge of the industry and, in some cases, on their knowledge of both the industry and the conditions in the country. As judgment is an important part of this phase of the screening, it is essential that as many informed and industrially experienced people as possible should review the collection of possibilities. Those reviewing the cards at this point should include not only those who have worked to prepare them, but also government officials knowledgeable about existing industry and resources; and particularly private businessmen who are familiar with the realities of the local market, local manufacturing conditions, and, in some instances, world markets. That an individual businessman who has such a preview may take advantage of project ideas on the list is not harmful. After all, the purpose of the exercise is industrial development, and the sooner anyone picks up any idea generated in the screening process, the sooner new plants will be built. This phase of the screening process should eliminate more cards and leave the collection ready to go into the stage of more detailed analysis.

The purpose of screening is not to make detailed feasibility studies; it is to identify a substantial number of product manufacturing possibilities which, on the basis of preliminary examination, appear to warrant detailed investigation either by potential investors or by the industrial development agency. Before the list is ready for promotion or feasibility study work, a preliminary reappraisal of each product possibility should be made. This is necessary because the original mass collection of information and the subsequent filling in of bits and pieces have undoubtedly left large holes in the information on some of the possibilities. Now is the time to fill in the blank spaces with a minimum amount of new research and inquiry. How much new work should be done at this stage on each of several hundred possibilities is a debatable point. Clearly, enough should be done so that no possibility is allowed to remain on the active list with a major question mark on some important question which could easily be answered by an hour or two of investigation. There will be many important question marks on the cards as a result of the review described above. Some of them may be answered by a phone call or an interview with the right person or with a moderate amount of statistical research. By the end of this stage no question about any possibility which can be answered quickly should be left open. Warning signals which may indicate potential weaknesses of the market or material availabilities should receive fairly careful attention. At this stage definitive answers should be obtained on the current status of all pending projects so that those definitely committed can be removed from the active list. By the time this collection of missing data has been completed and the completed cards have been finally reviewed by all concerned, it is probable that the list of active possibilities has been narrowed down to something under two hundred, and perhaps to one hundred. The list of product manufacturing possibilities is then ready for preliminary promotion efforts or for detailed feasibility studies where they appear to be needed.

7

Feasibility Studies

Feasibility studies are important aids in industrial investment work, but their role is usually either overrated or practically ignored by those who are responsible for industrial development. Those who have become fascinated by this development tool tend to regard a feasibility study as a necessary prerequisite for any industrial promotion effort, while those who are not feasibility-study-minded often ignore its value completely. Neither of these extremes is justified, but between the two lies the selective use of feasibility studies of various kinds in situations where they can be of real value.

If we use the term feasibility study in its broadest sense, it is obvious that there must be a feasibility study to precede every decision by anyone to invest in an industrial project. There may not be a document labeled "feasibility study," but the essential elements of a feasibility study will exist, even if only in the mind of the investor. Before making the investment decision, the investor will have studied the project sufficiently to satisfy himself that a market exists for the product, that materials can be obtained at reasonable cost, that labor and infrastructure services are available, that a plant of a certain size and kind and cost will be appropriate, and that revenues will exceed production costs by a sufficient margin to provide a satisfactory return on the investment. If the project is a large one, these and other relevant factors will have been analyzed in detail and the results recorded. If the project is a very small one, less formal study may have been involved. In some cases, there may not have been a systematic analysis or a detailed recording of information. But formal or informal, documented or not, feasibility calculations will have been made by the investor as a means of arriving at the investment decision. This is a feasibility study in the form closest to the point of investment commitment.

The use of the term feasibility study in the industrial development business generally implies a study done by someone other than the investor who makes his own calculations to arrive at his own investment decision. It often means a study done by an industrial development agency or by someone for such an agency. Frequently the studies are done without any specific investor in mind; but sometimes they are done exclusively for an interested prospective investor, and occasionally they are done in close association with him. Feasibility studies may be made by the staff of a development agency or by consultants working for it. Under a program of the United States Agency for International Development, the making of feasibility studies by or for a prospective investor is encouraged by an arrangement whereby AID will pay half the cost on condition that if the investment is made, the investor repays AID for its share of the cost; but that if the investment is not made, the study becomes the property of AID and can be promoted to others.

The vital essential of a feasibility study is that it be completely objective and unbiased. A feasibility study is a scientific exercise which combines engineering, economic, and financial analysis to determine whether a specific project is sound in every way and to measure its commercial and economic value. Unless a feasibility study is approached from this viewpoint, it will be worthless or worse. The underdeveloped world is often victimized by salesmen who offer "feasibility studies" which purport to analyze the technical and economic aspects of projects but whose real purpose is to sell machinery to unsophisticated governments. Any study which is made or financed by those who stand to gain by its conclusions, through the sale of either equipment or service, must always be suspected as lacking objectivity if not as being fraudulent. A feasibility study which lacks the essential element of independent and professional-quality authorship will have little or no value for attracting private investment, for nobody will believe its contents or its conclusions.

In addition to objectivity, a feasibility study of any kind must be technically sound, or it will have little value. What it covers it must cover thoroughly. The facts must be comprehensive and internally consistent, and the conclusions must be soundly based in logic and in the information presented. This implies that any feasibility study must be made by people who know the industry and who are competent to analyze all aspects—engineering, financial, and marketing. Usually this means that more than one specialist will have to contribute to the study, for rarely is an engineer, an economist, an accountant, or a marketing specialist competent to deal professionally with all the aspects of a project's technical and commercial soundness.

When Feasibility Studies Are Needed

There are some industrial investment situations for which there is no need for a development agency to make feasibility studies and for which feasibility studies, if made, would only represent a waste of time and money. In this class we have many of the branch-type projects built to provide products which will be sold by the parent company through its established market channels in the parent company's home country. Here it is obvious that there is no need for the country seeking the plant to make a market survey, for the market is well known to the prospective investor. Nor is there any need to examine alternative processes or equipment requirements, for the prospective investor knows the technical end of his business intimately. This is the situation which Puerto Rico faced in regard to many of its industrial possibilities, and consequently feasibility studies were not made there for projects of this kind. It was obvious that there was no point in explaining how to make brassieres to an established brassiere manufacturer who was interested in Puerto Rico as a location where he might make his product more cheaply for his established markets. In this situation the prospective investor needed only information on labor availability, skills, and costs; transportation costs; and other factors affecting the feasibility calculation of production costs in Puerto Rico compared with alternative locations. For other places which are trying to attract industry of the branch-plant kind to produce for export markets well known to the prospective investors, there is likewise no point in making complete feasibility studies.

Feasibility studies need not be prepared by industrial development agencies in some situations. Much depends on the kind of investor needed by a project. If the financing is to come entirely from a manufacturing company which has long been a producer of the product, there is obviously no point in a study which explains alternative production processes and goes into great detail as to the equipment needed or its cost. These things will be known by the prospective investor. However, if financing is likely to be sought from a bank or other financing institution, the technical part of a feasibility study may be very important, for financial agencies are usually not sufficiently technically oriented to understand or evaluate these aspects of a project unless they are thoroughly set forth in the project papers. If the product of a project is to be marketed abroad through the marketing channels of the prospective investing company, there is clearly no need for a feasibility study of the markets.

The differing needs of various prospective investors in regard to project information and analysis suggest that there should be considerable flexibility in the content of the feasibility studies. It should not be a question of a complete, standard feasibility study or none at all; rather, it should be a decision as to what kind or degree of feasibility study is appropriate in a given investment situation. In one instance everything but the technical or engineering part will be needed; in another, everything but the market analysis. In the case of a project for a company experienced in the field to make its product for the local market in the developing country, all that may be needed is a market survey plus an analysis of factors affecting local production costs. The company can then design its own plant and make its own investment and production cost calculations.

It should be recognized that in the great majority of cases, the prime mover in an industrial investment in a developing country will be a manufacturing company which knows its business well. The objective of the industrial development agency should be to provide the prospective investor with whatever information is needed to arouse his interest in the opportunity and to supplement information already known to him so he can arrive at an investment decision. To provide more than this is a waste of time and money. To provide less may cause the prospective investor to lose interest or to arrive at a negative conclusion based on inaccurate or incomplete information.

A complete feasibility study, containing all the elements which will be outlined below, is most often needed for larger projects whose financing will come from a combination of several interests, some of whom lack information on some of the feasibility elements which may be well known to other participants. A large project, for example, may have a technical partner who knows the engineering aspects of the industry thoroughly, but it may obtain part of its financing from a local industrial development bank and part from an international industrial financing company who may want to see a comprehensive feasibility study before they will join in the financing.

The essential point about feasibility studies prepared by or for industrial development agencies is that they are a presentable packaging of information and analysis about a project in a form suitable for the investment promotion situation which is foreseen for the particular project. Whether they are complete or only partial feasibility studies is not the important thing. Regardless of their scope or content, feasibility studies represent an orderly collection of accurate information bearing the seal of authenticity of independent and objective analysis and prepared in such a way that there is maximum impact on the prospective investors to whom it will be taken.

Some people have taken the view that the chances of an investment's being made are increased substantially if a specific investor for a project is identified first and if he participates in the work of making the feasibility study. This was the approach taken with moderate success by the Rockefeller Brothers Fund in their feasibility study work in

Nigeria. It is also the idea which is basic to the AID program of sharing the cost of feasibility studies with the prospective investor. There is no doubt that a company which has become interested in a project to the extent that it will invest time or money in making the feasibility study is already half-committed to the project. If the conclusions of the study are positive, it is more than likely that the original prospective investor will follow through and make the investment. While it would be advantageous for a country to have more than one prospective investor interested in each project so that a minimum of concessions or subsidies would have to be given, this is a situation which is not likely to be realized in many cases. If it is possible to get one prospect interested in a project to the point of participating in one way or another in the study, this is all to the good and may be all that can be expected in most cases. The promotion problem may have been solved by doing the promotion first and the study second. But often it will be found that no prospective investor can be readily interested in a project which has not been studied and found attractive. Then the procedure is to make a "cold" feasibility study which, if it comes out positive, can be used to arouse the interest of prospective investors. An industrial development agency should not restrict its activities to one of these approaches or the other. Where it can interest a prospective investor in sharing in the cost or work of doing a study, it should do so; and it can regard projects handled this way as being already more than half promoted before they are studied. It should also go ahead and make feasibility studies of other opportunities which appear promising even though no investor prospects are in sight.

Feasibility studies are sometimes useful in forcing a company which had previously studied the project and failed to act to make an investment commitment to avoid the danger that a competitor might get interested in the opportunity when the feasibility study is released. The fact that a study is being made focuses attention on a project, for if it is likely to be strongly positive, it can be assumed that investment will be forthcoming from somewhere.

What Feasibility Studies Should Contain

While recognizing that partial feasibility studies may be all that is needed in many situations, the full scope of a complete feasibility study should be kept in mind to ensure that nothing is left out unless there is a good reason for doing so. The methods of developing and analyzing an industrial project in its technical, commercial, and economic aspects were described in my previous book [1] and will not be repeated here.

---

[1] Murray D. Bryce, *Industrial Development: A Guide for Accelerating Economic Growth*, McGraw-Hill Book Company, New York, 1960.

The presentation for the financing of projects was explained there, and the following items were suggested for inclusion in the project prospectus:

Introductory summary
Project history and sponsors
Commercial aspects:
   The market analysis
   The competition
Engineering aspects
National economic justification:
   National economic profitability
   Specific direct benefits
   Indirect benefits to the economy
Financial aspects:
   Total project investment
   Financial structure proposed
   Earnings forecasts
   Cash flow estimates
   Debt service coverage
   Balance sheet estimates
The business climate
Appendix

The prospectus for financing a project which may follow an outline such as that given above is not exactly the same as a feasibility study, but it does resemble it. A feasibility study, if there is one for the project, comes first. It often contains a good deal of analysis of alternative processes, plant sizes, and costs at various possible locations. It may show calculations of return on investment under several assumptions as to possible financial structure, for at that point in a project's history there may be considerable doubt as to how the project will be financed. In other words, at the time of the feasibility study many important questions about the project may not yet be decided. The purpose of the study is to test the project and explore alternative ways it might be set up if an investor could be attracted. The prospective prime mover of the project, when one is located, will then make decisions on most of these questions and determine how he wants to set the project up. The project may then be described in a prospectus if outside financing is sought, particularly if it is sought from the public. The prospectus should therefore be thought of as the project description and financing plan in fairly final form.

There are no standard or even generally accepted forms for complete feasibility studies. Practically every one is different. However, it is possible to list the items which should be included and to explain them sufficiently to serve as a guide for preparing a feasibility study. Table 6 lists the various items in the order which would be suitable for many feasibility studies.

Table 6. Contents of a Typical Industrial Feasibility Study

1. Summary and conclusions
2. The product
3. Market analysis:
     Definition of anticipated market
     Market size
     Market growth trend and projections
     Competition
     Distribution channels
4. Production process and equipment (with alternatives)
5. Materials required, availability and cost
6. Fuel and energy requirements, availability and cost
7. Labor and management requirements, availability and cost
8. Investment needed (fixed assets and basic working capital)
9. Production cost estimates (for various levels of output)
10. Financial structure (with alternatives)
11. Financial estimates:
     Return on investment
     Cash flow
     Breakeven calculations
     Debt service coverage
12. Benefits to the economy:
     National income benefits
     Employment benefits
     Foreign exchange benefits
     Training benefits
13. Incentives or protective conditions required
Appendix: Major items of equipment required (with estimated cost)

As the methods of making the analysis and of calculating most of the items for inclusion in the feasibility study have been explained at length in my previous book, they will not be repeated here. However, several points deserve additional emphasis. The section on benefits to the national economy is one which is often omitted; but in my opinion this is not wisely done, for most projects require some concessions from government or temporary subsidies in their early years. The feasibility study is a good place to elaborate on the benefits the project should bring to the national economy as justification for the concessions or subsidies which are assumed in the financial calculations. A careful exposition of the benefits should pave the way for the project to receive the benefits which are warranted and to receive them with a minimum of delay. The explanation of the benefits should carry more weight if it is given by the independent technician who prepares the feasibility study than if it is expounded by investors who stand to gain personally from the concessions or subsidies.

The foreign exchange benefit calculation is of special importance because of the difficult foreign exchange position of most developing countries. The estimate of foreign exchange earnings or savings should include all prospective foreign exchange earnings of the project through anticipated sales abroad; all foreign exchange expenses such as purchases of imported materials and spare parts, salaries and expenses of foreign technicians if paid in foreign exchange, fees for licenses or royalties or management, anticipated remittances of profits, and similar items. The withdrawal and repatriation of the foreign capital originally brought in should be treated as an offset of the original capital inflow and not as a current foreign exchange expense. The net foreign exchange cost of the project, year by year, obtained by deducting foreign exchange earnings from foreign exchange costs, should be compared with the foreign exchange saving, if any, arising from producing the project's product locally instead of importing it.

The estimate of the benefits which a project may bring a country through training workers in industrial skills is more difficult to calculate, but in many cases it is the most important of all benefits. One way to arrive at an approximation of the value of this benefit is to estimate how many workers will be trained per year and multiply this number by an estimate of the alternative cost of providing them with a similar amount of training in an industrial or technical school. Though the nature of the training in a factory differs from that in an industrial school, it might well be argued that the more practical nature of training on the job and the experience in working under real factory conditions would equal in many cases the theoretical training which would be given in a school.

On the basis of the needs of the project as revealed in the financial calculations and the benefits to the economy which can be quantified, it should be possible to state what incentives or subsidies the project should have to meet the legitimate requirements of the investor and the economy as a whole. Too little return which might arise without incentives or subsidies of any kind would result in many instances in no investment. Too-generous incentives or subsidies could result in a project's being "bought" by a country for more than it is worth. Direct and indirect economic benefits can usually justify some degree of subsidy for a new industry; but there is a limit to how far a country can go in subsidizing industry, even industry which will be basically sound in the long run. The feasibility study is a good place to evaluate the worth of a project to the country as well as to the private investor and to arrive at an objective analysis of what support the project should have.

8

Promoting Industrial Investment

Why Promotion Is Necessary

One of the most widespread and dangerous illusions in the under-developed world is the belief that large numbers of eager would-be investors are waiting impatiently to be allowed to invest in industry in the developing countries. Those who oppose private investment in industry, especially investment by foreigners, often draw a picture of vast hordes of determined but unscrupulous capitalists conspiring with right-ist politicians in deals which will permit them to invest in industry which will be highly exploitive. This is the threat which extreme nationalists point to as the new colonialism which may destroy the fruits of independence. Like most highly emotional views of economic situations, this one contains elements of reality; but it is overdrawn and over-simplified to the point that it is nonsense when applied to the main field of private foreign industrial investment in most developing countries.

While there is an overabundance of industrial salesmen who refer to themselves as investors in most developing countries, there is scarcity of real investors who are prepared to risk their own capital in starting new industries. The scarcity is simply a reflection of the fact that there are some fifty-odd underdeveloped countries competing for industrial investment, not only against each other, but also against the more in-dustrialized countries which offer distinct advantages to the industrial investor. The investors whose participation is so widely sought are not unlimited in number. In theory, anyone in the world with capital and some industrial know-how might be considered a potential investor in foreign industrial projects; but in reality, only a small fraction of such people or companies represent active prospects. Many industrial firms prefer, for various good reasons, to limit their operations to their home country. Only a few are interested in even considering the possibility of a foreign operation, especially in a country as remote as one in Africa, Asia, or Latin America—areas which bring to the minds of most American or European businessmen visions of riots, revolutions, or primitive backwardness.

Nobody knows how many industrial companies in the developed world would give serious consideration to a well-promoted and sound foreign opportunity. The number is growing as more and more businessmen learn about the opportunities of foreign operations and about the developing countries and their advantages as well as their hazards as locations for industrial activities. The number of American industrial companies which have carried their interest in foreign operations to the point of actually investing in manufacturing plants outside North America appears to be fewer than 1,000. Most of these firms have ventured into Europe, not into the underdeveloped world. Probably not more than a quarter of these American firms have participated in industrial projects in Latin America, Africa, and Asia. If, as a guess, we assume that two to three times as many European firms have invested in projects in the underdeveloped areas of the world, mainly because of colonial connections, we have a total of about 1,000 experienced industrial companies which have invested in manufacturing operations in developing countries. These are not the only companies which might be attracted to the right opportunity, for the list is continually growing; but they serve to quantify in an "order of magnitude" sense the statement that the number of potential investors for all the developing countries to approach for industrial capital and know-how is far from unlimited. We might summarize the equation by suggesting that we have about fifty underdeveloped nations seeking industrial participation from perhaps 1,000 internationally experienced industrial investors and from potentially an equal number of investors who have yet to make their first foreign venture, but who might do so in the next ten years if properly approached with the right opportunity.

The American or European company which can be regarded as a potential investor because of its resources of funds, staff, markets, and know-how for industrial projects in the developing countries is faced with a bewildering array of alternatives. Not only are there some fifty countries which might conceivably be considered as locations for an overseas manufacturing project, but also there are competitive alternatives in the industrialized countries where economic growth rates are higher than in most underdeveloped nations and where risks are lower and facilities better. We must face the fact that most of our prospective investors will decide that they can do better, all things considered, by placing all or most of their available resources in investments in Europe or North America. For most of the companies which reach this conclusion, it is probably the right investment decision in terms of safeguarding the interests of their shareholders. Let there be no illusions about the possibilities of private investors risking their capital in underdeveloped countries for motives of philanthropy or even of participation in the economic competition of East and West. They will invest only when and if they are convinced on grounds of cold financial calculation that the investment represents the best possible use of their capital and other resources, taking into account all the foreseeable financial advantages as well as the risks. To invest on any other basis would be a default of the duty of the company officials to the firm's shareholders who have invested their funds in the company in the expectation that they will be used to maximum effectiveness.

With a limited number of potential investors on the one hand and heavy competition for the capital both from some fifty other developing countries and from the thriving industrial economies of Europe and America on the other, any one country seeking to attract industrial investors is faced with a great challenge. The situation is far from being as hopeless as it might appear, however, for those developing countries which actually have industrial investment opportunities and which are serious enough about industrial development to embark on well-organized programs to develop specific investment opportunities and attract capital to them. While a number of developing countries in this category —probably not more than two dozen—will create conditions suitable for industrial development and will make a serious effort to attract private capital for industry, the majority will not do so. The number of countries which might have a chance of attracting any individual prospective industrial investor will be further reduced by the nature of the firm's international interest and by the kind of specific industrial investment opportunity being promoted. Even when the field is thus limited to the point where it can be seen that the competition for capital is not unlimited, the fact remains that the firm seeking investment opportunities has plenty of alternatives in both the developed and the undeveloped worlds and has no need to stand in line pleading for any one country to permit it to make an investment. The more realistic picture is that of a company which is ready to consider a foreign investment and which makes limited explorations in a few countries. It is then very ready to give special attention to any reasonable approach by a country which shows its receptivity by going out of its way to take the initiative in promoting a sound, well-prepared project which is ready for investment.

For the countries to whom this book is addressed—those who are serious about wanting industrial development, who have opportunities, and who really welcome foreign industrial capital and know-how— effective industrial investment promotion is the key to industrial development. A good industrial development program has many aspects, and they are all important. But if one part is more important than any other, it is investment promotion. To be sure, investment promotion cannot be done with much success unless the investment climate is reasonably attractive; and its effectiveness will be limited unless it promotes specific projects. This requires identification of opportunities and testing of feasibility. No matter how good the other parts of the program may be, the program is likely to fail if considerable emphasis is not given to a highly organized and hard-hitting promotion effort. There are many examples which support this conclusion. The industrial development of Puerto Rico, the most successful program so far in the world in attracting large numbers of outside investors, has been largely based on good promotion. Many other places have spent scarce funds in feasibility studies and industrial research. Nevertheless, they have achieved little industrial development because the industrial studies, however well done, accumulated dust in libraries for lack of a promotion program. Investment promotion is the last and most important link in the chain which constitutes a comprehensive industrial development program. No matter what else is done, or not done, or done inadequately, my advice is to emphasize the investment promotion part of the program. It is only through finding the investors with the money and the industrial experience that the industrialization of the country can be speeded up, and no expense or effort should be spared to make this vital activity successful.

The Two Kinds of Industrial Investment Promotion

Most countries which have realized the need to attract foreign investment to industry and which have taken the first step in setting up some kind of investment promotion activity have failed to realize that there are two different kinds of investment promotion: general promotion and project promotion. A clear understanding of the differences between the two approaches is basic to setting up a successful program which should involve both kinds of promotion, in proper balance and relationship to each other.

The most common kind of investment promotion is the general type. It consists of publicizing internationally information about the country which is thought to be of value in convincing potential investors that the country welcomes foreign capital, that it has a good investment climate, and that it has plenty of industrial opportunities based upon the size of the local market or upon some special feature such as low-cost power or skilled labor or good transportation facilities. In this kind of publicity emphasis is usually given to tax and other incentives offered and to the eagerness of the development agency to assist prospective investors. General promotional publicity rarely mentions specific project opportunities because programs of this type are usually operated by agencies which have never identified specific projects and which have never examined the feasibility of specific projects. The promotion effort may be all that there is to the development activity, and it may be run by people who have no knowledge of the technical or economic elements upon which industrial investment decisions are based. If outside assistance is used in this kind of effort, it is usually provided by public relations people who also lack the capability to discuss industrial investment on a project basis with potential investors. Often the general promotion program consists almost entirely in preparing attractive general promotion literature which is mailed to those who respond to generalized promotion advertisements in magazines and newspapers either of the mass public circulation type or of the general business periodical variety.

The other kind of industrial investment promotion is project promotion. It is completely different from general promotion in its approach and its methods. Project promotion, as the name indicates, is focused on specific projects which have been identified as opportunities for investment in a defined manufacturing facility to produce a product or a related group of products. The project has not merely been identified as an idea or a vague possibility. It has been investigated, tested, and evaluated to measure its feasibility as a commercial private investment and as a project which would be worthwhile to the economy of the country, thus justifying the expenditure of public funds in its promotion. As explained in the previous chapter, the degree to which it is necessary or worthwhile to carry feasibility studies varies from one project to another; but we assume the project has been examined in sufficient detail in the preinvestment phase. In short, the project has reached the stage where it can be classified as "promotable." This means it is ready to be taken to a prospective investor and that it has sufficient evaluation and information to attract his interest and win his confidence in a project which the country's development agency has concluded is sound and highly desirable. Project promotion cannot be done by itself, as general promotion can; it must be a part of a comprehensive industrial development program which involves identifying opportunities and examining their feasibility as described in this book.

Most of this chapter will deal with how to do project promotion. But first we should consider why this kind of promotion is recommended for emphasis despite the obvious fact that it is more complex than the general method of promotion. Like any selling program, an approach to promoting investment in industry in a country should be based upon some thoughtful analysis of some basic questions: "Who are the potential customers?" "What is likely to catch their interest so they will give serious consideration to what we are trying to sell?" "What kind of information or persuasion will be effective in bringing them to an affirmative decision?"

The objects of industrial investment promotion efforts are people who are in key positions to make or influence decisions concerning the investment of capital and the commitment of resources to specific industrial projects. Note the stress on the words "specific industrial projects." Private investments are made in projects, and it is only incidental that the projects happen to be in countries. Naturally, consideration in the project investment decision is given to the investment climate of the country, and often this leads to a negative decision. A positive decision is made only if the project is right and if the country is too. As a matter of promotion strategy we could try to create a favorable investment climate image of the country first and then, when the potential investors are in the right frame of mind, come up with specific project opportunities. Alternatively, we could combine the presentation of project feasibility information with investment climate publicity in the belief that a "package" presentation would have maximum impact. It is probably better to make a judicious combination of both approaches—use some general publicity to try to create a favorable image of the country as a place for industrial investment and then supply further evidence of investment climate advantages along with each presentation of a specific project opportunity.

The investment decision maker who is the target of any kind of investment promotion is usually specialized in his interests. He is not so much concerned with generalities of the investment climate in thirty different countries which would like him to invest as with a series of economic and technical questions which might attract his attention, and possibly eventually his capital, to a project to manufacture the specific product in which his company has special experience. He will rarely have the time or inclination to make world-wide examinations of details of tax-exemption plans or other attractions various countries are publicizing. He will want much detail on tax and legal and other investment climate matters only for the few countries which he has come to regard as being locations worthy of serious consideration, no matter how he came to regard them as such. It is my opinion that a large part of the industrial promotion budget and effort should be devoted to identifying specific potential investors for specific projects and to placing before them sufficient detail on the projects in which they have reason to be interested to bring them to the point of personally examining in detail both the project feasibility and the investment climate.

While the project method is highly selective both in identifying the prospective investors and in dealing with them on a personal and individual basis, the general promotion method is so diffuse that it has serious disadvantages which limit its usefulness. Project promotion for a country in any given year might concentrate most of the attention on promoting a limited number of projects which have been found to be highly attractive commercially and of high priority for the country. Perhaps only ten or twenty projects will be actively promoted. There may be an average of only 50 to 100 companies which can be considered as being possible prospects for each project. Thus we would have between 500 and 2,000 potential investors to whom the projects would be promoted during the year. Consider the vast difference between a promotion effort of this nature and a general one in which broad investment climate information is communicated to the entire business community of a country such as the United States in the hope that someone who sees it will be sufficiently interested to respond by seeking help in exploring factors which would enable him to decide whether the country is a suitable location for the project he has in mind. The difference between the two approaches can be calculated in terms of cost versus benefits. A general promotion campaign is costly because it is based on carrying a message to vast numbers of people in the hope that it will reach the few who will be interested and who are in a position to invest. Usually it is based on advertising in mass-circulation periodicals whose rates are high. It is my opinion that advertising in newspapers or mass-circulation magazines may be much more appropriate for selling automobiles or clothing or food products for which almost every reader is a potential customer than for promoting an underdeveloped country as an industrial location; at most, only a few hundred of the potential readers are potential investors. Thus the advertiser of industrial promotion would be paying for reaching a huge audience of which perhaps not even one per cent would be potential prospects. This is obviously an extremely wasteful way to spend industrial investment promotion funds. Advertising in newspapers or general circulation magazines may be warranted if a country has had a bad investment climate and must change its foreign image before it will receive consideration as a location for industry. It may also be justified for a country whose total industrial investment promotion program is large, especially if a very wide range of manufacturing opportunities exist. It may be worthwhile if the industrial advertising which creates a favorable public image of the country is important for tourism promotion or for building up international goodwill for political or defense reasons or for creating broader acceptance of the country's exports. Puerto Rico, for example, has consistently engaged in an expensive program of image advertising in mass circulation magazines, but this has also served the needs of tourism promotion and the rum export program.

The situation is different for a country whose total budget for promotion in the United States may be less than one-tenth of the amount

Puerto Rico spends for its combined industrial, tourism, and rum promotion campaign. A country seeking the maximum industrial investment on a small promotion budget can hardly afford a general type of promotion program, for it would be so small that it would be unnoticed and it would be prohibitively expensive in terms of advertising cost per prospective investor brought in. A country spending only for industrial investment results must consider its alternatives by measuring the cost per investor contacted, or better yet, the cost per industrial investment actually made.

Advertising in newspapers and magazines is only one part of a typical general promotion program which is overly costly in terms of the results which may be expected. Other activities, such as the preparation of expensive promotional literature to be mailed to large and not very selective mailing lists and in response to replies to advertisements in newspapers and magazines, can be costly and are apt to produce little by way of investment results. A large part of the requests for literature advertised in mass-circulation publications is likely to come from high-school students and others who may be curious about the country but who are not investment decision makers. Series of conferences, large meetings, or luncheons to which large numbers of businessmen are invited to hear about "Industry in the Republic of _____" are also unlikely to pay their way in investments, for they tend to attract a wide variety of businessmen—traders, would-be consultants and contractors, machinery salesmen, bankers, and such—who may be useful contacts but who are not in a position to make industrial investments. My conclusion is that for a country with a small industrial promotion budget, say less than half a million dollars a year for industrial promotion in the United States, the general type of promotion is almost always quite unproductive of results. The chances of investment results with a small budget can be improved by making the promotion program highly selective on a project basis, giving little attention to the enormously difficult task of educating the general public about the country.

How to Identify Prospective Investors

There are two essential things to be done in a highly selective industrial investment promotion effort to attract investment to specific projects: One is to have a good group of promotable projects with enough evidence as to their feasibility, and the other is to do a thorough job in identifying as many companies as possible which appear to have good reason to be interested in one or more of the specific projects being promoted. At this point we can assume that the industrial development agency has come up with a reasonable number, say at least ten, of promotable projects, through the use of methods previously described.

The next step is to identify the companies which should be contacted to test their interest in even considering a specific project.

Building up a list of investor leads for each project requires an appreciation of the different types of potential investors which exist, for they will be found in different places, they have to be approached differently, and they can play different roles in the process of putting together the financing or sponsorship of a project. The manufacturing companies comprise the largest and most important group. They possess most of the technical and management know-how which is needed as much as capital for setting up new industries. They are the ones most likely to take the initiative in sponsoring projects, finding supplementary financing, making market connections, promoting production efficiency, and providing the business management for the new industry. For any project most of the good investor prospects are likely to be in this category. Financial institutions, whether they be private corporations associated with commercial banks, wealthy individuals, or governmentally sponsored international financial institutions, are important, but in a lesser and different way. They will rarely take the initiative in sponsoring a project or in managing it, which is natural as they are primarily financiers, not industrialists. They may help in finding a technical sponsor or in locating additional financing for a project. Their role may be crucial in putting together a project, but rarely is it as primary or as central as the role of the entrepreneur, which is often played by a manufacturing company. Usually the financial partner will not have the industry-specialized know-how to set up the project or operate it, nor will he desire to supply these elements. They must come in most cases from the manufacturing company which knows the field. Occasionally, those interested in selling equipment or obtaining construction contracts for the project may be potential investors in a project, although usually on a minor scale. Their main interest is in sales and perhaps in a management contract for operating the new industry in its early years. Although they are hardly real investors, companies of this kind may be useful in helping to find technical or financial sponsors or partners for a project in the hope that this may lead to opportunities to sell equipment or services. Efforts to promote the setting up of an industrial project should involve contacts with all three types of potential investors; but the emphasis, particularly at the start, should be on finding a manufacturing firm which could become the project's sponsor and operator. Financial institutions and equipment sellers and contractors may help locate the manufacturing company for the central role of sponsor, but their real participation in the process of putting together the project is likely to come later.

Prospective manufacturing company sponsors for projects usually have several of the following characteristics:

1. They are making the same kind of product as the one identified as an opportunity. They have specialized know-how in producing and marketing the product. They often have patents or designs or other special advantages for the particular product.

2. They are big enough and in sufficiently good financial condition to warrant attention. These points can be determined by checking the Dun & Bradstreet record of each firm.

3. They are already manufacturing outside their home country, either on their own or in some kind of partnership with others. They are therefore more experienced in all aspects of international operations than the average firm and have shown their willingness to make foreign investments.

4. They are expanding their operations, which indicates that they have capital or access to funds, that they are successfully managed, and that there is growing market acceptance for their product.

5. They have the nonmoney ingredients for successful overseas investment: both technical and managerial staff to cope with expanding foreign operations, markets for their product, and technical backup capabilities such as research facilities.

6. They are making goods which have the prospect of long-term growth rather than decline.

7. They are already selling their product in the country seeking the investment and therefore have a stake in protecting their market by producing on the spot. Or they are strongly competitive with firms whose products already dominate the market and may wish to get ahead of the competition by setting up local manufacturing facilities.

8. They are already using some of the country's raw materials in their manufacturing operations elsewhere. Therefore an investment to upgrade the material in the country would be a logical move in integrating their operation.

Once an investment promotion staff has identified the products whose manufacture represents the promotable projects, it is in a position to build up its lists of leads—companies which must be contacted to determine their interest in further discussion about one of the projects. Keeping in mind the characteristics just described, research must be done to identify the worthwhile investment prospects and their key officers and to learn enough about the companies so they may be approached thoughtfully. Some of the best sources for finding leads are:

1. *Directories of firms manufacturing or distributing their product outside their home country.* The listing of United States firms in this category is *Directory of American Firms Operating in Foreign Countries,* published by World Trade Academy Press, Inc., 50 East 42nd Street, New York, N.Y. This book lists companies, their products, and the countries in which they operate.

2. Mailing lists. These may be purchased and give names of firms which manufacture products in various product groups.

3. Lists of foreign firms manufacturing or operating sales subsidiaries in various countries. The United States Government publishes such lists of American firms operating in most countries; the Puerto Rican Economic Development Administration publishes a directory of manufacturing firms with home office addresses; chambers of commerce of various foreign groups in some countries publish directories of their members who have manufacturing or sales operations.

4. Membership lists of trade associations, manufacturers associations, and chambers of commerce. Sometimes these list firms by product.

5. News items of firms setting up manufacturing plants abroad. American companies in this category are often given in such publications as *International Commerce* (published by the U.S. Department of Commerce), trade journals for the various industries, and business newspapers such as *The Wall Street Journal* and the *Journal of Commerce.*

6. Directories of manufacturing firms which indicate their products. For United States firms there are three important directories which are basic reference works in any promotion effort aimed at United States investors. The *Million Dollar Directory* lists over 6,000 manufacturing firms with assets over $1 million, and *The Middle Market* lists nearly 1,000 manufacturing firms with assets between $500,000 and $1 million. Both are published by Dun & Bradstreet, Inc., 99 Church Street, New York, N.Y. These directories give product, sales volume, number of employees, location, and names of company officers for each firm listed. *Moody's Industrial Manual,* published annually by Moody's Investors Service, Inc., 99 Church Street, New York, N.Y., contains more detailed financial and operating information on most American and some foreign companies.

7. Banks interested in developing business in a foreign country. Sometimes these are prepared to identify companies who might be interested in investment and manufacturing opportunities.

8. Contacts with trade associations. These may supply names of members who should be contacted with project opportunity information in regard to various products.

Methods of Investment Project Promotion

The process of promoting industrial investment selectively by the project method may be summarized as consisting of three phases:

1. Identifying leads. Through the use of sources of information on companies which should be considered for classification as "investment leads," lists are developed of companies to be contacted. At this stage enough information should be obtained about the companies to judge whether they warrant inclusion on any promotion list.

2. Testing leads. The next stage is to contact each firm to determine whether it has any interest in learning more about the project opportunity which has been mentioned. This contact may be made by a personal visit to the key official by an industrial promotion officer who has made an appointment in advance by telephone. During such a call the promotion officer will describe to the company official the project being promoted, offer him a feasibility study or whatever specific promotion document is being used for the project, describe the main features of the investment incentive and assistance program, and present him with a brochure describing the main features of the country as a location for industry. This is the best way to test leads as it almost forces the prospective investor to give some consideration to the country and the selected project. It is also the most costly and time-consuming way to do the job. It may even be somewhat wasteful because dozens of nonproductive calls will be necessary for each case in which a serious interest is developed. On the other hand, this system avoids the danger of wasting leads which may be important if only a small number of company leads can be discovered for a given project. This is the method of treating each lead as potentially being of great value. A less personal and therefore less effective way of testing leads is to mail to the appropriate company official a copy of the feasibility study or a summary of it or other information on a project, and a brochure on the investment incentives, together with a letter offering to discuss the investment opportunity should he indicate his interest. An alternative to this method is simply to send a letter saying that a feasibility study of an investment opportunity to make _____ product in _____ has been prepared and that an investment promotion officer will be available to discuss it if the company indicates an interest. A telegram conveying the same message might be more likely to attract attention and bring forth an invitation to come for a presentation. A third approach, which is least expensive and probably also receives the least attention from company officials, is the telephone call in which the promotion officer describes the opportunity and asks for an appointment to present detailed information. This approach sometimes works well, especially when the call is made from another city; but there are undoubtedly cases where the call is an intrusion, and serious attention is not given to the project discussed. Whatever the means used to contact the companies on the list, the end result of the contact should be that the investment promotion officer decides either to drop the company from the list because there is no sign of interest in further discussion of the project being promoted or, if there is any interest shown, to place the company in the category of "investment prospects."

3. Following up on prospects. Once a company has shown interest in hearing more about an investment project, it is the responsibility of the investment promotion officer to supply whatever information the prospective investor wants about the project, the investment incentives and industrial locations, the cost factors, and other investment considerations. This is not only the period for supplying requested information. It is also the time for persuasion. The investment promotion officer will have to "sell" the positive industrial environment which has been created. He will have to use the salesman's skills in the rebuttal of objections and problems raised. At some stage in the contact with the prospect, he should be urged to visit the country and see for himself the favorable conditions which exist for new industry. If the manufacturer agrees to make the trip, it should be tactfully suggested to him that he should bring with him detailed information on production costs in his present locations so that he can calculate on the spot the economics of locating a plant in the country. At some point, the prospective investor should also be asked to supply basic data about his firm which will be needed to determine eligibility for some of the incentives and for local financial participation in his project. By the very act of providing such information, a firm has taken one step toward a commitment to invest.

The technique of the "red carpet treatment" for the prospective investor warrants careful attention. At every stage the prospect must be made to feel that he is really wanted and that nothing will stand in the way of his being given every conceivable kind of assistance in setting up his industry. It may be appropriate for the prospect to be sent a letter or cable of personal invitation from the President, Prime Minister, or Minister of Industries. Persuading the prospect to visit the country is the most critical stage in the process of promotion. If he decides to make the trip, he should be met at the airport by suitable senior government officials. After an opportunity to rest up from the trip, the prospect should have an initial discussion of the project with top officials of the development agency and possibly with other key officials of the government. He should be received by the appropriate minister on his first business day in the country. He should be guided to local manufacturers who can be counted on to give a favorable account of their operating experience. He should be assured of all possible assistance in making his examination of factors affecting the feasibility of the project and in making application for all benefits the investor would be entitled to under the new industries incentives laws. The development agency should offer to do market studies, transportation cost analyses, or other research needed to complete the picture for the investor. He should be shown rental buildings and factory sites and assured of assistance in recruiting and training labor should he desire it.

If an investment prospect has reached this point and continues to show interest in investment, he has entered the stage of negotiation. This can be verified by noting the prospect's detailed questions as to the availability of local financial participation, the amount of import duty relief he could get, or the tariff protection which might be granted for his product. He is at the point where he considers the project investible provided he gets the package of benefits which in total meets his expectations. His objective will naturally be to enlarge as far as possible the value of the package of incentives by bargaining for more than he really expects to get. He will, of course, magnify his problems and difficulties. The negotiator's objective is to persuade the prospective investor to make an agreement with the government or some other firm commitment to proceed with the project while minimizing both the amount of the incentives and the risk of losing the prospect.

Literature as a Tool for Investment Promotion

The process of selective promotion of investment for specific projects just described depends in part on the skill of the investment promotion personnel, but it also depends on several tools and supporting services which will now be discussed. These include literature, advertising, and public relations support.

Suitable industrial investment promotion literature plays a key role in a good promotion program. There are two basic items: a general industrial brochure and a detailed fact book or handbook. The general brochure, which is frequently the only ammunition for a general type of promotional effort, is also important in a project type of promotion program because it will contain basic information which is relevant to all industrial projects. This brochure should include the following:

1. Concise descriptions of the country, its economy, its market, its industrial and business structure. This introduces the prospective investor to the country.

2. Brief explanations of all the benefits, incentives, and other forms of assistance or special treatment given to new industries, including the conditions under which projects are eligible to receive the benefits and the procedure by which the benefits are granted.

3. Summarized material on the general conditions affecting all business, such as taxes, labor legislation, etc.

4. An evaluation of the country as a location for industry which emphasizes the positive features but which also gives the negative aspects.

5. A statement of the government's policies concerning industrial development—attitudes toward private and foreign investment, its record on these questions, policies on protection or other special considerations for industry.

The general investment promotion brochure must be highly attractive in design and printing as well as persuasive in content. It should contain pictures. Some of these should show successful industries already operating; others should show evidence of progress and modernity and good living conditions for foreigners who may come to manage the new factories in their early years. The competitive standard of investment promotion material is now so high that no country can afford to use a dull or old-fashioned-looking booklet, no matter how well written its content. Frequently this brochure will be the first thing a prospective investor has ever seen from the country which is seeking his investment, and he may judge the level of development of the country and the sophistication of its leaders by the first impression made by this document.

A second general publication that is required in a promotion program is a much more detailed reference book which is given a restricted circulation. It is sometimes called a "Fact Book" or an "Industrial Handbook." Since it is a reference book, not one intended to be read in its entirety by a prospective investor, it should aim at thorough coverage of all subjects of general interest to anyone considering an investment. The subjects to be covered should include:

1. General information: Geographical facts, historical summary, climate details, population statistics, public holidays, currency (and conversions to leading international currencies), names and addresses of banks, weights and measures, information on postal services and rates, cable service and rates, newspapers, radio and television services, schools, libraries, suitable clothing, taxi and drive-rental car rates, driver's license procedures, names, addresses, phone numbers and rates of hotels, sports facilities, social and cultural activities, names and addresses of associations, clubs and leading societies, details concerning immigration and customs regulations.

2. The economy: Economic history, main sectors of the economy, development plan, industrial sector (in greater detail), progress in industrial development, lists of main industries with names and addresses of principal firms, list of main foreign companies involved in manufacturing, exports and imports in detail for several recent years, indexes of price levels and cost of living.

3. Industrial development: Industrial development plans and program, development agencies, incentive legislation in full, incentive procedures, financing available for industry, protective tariffs, industrial estates, industrial buildings available for rent, industrial land availability and cost.

4. Government: Constitution and organization of government, functions of major government ministries and agencies, government financial statistics, addresses and phone numbers of principal government offices.

5. Transportation services: Transportation services available by road, rail, sea, and air; names and addresses of transportation companies; routes, rates, frequency of service; port and airport freight facilities; shipping agents.

6. Utilities and fuels: Details concerning nature of service: cost of electricity, gas, water; cost of fuel oil, diesel oil, kerosene, etc.

7. Agriculture and natural resources: Land tenure system, agricultural production, soils, minerals, land use and vegetation, animal life, fisheries.

8. Income and other taxes: Tax rates, main principles of the tax system, deductions and exemptions allowed, international tax credit arrangements.

9. Labor: Size and composition of the labor force, growth in the labor force, employment by occupation, unemployment, union organization, strikes, industrial relations machinery, social security system, legal minimum wage rates, actual wages by occupation or industry, technical education.

10. Tariff and import regulations: Tariff rates on major imports of interest to industry such as equipment or materials, tariff rates on products which are or might be manufactured locally, import regulations and procedures, import licensing.

11. Company legislation: Laws affecting the registration or incorporation of partnerships and corporations, operations of foreign companies, trademark and patent protection.

In addition to the two general kinds of literature tools for investment promotion which have just been described, there are other printed aids which are also useful. In the comprehensive Nigeria industrial development program set up by the Arthur D. Little team, a valuable device was a series of booklets which were widely distributed to potential investors. The first booklet, which was entitled *One Hundred Industrial Possibilities in Nigeria*, contained a paragraph or two on a large number of products or groups of products which preliminary examination had revealed as promising for more detailed investigation. The basis for selecting the products was apparent feasibility resting, in most instances, on an analysis of import statistics which showed a local market of significant size for the item. The screening process which led to the choice of the products listed involved more than two hundred possibilities at one stage, but many were eliminated when it was found in some cases that projects were already committed to fill the need or when it became known that the market size was too small for a minimum-sized plant. In addition to the brief explanations of the basis for placing each product on the list, the booklet contained a summary of investment climate information, such as descriptions of incentives, taxes, and the labor situation. The booklet played an important role in the early stages of investment promotion before more detailed feasibility studies could be prepared. The wide general distribution of the booklet brought forth many enquiries from manufacturers whose interest was aroused by a specific product item which they could consider producing. The booklet was a general one in that it contained material not specific to any one project, and it covered the whole range of industry. But the response it brought forth was highly specific since each prospective investor focused on the one opportunity of greatest interest to him.

The other publications in the Nigeria series of investment booklets were more of a general background nature, providing information of interest to almost any investor considering Nigeria as an industrial location. But they were also studies in depth on important questions, not superficial generalities. The second booklet in the series was a *Directory of Industry in Nigeria,* the most complete list of manufacturing establishments which had been compiled. The plants were classified by product according to the *United Nations Standard Industrial Classification,* and each product group was listed by location, first by regions, then by cities. For each factory the directory gave the name of the company, the address, the year established, and the approximate size as measured by numbers of workers and indicated by code letters for size groups. The directory had considerable value in feasibility study work because it showed potential markets for industrial supplies and intermediate products and also sources of supply for items a new plant might wish to purchase. As an industrial investment promotion tool the directory had value in showing the existing competition already manufacturing any product, the success Nigeria had already had in attracting specific kinds of manufacturing plants, and the names of firms a prospective investor might wish to contact for discussions of factors relevant to the project under consideration.

Another booklet was *Labour for Industry in Nigeria,* a comprehensive and objective evaluation of labor availability, skills, costs, and productivity. It contained detailed wage rates for most types of labor, an appraisal of the trade union situation, a summary of labor legislation, and the cost of fringe benefits. It contained most of the information on labor which a prospective investor would require before making an investment decision.

Several additional booklets in the series were also prepared: *Transportation in Nigeria,* a detailed collection of information on freight rates and available freight service for various kinds of cargo by road, rail, sea, and air, both within the country and between Nigeria and African and overseas markets and sources of supply for equipment and materials. *Sites for Industry,* a detailed study on the availability and cost of land for industry in various parts of the country with specific suitable plant sites identified and priced. *Incentives for Industry,* a detailed description of tax exemptions, tariff policy, and other incentives for industry, with an evaluation of when specific incentives are normally granted, how long it takes to secure the benefits, and how a prospective investor should proceed to obtain them.

The booklets in the Nigeria series served various purposes in the investment promotion program. *One Hundred Industrial Possibilities* was frankly intended to attract the interest of investors to specific opportunities at a time when more detailed project material was not yet ready and when only preliminary work had been done to identify the most feasible projects and find out which manufacturers were the best prospects for them. The *Directory* was a basic reference book of value at every stage of the industrial program. The other booklets served the needs of prospective investors when they had reached the stage of exploring an investment opportunity. By providing a wealth of detailed information on important questions, a great deal of time was saved for both the investors and the industrial development team as the details common to a wide range of projects had already been collected and sources were recorded from which further information could be easily obtained.

Valuable support for an investment promotion program can come from the preparation of an appraisal of a country as a location for industry if the analysis is done by an organization or even by an individual whose name carries assurance of objectivity and independence. Only if the analysis does carry this assurance will it be of much value. A description of the investment climate by an advertising or public relations firm will be discounted heavily by most prospective investors, for they will realize that it is only advertising material prepared by people who will publicize any product when paid to do so and who in any event have not the technical or economic competence to make a serious evaluation of the factors important to industrial feasibility. An evaluation of a country as a place for industry must be done by a group who have a reputation for professional work of a high standard and who are well known in the country from which investment is to be sought. The name of such a group lends authenticity to what is reported, for it will be realized that a firm of this kind cannot afford to have its name associated with information which is exaggerated, unreliable, or in any way misleading to investors.

Once a country has been successful in attracting a number of industries which are operating well, it should make the most of the results and use the first plants to attract others. This is the "success story" technique—probably the most powerful device which can be used to attract investment. The very existence in a country of a group of successful new industries is the proof that the country has an investment climate which is good for industry and that its labor is capable of meeting industrial requirements. For a potential investor who is contemplating the possibility of an investment, information about successful new industries is tangible proof that the promotional claims about the desirability of the country as a place for industry are valid. Naturally, the bigger and the better known the established industries are, the more persuasive the success stories will be to similar firms which are being sought. The success story approach should be used in the form of an illustrated, highly attractive brochure printed on glossy paper. It should contain brief and readable stories on a number of the more important and successful new industries. Something between five and fifteen success stories of this kind would make a suitable brochure. Each success story should contain one or two good pictures of the factory and the essential facts about the size of the plant, the investment, the sources of the capital, and, if publicly available, the profitability of the enterprise. It should contain direct quotations from the manager or other top officials concerning their experience in the following: the availability and productivity of labor, the generosity of the incentives offered to industry, the cooperative attitude of the government in helping new industry, the community attitude toward industry and toward foreign technical and management staff. It should also include the manager's comments on the attractiveness of the country as an industrial location and on what living in the country is like for a foreign plant manager. The success story brochure is not something to be distributed in large quantities even though it is a general piece of promotional material. It should be used to supplement feasibility studies or other more technical investment literature when presenting a prospective investor interested in a specific project with background information. It may also be used for distribution when groups of businessmen are being approached in more general promotional campaigns. The materials used in each success story in the brochure can be used for advertisements in a promotional campaign in which paid publicity is being placed in trade or business journals.

The Role of Advertising Agencies and Consultants

Many industrial investment promotion programs are started with the assistance of either advertising agencies or public relations firms. This is not surprising, for many firms of both kinds are active in promoting their services in this field. Both types of organizations can play a useful role in industrial promotion in some situations; but it is my opinion that programs which rely exclusively on such help, especially at the beginning, are likely to be relatively unsuccessful because usually neither advertising nor public relations firms have the technical capabilities or reputation which is needed for promoting specific projects. Their efforts therefore tend to be general and to consist in publicizing the investment climate rather than the project opportunities, which constitute a stronger basis for attracting investors. The difference between advertising agencies and public relations firms should be understood. The former are organizations which place advertisements in periodicals and receive most or all of their pay in the form of commissions from the newspaper or magazines used in the campaign. They may also design and prepare advertising material, sometimes on the basis of additional charges to the client, that is, the development agency which employs them. Public relations consultants sometimes also place advertisements and obtain commissions from the publications; more often they serve their client in a variety of other activities. These usually include the preparation of press releases or background feature stories which are distributed either on a general or a selective basis to periodicals which may run them free of charge in their nonadvertising space. Their activities may also include representing the foreign development agency at meetings with prospective investors or in general conferences with people interested in the country. They may also involve efforts to get conventions or other groups to visit the country and contact work to interest editors in publishing material or radio or television stations to carry background material of publicity value.

If an investment attraction program is to include advertising in newspapers or magazines, the advertisements should be placed through an agent. He will provide some useful services, and the advertising will cost no more than if placed directly because the commission is paid by the periodical. This does not mean that the agent has any particular competence in advising on how big the advertising program should be or how it should relate to the rest of the promotion program. His interest will naturally be to secure as large a volume of advertising as possible for correspondingly large commissions.

The public relations consultants are in a different category and may play a larger and more useful role in an investment promotion program. In preparing press releases and feature stories and getting them published in free space in a variety of periodicals, they may be able to get more useful publicity for a country's development program for the money than if the funds were spent entirely on buying advertising space. Moreover, the publicity may carry more weight with the reader. While a paid advertisement is always suspect and is often discounted by a reader, especially by those sophisticated enough to be in positions to make important investment decisions, a feature story in the general columns of a newspaper or a magazine is normally given more credence as it carries at least the implication that the editor has read it and accepted it as factual.

A third form of outside help in a promotion program may come from industrial research and consulting firms. Such firms normally do not do promotion work in the usual sense because they must be very careful to protect their reputation for independence and integrity. Sometimes, as the Arthur D. Little firm did in the early stages of the Puerto Rico program and recently in the Nigeria industrial program, they are prepared to play a promotion role, provided it is a limited one. The terms are that promotion be limited to projects which they have evaluated and consider to be sound and legitimate. For such projects they are prepared to identify companies in the specific manufacturing field which would have a reason to be interested in the opportunity and to place before such prospects the technical and economic details which could provide the basis for a decision on whether the company wished to investigate the opportunity further. In the case of the Nigeria program, the consultants were also able to offer prospective investors assistance in gathering any additional feasibility information requested and in helping the prospective investor apply for any concessions or incentive benefits he might require and be entitled to. The assistance of research-based consulting firms in a promotion program requires that they also be involved in analyzing the opportunities; otherwise, they would not accept a promotional role. But if this involvement exists, their role can be an important one, especially in the early years of a program when the country does not have the staff or facilities to do selective foreign investment promotion itself. The use of a consulting firm of this kind does not, of course, imply that no role remains for advertising agencies or public relations consultants. The work of all three kinds of organizations tends to be complementary rather than competitive, and all may be needed in a major program. The most desirable arrangement would be to use all three as a team, with each taking care of that part of the work for which it has special competence.

9

Assisting New Investors in Industry

When an investor large or small contemplates the possibility of making his first plunge into a foreign investment, especially in the under-developed world, he is beset by fears of the unknown. He is considering taking capital and management resources from a place he knows well, where they can be safely and profitably employed, and putting them into a situation which seems hazardous. The prospective investor's fears are magnified by his realization of how little he really knows about the country where the investment may be made. He will fear that he will be going as a stranger without friends into an unknown and possibly hostile environment. Like a prospective immigrant who thinks of moving to a remote land in the hope of making his fortune, he is held back by his familiar ties but even more by his fear of the unknown.

What the immigrant and the investor need are reassurances and assistance. The fears of the unknown can be removed by making the new land known. The doubts as to whether he will be welcomed and treated as a friend are psychological in origin. They can be removed only by giving the newcomer ample evidence that he is wanted, that he will be welcomed and treated not only fairly, but cordially.

The message of welcome which many developing countries genuinely intend for foreign companies and individuals who can bring the urgently needed industrial capital and know-how is often not communicated to the prospective investor.

The fear of the unknown and possibly unfriendly environment is something which varies greatly depending on the investor and his past experience. Companies which have operated manufacturing facilities for many years in various parts of the world will face another new country with the confidence which flows from successful experiences in similar situations in other places. The need of such investors for reassurances and assistance will be minimal. Many companies which have the resources and industrial experience needed by the underdeveloped countries have had no such background. Few of them, much less than 10 per cent if we take American firms as an example, have ever ventured abroad, even to developed countries where the environment is similar to home. Almost everything about the foreign country being considered is strange, and many things appear threatening. The company will have doubts as to whether foreigners and their capital are really welcome. It will wonder what dangers may lurk beneath the local political scene. It will lack much of the information which it normally uses to evaluate an investment situation. It will not have the local associates such as lawyers, accountants, and construction contractors, in whom it can place trust easily. It will lack familiarity with business methods and customs and will fear that costly mistakes may be made.

Since they are faced with a maze of unknown and potentially dangerous factors, it is not surprising that few of the companies which could go into manufacturing in developing countries ever make the plunge. That they do not go abroad means loss of potential gains for the companies, but even more important, a loss of industrial resources and experience for the developing country. To the investor who stays home the loss will not be critical. He may just make a lower rate of return on his capital. To the country which needs the industry, the loss is much more serious. It means losing the new industry it needs to raise living standards and train its people in industrial skills.

The big investment promotion problem facing the underdeveloped world is not that of getting the experienced international companies to go abroad. They are already abroad on a large scale and are always ready to consider setting up a plant in another country when a project is feasible and the investment climate is acceptable. The problem is how to multiply several times over the number of experienced manufacturing companies who do go abroad. Instead of about 300 American companies manufacturing in Latin America, Africa, and Asia, what is needed is 5,000 or more, each making its contribution to industrial development. There should be at least an equal number of industrial companies from other countries. Promotion alone will not bring about such a massive flow of industrial resources. At most, all that promotion can hope to do is to attract the interest of potential investors to a country and bring them to the point where they are prepared to learn more about the country and its industrial opportunities and to consider the feasibility of a specific project.

It is at this point of initial interest that the program of assistance to new investors takes over from the promotion program. In the sequence of events the promotion phase usually ends when the prospective investor gets on the plane in his home country and starts on his way to investigate on the spot the investment opportunities in the foreign country. He will take that step only when he has had his interest aroused to a high degree by effective promotion or by his own preliminary studies. Once he starts the trip, he has taken a big step toward commitment of an investment. He has let it be known to his associates that he considers a first-hand look at country X is justified on the basis of his studies of the situation up to that point. He is saying that in his experienced business judgment the place looks promising. In going this far he has not taken an irreversible step; but he has made a tentative endorsement of the country as a place where the company should consider operating. It will be psychologically easier from that point to go forward than to back out and have others feel that his first decision was based on inadequate study or poor judgment.

Why is it then that a high percentage of potential investors who go to underdeveloped countries to look into investment possibilities go home and never make the investment? And there is no doubt that the percentage is high. In some instances, of course, the so-called investors are not really investors at all, but salesmen. In other instances investors find evidence of unfeasibility which forces them to abandon their projects. I believe that in many cases the prospective investors fail to make their investments because they are not given the cordial welcome, the reassurances, and the practical assistance which they need to feel secure in making their commitments.

The Kinds of Assistance New Investors Need

The first need of a prospective investor who has reached the point of giving serious consideration to an investment possibility is information. He needs much information, and of course it must be accurate and up-to-date. What he will want to know about the country and about his project will usually go far beyond what has been prepared for investment promotion purposes and often far beyond what anyone in the country thinks is really needed. In providing information for a potential investor, no effort should be spared to give him the information that he needs or thinks he needs. The prospective investor usually will not find it easy to obtain information on his own. He normally does not have the local staff to help him with the detailed research, and he does not know where to go for reliable facts or sound opinions. He may not be able to spare the time required to find the needed information. He will want a seemingly endless flow of details on such questions as markets, plant sites, taxes, labor availability and costs, tariffs, raw materials, transport facilities and rates, credit sources, power rates, fuel costs, and distribution channels. That facts on many of these feasibility elements have already been provided in earlier reports should not discourage anyone from rechecking to obtain later or more precise facts, for it is only through the combination of such details that the investor will arrive at a positive investment decision.

Sometimes the mere collection of raw data is not sufficient if it is desired to give the maximum assistance to the prospective investor. He may need and welcome an analysis of the facts so they will be directly usable in evaluating whether to invest in the project under consideration. If a full feasibility study has not been prepared on the project, this may be the form the analysis type of assistance should take. Such a study may be done exclusively for a specific investor and made available only to him; but usually this should be done only with the provision that if he fails to act within a reasonable time, say six months or a year, the report will then be given to other potential investors. The fact that he is offered a project ahead of his competitors, but with the knowledge that if he does not move quickly they may take the project away from him, is often a spur which produces a prompt investment commitment. A "tailor-made" feasibility study made in response to a show of interest by a specific investor may be made by the industrial development agency independently, or it may be made jointly with the prospective investor. He or his people may work with the development agency staff in making exactly the kind of study which fits the needs and interests of the company concerned. This may be the most valuable kind of study, for it can avoid wasting time on matters not relevant to the particular company, while concentrating on the points of greatest importance in bringing about an investment decision. A study done partly by company staff has another advantage: participation of this kind is another step in the sequence of steps leading to a commitment. Having helped make the study, a company will find it harder to put the report aside or take a critical attitude toward its assumptions or conclusions.

In many cases there is no need to make a completely new feasibility study as part of the assistance to an investor. If a study exists, it may only be necessary to update it. If it is weak on some aspect of the problem, it may be desirable to do a part of the study over again. The investor may hesitate to invest because of inadequate market information; in this case, a thorough market survey may be all that is needed. The investor may not be confident of his cost calculations; in this instance, an investigation of the cost of materials, labor, and other elements of production may be required. The problem may be a lack of needed information or doubts as to the accuracy of available data. In other instances, the information may be readily available to the industrial development agency but needs to be communicated to the potential investor, who must be convinced that the information is reliable.

Assistance in evaluating alternative locations within a country is frequently an important part of testing a project's feasibility, as the profitability may vary considerably depending on location. Because they know the country better, especially its transport facilities and its markets, the staff of the industrial development agency may be able to analyze accurately the costs and benefits of alternative locations for a foreign investor.

The selection of a suitable site for a proposed factory often comes up at this point, even though a project which is otherwise completely feasible is rarely lost to a country because of lack of a suitable site. Usually a country can offer several alternative locations and pieces of land which will meet minimum requirements. In a developed country such as the United States, attracting industry to a community often depends on having choice sites available. Industrial development work emphasizes the readiness of good industrial land, and promotion often centers around the availability of sites. A community which lacks good industrial sites will lose new industry to other locations offering better sites. While this may be true within a developing country, it would be a rare case if a new investment were lost to another country because of lack of a suitable place to put a factory. Nevertheless, providing assistance to a prospective investor in finding a good selection of alternative sites, in evaluating the advantages and disadvantages of each, and in obtaining options on suitable land, is an important element in the process of bringing a project closer to final commitment.

To assist the new investor in dealing with a government which is strange to him is one of the most important kinds of help which should be given. That the country has set up various incentives to attract and assist new industry is an important step toward industrial development. In most countries there is a big difference between incentives on the statute books and incentives granted to a new investor. Sometimes the gap is so great that investors consider the difficulty of getting the benefits greater than their value, so they make their investment decision as though the incentives did not exist. A country which is serious about industrial development and which really means what it implies by passing incentive laws has a great opportunity to maximize the attraction power of good incentives by providing the means by which the new investor can obtain the benefits due to him quickly and easily. Incentive granting in almost any country can be speeded up for the foreign investor by an active system of expediting by the industrial development staff.

Giving a new investor assistance in relations with the government starts with telling him exactly what benefits and concessions he should be able to get. This will enable him to make his feasibility calculations and also to estimate how far he can expect the government to go in giving him tax holidays, import-duty relief, or tariff protection. It is important at this stage to avoid giving a prospective investor the impression that he may get more benefits than he is actually likely to receive. The disappointment of being turned down in requesting something which he had come to expect as a right is sometimes enough to make an investor abandon his project and feel he has been told he is not wanted. The development staff should counsel the investor not only on what incentives, subsidies, or other benefits to ask for, but also on how to ask for them in the most effective way. The investor should be made to realize that the benefits and subsidies cost the country something, in some instances a great deal. He should realize that costly benefits are not granted without consideration of the offsetting benefits the country hopes to receive. He should then be helped to prepare a convincing case which sets forth in quantified terms the benefits his project will bring to the economy. Once the necessary forms are properly prepared with appropriate supporting material, which should eliminate the danger of the incentive applications' being returned for more information, the development staff must swing into action to push the applications through the ministries concerned with a minimum of delay. In most places this is simply a matter of carrying the papers around, sitting with officials while they review the applications, answering questions, and pressing for decisions. When procrastination at lower levels delays the progress of incentive applications, pressure must be applied at whatever higher level is necessary to get action. Obtaining the most rapid possible review of and decisions on all matters affecting an investment application should be a matter of pride for a development agency staff and one of their highest-priority jobs. They must earn the reputation of being "people who can get things done—and done quickly." If they can expedite action in all matters on which an investor must go to the government, the investor will be most favorably impressed with the country and its efficient government, and he will feel that he is really wanted. This impression may be more important in bringing him to a decision than the cash value of the incentive benefits he has requested.

Giving a prospective investor fast action in letting him know where he stands on incentives and other concessions does not imply that he should be given anything and everything he asks for. Investors tend to ask for more than is reasonable and for more than they expect or need to get. The time to talk them out of unreasonable demands is before they have formalized them into firm applications and thus put their pride at stake. Once a reasonable request has been made, and the development staff has agreed that it is a reasonable request, the investor should get his approval without delays which might raise questions in his mind as to the reasons for the delays or doubts as to the wisdom of the project.

It must always be remembered that the prospective foreign investor may be a complete stranger in the country and that the country may constitute a completely new experience for him. He needs to get into personal face-to-face contact with a wide range of people—government officials at various levels (usually the higher the better) and business and industrial executives (both local nationals and foreigners). At a minimum these contacts should be businesslike. He should be able to get to see the right people quickly and feel that they are eager to see him and ready to spend whatever time is needed to deal with the business at hand. Nothing will cool off a potential investor more than to find when he comes to a country for the first time that it is difficult to get appointments with ministers or other officials. He will naturally be sensitive to even the slightest rebuff and may well form a negative impression and leave without a serious exploration of the project he came to investigate. The contacts with government officials and private businessmen should preferably be more than just businesslike. The stranger from abroad will want to get to know the key people on a more personal basis so he can evaluate their attitudes and ideas more accurately than may be possible in a formal interview. The time spent by a minister in having lunch or spending a social evening with a potential investor may easily be the extra touch which makes the investor a firm friend of the country and gives him confidence to go ahead with his project.

The final phase of assistance to new investors is to help the investor get his project established after he has made a firm commitment to go ahead. At this point the investment is assured for the country; but the right kind of assistance may result in getting the project into production more quickly so that its benefits for the country will start flowing at an earlier date. In addition to the direct benefits, getting the project into production quickly is also important as an example to potential investors that things can be done rapidly and that the government and its development agency are ready to follow through and help a new company get firmly established. This is one more way of showing that foreign industrial investments are really wanted. The success of one enterprise is the most powerful attraction for others. Assistance in this phase may involve many things. The new company may need help in getting incorporated, in buying or leasing a suitable plant site, in finding qualified professional associates such as lawyers or public accountants, in recruiting local management and technical staff, and in selecting and training workers. All of these may be important, but the building of a good labor force may be the most critical. Action by the development agency may be extremely valuable in this area. If, as in most developing countries, few of the available workers have had factory experience, the lack of trained workers may be the greatest obstacle to efficient operation in a new factory. More countries could well follow the example of Puerto Rico, which has long made worker training for specific projects an important part of its industrial development package. Under the Puerto Rican system, the development agency is prepared to set up in advance of the opening of a new plant a special training operation to give carefully selected applicants the necessary pretraining so they can enter the new factory with at least the basic starting skills. Help to the industry must take many forms over a period of months or even years. The development agency should stand ready during this period to work closely with the new industry in solving its problems. Some problems will be technical ones such as a consultant might handle; others will be governmental. The new company may need tariff revisions or government loans or other forms of help within the power of the government to give. It will be up to the development agency to help the new industry get what it needs to survive and to prosper.

How to Give Assistance to New Investors

A government development agency which seeks to give assistance to new industrialists must play a role which is different from that which is customary for most government offices. In some ways the help-giving agency must serve the prospective investor as if it were a consulting firm serving a client. The investor needs help; the agency defines what kind of help is needed and then proceeds to give it, keeping in mind that in this task it is working for and serving the client as best it can. Such a role, within reasonable limits, is no contradiction of the agency's responsibility to the government, for the government looks upon the agency as a means to get more industry established. In other ways, the agency serves as a special kind of government office and becomes the contact point for the foreign investor, making it easier for him to find his way around in the government and to obtain what he needs for his project. One can look upon the industrial development agency as a kind of middleman between the new investor and the government. It interprets the government's policy to the foreign investor so he will not ask for the impossible. It interprets the investor's requests to the government to expedite the granting of whatever concessions are appropriate. Through facing both ways, the agency is able to bridge the communications gap which would otherwise exist between the government and the new investor.

In order to serve both the new investor and the government properly, the agency which helps the new industrialists should be somewhat more independent and more business-oriented than most ministerial bureaus usually are. The agency should be promotion-minded and action-motivated. The challenge is to get things done and done quickly. The success of the whole agency is measured by the amount of new industry it helps get established, and the service to new investors is an important link in the chain. The agency will be able to do its job most effectively if it can adopt some of the initiative of consultants and do as they do in seeking out clients to help and in finding ways to make their assistance to them as practical as possible.

The requirement that assistance to new investors be action-based and operate with pressure for results means that the agency performing this work should be staffed by people who are somewhat different in their outlook and work habits from most civil servants. In regular government work in the ministries the stress is on careful review of each problem in order to protect the government and the civil servants from errors. In assistance to investors the emphasis is entirely different. The need is for promotion up to the point where an investor makes his commitment. Then it is for assistance to get the new plant into successful operation quickly. The man who will be successful in helping investors arrive at decisions will be one who can move quickly but reliably and who will not hesitate to push a reluctant or slow-moving official to act—in short, a man "who can get things done." A government can usually rely on its traditional machinery to put enough of a brake on action to ensure that nothing is done too hastily. From the development agency must come the drive to get things done fast enough to impress the prospective investor and to get him to the investment decision before he changes his mind.

The comments made earlier about the importance of foreign investors' being well received by senior officials in more than a formal business way apply also to those who provide assistance to the new investor at the working level. The development agency should not see itself as merely a fact-gathering and question-answering machine. It might perform this part of its work with the utmost efficiency and yet fail to do what is more important—impart to the prospective new industrialists the feeling that the country has a group of able, honest, and sincere people who not only are ready to perform all needed services but who also are personally friendly to the stranger from abroad and ready at all times to go beyond the call of duty in giving assistance. The potential investor will judge the country, its people, and its government to a large degree by the people from the development agency who work with him. If they give him the added human touch of friendship and cordiality, they will do much to win both a friend and an investor for the country.

Most developing countries do surprisingly little to help the potential investor either before or after he makes an investment commitment. In many countries he is often left to his own limited resources to put his project together and to put his enterprise into operation if, despite all the difficulties, he decides to go ahead. There are some notable exceptions, of which three examples may be useful: Puerto Rico, Taiwan, and Nigeria.

Puerto Rico pioneered the business of working closely with potential new investors up to their point of decision and also afterwards while they set up their projects. The Puerto Rican industrial promotion program operation is based on helping the investment prospect reach a detailed evaluation of how his costs would be affected by producing on the island. Partly this is done on the mainland but as soon as he shows evidence of serious interest, an attempt is made to persuade him to visit Puerto Rico for an on-the-spot evaluation of the situation. If possible, a breakdown of his costs at present locations is obtained and analyzed so he can be shown the change in costs which might result through having a plant in Puerto Rico. He is urged to take enough data with him to the island so that he can make comparisons for himself. When he arrives in Puerto Rico, he is given the "red carpet treatment," which includes visits to successful plants where he can discuss the industrial climate with factory managers who have been through the experience of setting up new industries on the island. The development agency is then ready to undertake whatever other fact gathering or analysis the investor may need. When he decides to apply for tax exemption or training benefits or other special incentives, the agency sees that he gets prompt and reasonable action. When he decides to invest, the agency follows through in getting a plant site or leasing factory buildings, in recruiting and pretraining labor, and in other ways which may be helpful.

A similar program of service to investors has been operating for several years in Taiwan, whose industrial development program benefited from Puerto Rico's experience in this field. More recently Nigeria, through the assistance of a team from Arthur D. Little, Inc., provided under the United States Agency for International Development, has embarked on somewhat similar activities, which provided the direct experience upon which many of the ideas in this chapter were based.

10

Financing Industrial Development

It is a basic theme of this book that in developing countries which rely on the private sector to any substantial degree, most financing for industry should come from private investors. This is not an expression of ideological bias, but simply a recognition that in most situations this is the practical solution which works best for a variety of reasons. Much of the investment for economic development must go into the infrastructure—into highways, railways, ports, power facilities, educational facilities, and similar supporting services. The cost of these investments is enormous: it is almost always far beyond the capacity of the government to finance properly, even with a substantial amount of foreign loans obtained from international agencies and friendly governments. At the same time there are great resources of capital in private hands, in the world, and even in most developing countries, which can be drawn into financing national development. These private funds may be made productive by attracting them to the industrial sector of the economy.

Any diversion of government funds from infrastructure investment to industrial financing is likely to have two adverse effects on over-all economic growth: First, there will be a reduction in the total amount of economic development because scarce resources will have been invested in industry which generally is of lower priority than infrastructure and therefore the growth of industry itself will have been impeded because of failure to develop the foundation needed for sound industrial development. Second, the total investment for development is likely to be less because the amount which might have been drawn from private investors for industry will not have been brought forth.

Reliance on the private sector for financing industrial development is justified by other factors beside conserving the scarce government

157

resources for financing the building up of the infrastructure. For new industry to make its proper contribution to a country's economic advancement, it must be soundly conceived in the first place, and it must be efficiently managed. Experience in dozens of developing countries has shown that usually these objectives are most likely to be realized by private financing and management of industry. There are many good reasons why government may choose to establish state industrial enterprises; there are just as many reasons why inefficiency so often results and governments are forced to divert additional resources from development to subsidize their industrial projects. Since the pros and cons of government industrial development were discussed at length in my previous book, there is no need to repeat the arguments here. It is sufficient to observe that few governments in developing countries have either the funds or the management skills to spare for industry. What funds and skills they have are needed more urgently in other development work, and they are well advised in most cases to leave industrial development to the private sector.

The hazards of government in industry go far beyond the question of capability to manage a commercial manufacturing business. The dangers in the preinvestment phase may be equally great. Much that passes as "private foreign investment" in some of the developing countries is the thinly disguised purchase of industrial machinery by governments from salesmen who refer to themselves as "investors" on the basis that they can arrange for suppliers' credits to cover part of the machinery cost and that their companies will make an investment in the equity of the new industry. Such deals, usually arranged in connivance with a dishonest politician, may in fact involve an equity participation by the foreign interests, but generally it will be less than 25 per cent. The factories purchased are often well-engineered, soundly made, and able, if run properly, to produce the goods they were designed to make. But often the projects have no real commercial or economic feasibility, and sometimes they are completely unsuited technically to the needs of the situation. There may be inadequate market for the product, lack of materials, or no prospect of being able to manufacture at economic cost levels. The scale of the plant may be too large for the market or too small to produce at reasonable costs. The process may not be the best one for the given environment. Such projects are rarely based on an objective or independent study of feasibility, although sometimes the sales documents are labeled "feasibility studies" to imply an objectivity which they do not have. All too often, the motive is simply to sell the largest possible plant at the highest possible price regardless of its suitability or value to the country purchasing it. The so-called "participation" offered by the foreign machinery company should not lead anyone to believe that it represents a real investment of outside capital. More often the equity participation represents a small part of the excess profits due to overpricing and is put in as window dressing to conceal the fact that the arrangement is simply one to sell a plant at an inflated price. Projects of this kind are only possible with governments as local partners, for no private local businessman with an ounce of prudence would enter deals so obviously unsound. He would shop around and get the right plant at the best competitive price and accept equity participation only if it represented a real inflow of new capital to the project. The salesman's project is strictly for government. If it is of the kind described, it constitutes prima-facie evidence of collusion with local politicians or officials who are either corruptly involved or so naïve that they should not be allowed to spend public funds.

Another basic theme of this book is that in most developing countries much of the financing for new industry should come from foreign sources, especially in the early years of the industrial development drive. The more underdeveloped a country is, the more this is true. This is the way to achieve the most industrial growth in a short period of time and to make certain that the manufacturing sector of the economy is efficient and thus able to make its maximum contribution to the country's development. A major reason for heavy reliance on foreign capital is that the developing countries need industrial technology and management training even more than the capital, but they are unlikely to get the know-how they need so urgently unless it is associated with an inflow of at least part of the capital required. Another justification for attracting foreign financing for industry is that whatever can be obtained is likely to represent an increase in the total amount of resources available for investment in the country's development. Moreover, the foreign financing which comes in will be in the form of foreign exchange, which is usually the most precious resource in any development program.

Avoiding Excessive Reliance on Foreign Capital for Industrial Development

This book stresses the importance of attracting foreign capital for industrial development mainly because foreign capital will bring in industrial technology and management know-how which cannot be obtained in any other way. However, a developing country cannot afford to rely too heavily on foreign private investment for industrial development. If it does, it may be disappointed through failure to attract sufficient new industries to enable the industrialization process to gain momentum. While the creation of favorable conditions for industry and particularly for foreign investment is almost certain to increase the inflow of industry, this is no assurance that the results will meet expectations or needs. Despite increasing interest in the developing countries on the part of the leading manufacturing companies of the industrialized world, the number of companies actively investing their own funds in Africa, Asia, and Latin America is still discouragingly small. The number can be increased substantially by the developing countries if they will do even some of the things suggested in this book to improve their investment climate. Any individual country seeking industry can do even more, for it can benefit in the competitive situation from the inevitable failure of most underdeveloped countries to put their houses in order to attract foreign-sponsored industry. However, the fact must still be faced that maximum efforts to attract foreign capital alone for industrial development will not result in as much industrial growth as can be achieved if a country makes a massive simultaneous effort to mobilize domestic capital for industry. There is even a danger that emphasis on attracting foreign capital may result in a smaller total amount of investment in industry than would take place if there were a balanced mixture of foreign and local investment.

The desire of a nation, especially a new nation, for industrialization is based on much more than the hope that industry will raise the country's national income. A more fundamental motivation for industrial development in many countries is a deeply rooted desire of the people to show the world, and themselves, that they are capable of doing the work of industry, which requires more advanced skills than the work of agriculture or the extraction of raw materials. This is a natural and a highly meritorious human desire which has been at the root of much of the world's progress. It explains, at least in part, why developing nations want to "do it themselves" to the point of discouraging foreign investment in industry as well as the entry of foreign industrial technical and management personnel. One of the main themes of this book is that development of industry is primarily a transfer process from the industrialized countries to those seeking industry. At the same time, it should be recognized that the inflow of foreign capital and know-how for industry must be a temporary thing; otherwise it will conflict with the reasonable aspirations in every country that industry become national and not remain foreign indefinitely.

For any country which is realistic enough to recognize that a large-scale inflow of foreign-sponsored, foreign-financed, and foreign-managed industry is the key to a rapid start of industrialization in any mixed economy, the conflict between encouraging foreign industry in the country and holding the legitimate belief that industry should be something of the country is a real one. The success of the industrial development effort may rest on the way in which industrial policies are shaped to deal with this apparent conflict of interests. If a government does not base its industrial development program on the creation of conditions which attract foreign-sponsored and even foreign-controlled industry initially, it may not be able to achieve much industrial development. If it does not at the same time find an acceptable way to work toward the reasonably rapid "naturalization" of industry, it may find itself out of office, to be replaced in all probability by political extremists who promise industrialization on a national basis without reliance on the outside world. Short of a situation in which all or most of industry is state-initiated and run, with all the difficulties and disadvantages that such a course entails, the abandonment of the industrial transfer process is almost certain to represent the end of rapid or effective industrialization for the time being.

The reasons why any independent nation does not want industry to be permanently or indefinitely controlled by foreigners are many. The very idea of outside control suggests that decisions are made elsewhere and without proper regard for the real interests of the developing country. This was one of the most unacceptable features of the old imperialism, and it would be one of the most unacceptable aspects of a new foreign-controlled industrial sector. To see that such a situation is not acceptable one does not have to look to Africa or Asia. By the time that American interests came to own more than half the industry in Canada, public opinion reacted strongly and demanded that limitations be placed on foreign control, which they felt had gone too far. If this situation can develop in a country as advanced and as pro-American as Canada, it should surprise no one that newly independent and highly nationalistic countries in other parts of the world should also reject the kind of industrialization which implies indefinite or increasing foreign control.

The archaic sentiments of narrow nationalism which persist even in the sophisticated and apparently internationally minded Western countries are naturally more prevalent in countries which have had to stress their nationalism in recent struggles for independence. The nationalistic sentiments are emotional, not intellectual, and they blind people to the truth of basic economic facts of life such as the need for foreign capital for development. They lead people to feel that there is something exploitive and therefore unacceptable about foreign private ownership. People tend to ignore the fact that capital is one of the most international things in the world and that it will flow quite freely from one country to another if conditions are right to obtain slightly higher returns. They also forget that capital, whether local or foreign, must be paid its price, as determined by its alternatives in the market, if it is to go into industry. In this respect obtaining capital is no different from renting a piece of land or a building or hiring a laborer or an engineer. Each resource is available at a price and tends to go to the user who will pay most.

In purely economic terms it makes little difference to a country whether the capital for its industry comes mainly from foreign or from domestic sources. If it comes from foreign sources, the country can mobilize whatever domestic capital it has for other development purposes. It may be easier to obtain and use local capital for more traditional uses such as agricultural development, education, and public works, than for industry. If local capital is diverted to industrial development, the developing country may have to call on outside capital more heavily for infrastructure development. From the viewpoint of the consumer of industrial products it will make little difference whether the industries of the country are owned by local or foreign companies. Either may adopt policies which benefit the country and the people; either may do otherwise. There is no basis for the belief that foreign-owned industries are more likely to be monopolistic or exploitive than locally owned industries. Subject to the conditions which exist, any private company, whatever the origin of its capital, will try to maximize its profits. The public can find its protection either in developing competition in situations where this is possible or in imposing regulatory measures.

Despite the rationality of the arguments reiterated above as to the lack of logic in objecting to foreign-owned industry, it must be admitted that there are some valid arguments against foreign ownership of a country's industry. One is that real conflicts of legitimate interest can and do arise between international companies and the countries in which their subsidiaries are located. Many of the companies which invest internationally are those producing products sold on a world-wide basis. Their main headquarters and manufacturing facilities will usually be located in the country in which the company originated, but subsidiaries which are under the control of the parent company will be located in many other countries. Companies of this kind rarely commit the fault of following policies designed primarily to further the economic interests of their mother country. Usually they operate as if they were independent nations themselves, adopting policies designed to strengthen the company and advance its world-wide interests, irrespective of the national interests of the countries in which their offices and factories happen to be located. This is a trend which is increasing as more companies become "internationalized" in their activities.

In the normal course of business, conflicts of interest between the international company and the developing country are likely to be few. In most things there tends to be a harmony of interest. Both the company and the country want the industry to expand, to become more efficient, to diversify its operations, to develop new products, to use local supplies and raw materials, to train and upgrade local labor at all levels. Conflicts may arise if the company wishes to repatriate capital and earnings on a scale which is not compatible with a tight foreign-exchange situation in the country. They may also arise from less obvious but equally legitimate differences in views as to what the policies of the subsidiary should be. An international company faced by a decline in total world-wide demand for its product may decide to close down the subsidiaries which are the high-cost producers and to serve the market from the more efficient plants in its system. An international company may prevent some of its subsidiary plants from expanding into attractive export markets because the company has allocated the markets in question to other subsidiaries. Even in Canada, with its relative abundance of management personnel compared with most developing countries, foreign companies have sometimes failed to use local personnel in top positions to the extent which seemed reasonable to the public. These are illustrations of the kinds of conflicts which do arise when industry is foreign-owned. Most of these are disputes in which each party considers itself to be in the right. The existence of occasional difficulties of this kind provides useful ammunition to those who oppose foreign participation in the economy on nationalistic or ideological grounds. But on balance, my conclusion is that they are insignificant compared with the benefits which come from a substantial inflow of foreign industrial capital and skills. The alternative for most developing countries is unemployment and lower living standards due to less industrial development.

There are some other negative aspects to foreign ownership which underlie some of the emotional objections. Foreign ownership of industry necessarily implies an outflow of earnings to service the debt, to pay profits on equity investments, and to pay for royalties and other management costs. These outflows represent payments, often in scarce foreign exchange, which a country naturally should seek to reduce as soon as possible. The employment of foreigners in the better-paying key positions in industry may be an initial necessity, like the importation of capital, but it is also costly. Furthermore, the indefinite presence of foreigners in industry reduces the number of good jobs which local people should hold as soon as they are qualified. The temporary transfer of capital, equipment, and personnel may be wisely accepted as a transition phase, but there are economic as well as emotional reasons for making the phase as short as possible.

Policies in developing countries, as in the developed countries, are not made, however, by economists, by internationalists, or even by people who can be expected to weigh the pros and cons of foreign ownership of industry in an objective way. They are made by politicians subject to the push and pull of public opinion. Often the public is led or misled by small groups who rely on emotional arguments to distract the people from the real issues so the special interests may maintain their position. In most developing countries today, heavy reliance on foreign ownership of industry is politically dangerous to such a degree that it is not a policy which can be advised on a long-term basis. Essential though a foreign industrial inflow may be to almost every developing country, especially in its early stages of development, prudence dictates that great efforts be made from the start to mobilize local capital and get it into industry to the maximum possible extent.

Mobilizing Local Capital for Industrial Development

One of the greatest contradictions in the underdeveloped world is the remarkably large availability of local capital on the one hand and the relatively small use of such capital in industry on the other hand. There are few developing countries in which large amounts of capital are not already in existence. Much of it is privately owned and invested in the traditional ways—rural land ownership and urban real estate being two of the most common investments. From many underdeveloped countries vast sums have gone in flight to safe havens in America and Europe. Large amounts of capital have been built up in the pension funds of government employees in many countries and in reserves of local insurance companies in some nations which have reached a medium level of development. In many countries the amount of local capital which has been channeled into these uses far exceeds any possible requirement of capital for industrial development for many years to come. If even a small fraction of the wealth now lost to the economy or employed in low-priority uses could be rechanneled into industry, the problem of financing industrialization would be solved. How can it be done?

The redirection of existing locally owned capital into industry is not something which can be done easily or by any one act of government. The capital is in many forms and subject to many barriers which stand in the way of its diversion into industrial investment. Some of the funds are subject to law, and their use can be changed by altering the relevant laws or passing new ones. Most of the capital is in private hands and can be gotten into industry only through a combination of persuasion and pressure. In both cases what the government can do to divert capital to industry will be limited by over-all public feeling as to the safety and attractiveness of industry as an investment. The bringing home of local capital which local residents have placed abroad for safety is the extreme case. The money has gone because its owners feared for its security at home. It has therefore become almost "foreign capital" as far as the country is concerned. It can be drawn back only by the same kind of action which is necessary to attract new foreign capital—measures to improve the investment climate. This means creating conditions of reasonable political and economic stability even more than passing specific laws concerning convertibility and other matters. When invested abroad, most capital flight money does not earn a high return. Usually the prospects are that much higher returns could be made in industrial investment at home. Once a reasonable investment climate has been established, much of it will come home.

The repatriation of capital which has flown and the diversion of local capital from traditional uses to industrial investment both require the creation of new interests and attitudes in the minds of the private owners of capital. They must become industrial-investment-minded. That is, they must be attracted to industry by evidence that industrial investment offers better profit opportunities than alternative investments and that it does not necessarily involve unreasonable risks. Partly this is a process of publicizing industrial development. The idea of industrial development and the opportunities it offers must be given a great amount of publicity within a country if the right state of "industry mindedness" is to be generated. Part of the process is to develop a new generation of investors who accept industry as being as natural for investment as agriculture, real estate, trading, or moneylending. This is a state of mind which will grow as examples of highly successful industrial investments become more numerous in the country and as more and more well-known citizens become prominent in industrial investment or industrial management.

The diversion of capital from traditional uses to industry can be speeded up considerably by governments which realize the importance of doing so. The simplest and most effective method is to alter the tax situation so that investment in industry has more favorable tax treatment than other kinds of investment. For the wealthy in many countries one of the most attractive things about investment in land is that taxes on the earnings are low and often easy to evade. In contrast, investment in industry is often taxed more heavily, and the taxes are harder to evade. The government can bring about the reversal of this anomalous situation by imposing and collecting new high taxes on current earnings and capital gains from investments in land, while offering lower tax rates on earnings from investments in industry. Most governments, if they chose to and if they had the political and administrative strength to carry through their policy, could quickly channel large amounts of capital into more productive use in industry by implementing policies along these lines.

The passing of land reform laws in many countries creates an opportunity for a major diversion of local capital from land to industry. Under most of the land reform programs, the owners of large tracts of agricultural land are required to give up a substantial part of their land and are paid in the form of government bonds. The bonds are usually scheduled to be paid off by the governments which issued them in annual installments. A common term of land reform bonds is twenty years; thus 5 per cent of the face value of the bonds is to be paid off in cash each year. Some of the land reform bond repayment money may find its way into industrial investment without any special assistance. But much of the money may be invested in urban real estate or even in foreign securities unless a better alternative is provided. A means to encourage the direct conversion of land capital into industrial capital would exist if a system were organized through which an industrial development finance agency offered to accept land reform bonds in payment for industrial fund shares. The annual installment payments on the land reform bonds held by the industrial agency together with interest on the bonds would then go to the industrial agency, which would invest the proceeds in industry —in industrial shares or bonds, or better, in both. From the earnings of the industrial finance agency, dividends would be paid on the new industrial fund shares. The landowners would become the owners of industry through the device of owning shares in the agency which financed industry. The great attractions in this plan for the landowners are these: Instead of receiving bonds of fixed value which are likely to depreciate because of inflation long before they are fully paid off, they would receive shares in industry which would probably not depreciate in case of inflation, their dividends on the industrial fund shares would very likely exceed the bond interest they would have received on the land reform bonds, and their industrial investments would usually be relatively safe as they would be committed to a portfolio of many projects and not invested in a single project. From the point of view of the economy there would be several great advantages to the plan. The flight of the land payment capital would have been stopped, at least to the extent that the bonds were exchanged for industrial fund shares. The annual installments paid on the land reform bonds would be channeled directly and fully into a highly productive use, again only to the extent that the bonds were exchanged. A plan along these lines could be set up by one country. But if it were possible to include several countries in the system, the industrial financing fund could operate on an international basis, thus giving further diversification to the investment portfolio and offering an international assurance that the terms of the plan would be honored by all countries participating. Either a national or an international plan of this kind might be able to get into action more quickly if it could anticipate its annual receipts from the governments involved by borrowing the expected amounts a year or two in advance from an international lending agency.

In many developing countries which have reached a middle stage of economic advancement, large sums of capital have been accumulated in the pension funds of government employees. Sometimes these reserves are not used in a way which meets the nation's priorities for economic development. Normally the use of pension reserves is legally restricted, and in some countries they may not be invested in industrial securities of any kind. It is only right that pension reserves which represent the accumulated savings of large numbers of people, mostly in the middle- or lower-income groups, should not be endangered through being used in unsafe investments. However, if a country's industrial development climate is reasonably good and if the new industrial sector is developing successfully, there is no good reason why a portion of the capital in pension reserves should not be available for investment in industry. The use of such funds in industry should be to the mutual benefit of both the funds and the industrial sector of the economy. The portion which would be appropriate to allow for industrial investment would depend on the safety of industrial investment relative to other investments, and this would vary from time to time and from country to country. In many countries it would be reasonable to permit up to one-quarter or even one-half of pension reserves to be invested in industrial securities, provided that adequate diversification by industry and company were required to avoid the danger of a large loss in case of failure of one industrial company. For pension funds investments in bonds or preferred shares of industrial companies would be preferable to investments in common stock for the bulk of the funds involved, although the investment of a smaller amount in common stock in order to improve the overall rate of return would usually be desirable. The higher gains which pension funds should be able to make from a portfolio of industrial bonds and stocks, compared with returns obtained in nonindustrial investments, should appeal to the prospective beneficiaries of the funds as a good reason for a more liberal policy on pension fund investments. The application of a sound policy of drawing pension fund reserves into industrial investments will depend on the success a country has in establishing and developing some of the financial institutions to be discussed later —particularly stock exchanges and mutual funds.

Another pool of capital reserves which exists in some of the partly industrialized countries is to be found in the reserves of insurance companies, particularly life insurance companies which must accumulate large amounts for eventual payout to policy holders. During the period in a country's development when life insurance becomes popular, the volume of new policies written may increase rapidly and constitute one of the major forms in which capital is accumulated. Since most of those who take out policies are in the younger age brackets, the companies experience a low demand for funds for payment of death benefits. The use of the reserves which are thus built up is normally controlled by law. A change in law may be all that is necessary to encourage a shift of some of the investible funds to industrial investment. It might be justified in some situations for the government to require that a certain percentage of reserves, say 10 or 20 per cent, should be invested in approved industrial bonds, or perhaps better, in bonds or stock of a development bank or other financial intermediary which would provide both diversification of investment and professional management of the funds.

Various changes in the industrial investment situation are necessary in some countries before it is appropriate to make efforts to channel pension or insurance reserves into industrial investment and before it is possible to attract individual private investors to industrial investments. One of the most important is action to protect investors, particularly small, minority investors. Underdeveloped countries frequently do not have the kind of protection for the investing public which has developed in countries like the United States and which has helped to give the public confidence in purchasing the securities of industrial companies. This is understandable for in the past most companies in the less developed countries have been owned by families or by small groups of close associates. They have not been open to the general public as investments. As long as companies are closely held, that is, owned by a small number of shareholders, there is no particular need for government intervention to set standards. Once companies start to seek capital from the general public, either individuals or institutions such as pension funds or insurance companies, it is important that safeguards be established. One basic requirement should be that all companies accepting investments from the public must have their affairs audited at least once a year by certified public accountants who are independent of the company being audited. The auditor's report, together with reasonably detailed financial statements of the company's position and operations, should have to be published each year within a specified length of time, say three months, of the end of the company's financial year. The publication of false or misleading information in a company's annual reports should be a legal offence carrying a heavy penalty, and a simple way should be provided for any shareholder to complain about faulty or inadequate disclosure of a company's business. In addition, the government should establish an agency to supervise the affairs of all companies selling shares to the public. The agency should be required to review all prospectuses for new issues of securities and to grant or refuse permission for the new issues to be sold. It should also have the power to investigate a company any time it feels that incorrect or incomplete information may have been given in a prospectus or annual report. The agency should investigate complaints of unfair treatment of minority shareholders or other action by companies which is illegal or which represents discrimination against any shareholders. Specific unfair practices should be defined, and the agency should have the power to levy appropriate penalties on offending companies.

The development of investment in industrial securities also requires the creation of a stock exchange, which is nothing more or less than an auction market where those wishing to sell securities can meet with those who wish to buy securities and where they bargain, reach agreement, and make exchanges. Since it is impractical for large numbers of individual small investors to meet personally to trade securities, the practical operation of an exchange requires that there be an organized securities business with intermediary agents called brokers who will execute buy or sell orders for prescribed commissions. It is not necessary to wait until a large and active business in industrial securities develops before starting a stock exchange. In Lagos, Nigeria, for example, a stock exchange was started for trading in the shares of less than a dozen local companies. The exchange met only a few hours each week, but it served to establish a market and provided an opportunity for those wishing to buy or sell shares to meet and do business. Without a stock exchange, investment in industrial companies will not be attractive to most people because investments in shares will not be liquid. They may even be regarded as frozen by the individual who cannot get his money out when he needs it or when he thinks he could profit by investing it in something else. Once an active stock exchange is operating, industrial shares immediately achieve a new and most attractive feature: they become more liquid than most other investments. This is a characteristic of great importance to small investors. It is one that is not possessed by investment in land or buildings or in ownership of small, closely held companies. While stock exchanges are usually privately operated businesses in most countries, there would be nothing to prevent a government development bank or similar agency from taking the initiative in starting an exchange and in supervising it to ensure that it is honestly and efficiently run.

Once an organized stock market is in operation and a growing number of companies have issued shares which are available to the general public, the basis has been laid for other developments which are all part of creating an active capital market. One of these is the growth of investment firms which will sell new issues of securities, either bonds or stock, to the general public. It must not be assumed that the mere existence and availability of securities will automatically create a large demand for them. In a country where industrial securities have never been known, the ready customers will be few, even though the potential number of customers may be large. A satisfactory market for securities will come about only when securities are sold actively and aggressively. This is not likely to happen until the selling of securities has become an organized business, although there have been examples of a company selling its own securities directly to the general public. This was done in Argentina, where the Kaiser automobile company sold stock on a door-to-door basis and raised a large amount of capital from people who had never heard of industrial shares.

An investment dealer may soon go one step beyond selling new securities on commission: he may become an underwriter—buying a large block of bonds or shares from the company wanting the new capital, then selling the securities to the public as and when he can, for whatever price he can get. In this kind of an operation, the underwriter is like a merchant who buys the product—the industrial securities—at a wholesale price from the company which issued them, then sells them on a retail basis to a large number of individual customers. The importance of industrial security underwriting is great, and its development should be encouraged in most countries where it does not exist. It is a way of making substantial amounts of capital available fairly rapidly for an industrial company which is being set up or being expanded and of drawing in from a large number of private investors the capital needed to replace the funds already put up by the investment dealer. The fact that a reputable dealer has been willing to buy the stock or bonds outright when issued serves as an additional indication to the prospective small purchaser that the securities are worthy of consideration. Financing through such a mechanism is hardly available to small and medium-sized industrial firms, especially when they are new and unproved. Initially, the device fits the needs of the larger firms, especially those which have some foreign participation, preferably with a well-known brand name, and possibly the participation of a development bank or other local financial institution of good standing. That such partners are involved in the financing goes far to ensure that an investment dealer would be prepared to underwrite the new issue and that he could sell it successfully to the public.

The financing of new industry from local sources cannot rest only on new issues of securities purchased by individual investors and by pension funds and insurance companies, even if the capital market has been soundly developed through the establishment of a stock exchange, investment dealers, and underwriting firms. Much needs to be done by financial intermediary firms, and much that they do will help in the general development of the capital market. The kind of intermediary firm which is best known throughout the underdeveloped world is the development bank, which is usually owned by the government. A development bank, if it is to do its job well, must be quite different from a commercial bank. Its business will consist largely, if not entirely, in making well-secured term loans to productive enterprises, usually industrial companies, or in buying the shares of such firms. Its loans will usually be medium term (often defined as being of from one to five years' duration) or long term (often defined as being of more than five years' duration). This is in sharp contrast to the policies of commercial banks, which normally do not lend for more than one year. The difference between the two kinds of banks does not end with the duration of loans. The development bank, though interested in making a profit on its operation and in safeguarding its own capital, is primarily a development institution, or should be. Its main concern in financing a project should be the prospective value of the project to the national economy. At the same time it should require that projects meet reasonable standards of commercial profitability and offer reasonable security for the financing provided. A commercial bank quite properly insists on a higher level of security and must be reasonably certain that it can get back all the funds it has loaned within a year. This is important to safeguard the liquidity of the bank. Most development banks are also able to invest some of their funds in companies by purchasing their shares, usually as minority shareholders, leaving the management of the enterprises to the majority shareholders. This is especially important to a development bank in a country in which there is a likelihood of serious inflation which would depreciate the value of fixed loans to a serious degree and thus reduce the value of the bank's assets.

While most developing countries have development banks, many banks fail to meet the needs as well as they could. Some of them simply do not have the necessary investment funds to play an important role in industrial development. An expansion of the development bank is often the first step a country should take in embarking on a comprehensive industrial development program. The initial expansion of a development bank's resources may have to come from the government, and this is one of the most useful ways in which to invest government funds in industry. But any development bank which is well run should have no difficulty in obtaining long-term loans from the World Bank (through its subsidiary, the International Finance Corporation), the United States Agency for International Development, or, if it is in Latin America, from the Inter-American Development Bank. These international lending organizations look with much favor on development banks because they provide an ideal means by which development financing can be channeled into a multitude of small and medium-sized industrial projects. These could not be financed directly from an external lending institution because of the problems and costs of making and supervising large numbers of small loans. The local development bank which obtains a $2 million loan from an international agency and then uses the money for loans or equity participations in ten or twenty industrial firms, may be thought of as an institution which buys on the wholesale market and sells on the retail market. There is usually a spread of 2 or 3 per cent between the interest rate charged by the international agency and that charged by the development bank. In handling loans in the range of $25,000 to $300,000, and even smaller ones, the local development bank is able to provide a link of supervision and local knowledge which is superior to what an external lending agency could provide, as well as being more economical.

In reforming an existing development bank so that it may play a major role in industrial development, a country may well consider the possibility of making it less of a government agency and more of a joint venture with the private sector. Such a change might relieve the bank from many pressures to operate on a political rather than a purely economic basis and might bring forth greater participation from private investors. One step in making a bank less governmental is to provide that some of the directors be nominated by private industry and by the commercial banks. A more fundamental move is to provide a way for the private sector to join in financing the expansion of the bank's resources. This can be done by issuing new shares or bonds of the bank and making them available to the public. For private companies, insurance companies, pension funds, and other such investors, this provides an opportunity to invest in industrial growth on a supervised and diversified basis. For a private individual, who may be either a wealthy person or a member of the new and growing middle class, the availability of development bank securities might provide the ideal way to enter the field of industrial investing.

Another effective way to expand a development bank's resources and make it into a joint venture with the private sector is to invite the participation of some foreign private banks or financial institutions in financing the expansion. More than a dozen American banks and a substantial number of British and European banks have invested in the shares of foreign development banks. Their motives in doing so appear to be mixed. The prospects are usually good that the capital put into a development bank will be secure and that there will be a reasonable, though probably not a spectacular, return. A more important reason for participating may be that the association will lead to opportunities for related companies to invest directly in major projects and that the parent bank itself may benefit in contacts which will help to expand its international commercial banking. The participation of a foreign bank in a local development bank has another value which goes beyond the additional money provided: it is an assurance that the institution is well run, that it is operated on sound business principles rather than on a political basis, and that it does the job of evaluating the feasibility of projects well. Such an endorsement may go far in attracting both local and foreign capital directly to the projects which the bank helps finance.

In addition to the industrial financing done by a development bank, either wholly or partially government-owned, there is a real place in many developing countries for private industrial financing companies. In Latin America these are known as *financieras*. These companies are usually established by a group of local banks, insurance companies, and others interested in an opportunity to participate in industrial development financing beyond what they could do individually. Some of the *financieras*, like development banks, obtain loans from local or foreign or international financial institutions, and some of them also obtain equity participations from foreign sources. In many ways the private *financieras* are really private development banks, but their completely private nature enables them to operate with a freedom and a speed which are rarely possible for an institution which is largely or entirely governmental.

Somewhat similar to making available development bank shares for public investment is the creation of the kind of investment trust arrangement known in North America as the mutual fund. The mutual fund is a financial institution which sells its own shares to the public. Its assets consist of a portfolio of securities, usually mainly shares, of companies listed on the stock exchange. The mutual fund stands ready to redeem its shares, that is, to pay off its shareholders in cash, to the full current cash value as shown by the value of its portfolio on the stock market divided by the number of fund shares outstanding. The individual purchaser of mutual fund shares is thus assured of complete liquidity. He can obtain a full refund of his investment in cash on a day's notice. Through this device the small investor is able to "buy a piece" of a large portfolio which stands to have stability since it contains shares of several dozen companies, which are well diversified by industry. Mutual funds have been established successfully in several of the Latin American countries. This has proved their attractiveness to the private investor making his first investment in industrial securities, and it has shown that mutual funds are a valuable device in mobilizing local capital for industry. In Brazil, for example, the mutual fund managed by the International Basic Economy Corporation had assets equivalent to $26 million by the end of 1963, representing investments by nearly 45,000 people.

The Joint-venture Approach to Industrial Development

Some industrial development will come in most developing countries which is financed by purely internal private sources, if the right environment is created. There are few countries in which a substantial amount of privately held wealth does not exist. Gradually, as examples of profitable industrial ventures become evident and as knowledge of industrial opportunities and ways to approach industrial projects becomes more widespread, more private capital will find its way into manufacturing. Throughout this book many suggestions are made which can accelerate a movement of private funds into industry. In many countries forces are at work which will encourage this natural development. One of the most important is land reform, which may divert capital to industry when it can no longer be employed in land holding. Another is the decline of profitable investment opportunities in building houses, apartments, and office buildings as they become overbuilt in relation to the demand for them.

Industry will also come to most developing countries in the form of projects which are wholly owned by foreign investors, usually companies which wish to manufacture their product locally to protect a market which they have already developed. Much of this book is concerned with measures to increase the inflow of private foreign investment. In the recent past, few foreign companies were interested in any overseas investments unless they were entirely owned and controlled by the parent company. In view of the lack of capital available for industry in most underdeveloped countries and the virtual absence of local businessmen with industrial interest and experience who might be useful working partners, this attitude was only to be expected. Some of the world's leading companies, such as General Motors and Ford, still prefer not to invest abroad unless they have full control over the companies they establish. Their position may be well founded in experiences which they and others have encountered in situations where local shareholders have held views and demanded policies which conflicted with the world-wide interests of the parent company.

The wholly owned subsidiary company may still represent the most common form through which internationally minded companies set up manufacturing operations abroad, but since World War II the alternative of a joint venture with local associates has become increasingly important.[1] A joint venture may be defined as "any form of association which implies collaboration for more than a very transitory period." But I shall use the term to refer only to those joint ventures in which ownership is shared between one or more investors in a developed country, on the one hand, and one or more investors in the developing country, on the other hand. These are sometimes called joint capital ventures.

The joint venture in which ownership is shared for an indefinite period of time is so attractive to developing countries that some have gone out of their way to require or at least encourage this as the preferred form of foreign investment. There are several reasons for this preference. First, a joint venture goes far in meeting the aspiration of the people of most developing countries that development should be on a partnership basis in which the local partners share the benefits with the foreign partners. Inherent in this idea is the feeling that nonpartnership arrangements involve exploitation which is all too often reminiscent of colonial arrangements. Also involved is the idea that a partnership indicates that each party needs the other and has something to contribute to a mutual effort. Second, a joint venture is a means to draw local capital and management personnel into new industrial enterprises, providing experience in industry and the opportunity to grow into more substantial involvement as local strength is developed.

[1] Wolfgang G. Friedmann and George Kolmanoff (eds.), *Joint International Business Ventures,* Columbia University Press, New York, 1961.

Like any partnership arrangement in which two or more individuals or organizations are linked to undertake a common project, an industrial joint venture is bound to involve risks and difficulties which do not exist when one investor or one investing company proceeds entirely independently. There is the real danger that even with the best of intentions, disagreements may arise which are based on real conflicts of interest. To cite only one obvious basis of disagreement, the parent company may want the local project to fit into the company's world-wide business policies. For example, it may want the local enterprise to avoid selling its product in certain markets which the parent company can supply better from other plants. Such a policy may be directly contrary to the interests of the local partner, who may wish the local plant to prosper and expand by selling its product wherever it can do so profitably. Or, to give another example, the parent company may decide to suspend production at the local plant when business conditions decline and to supply the local market by importing the product from a plant in another country. This may be strongly contrary to the interests of the local partners, who may even want to insist on government action to exclude the proposed imports, even though they come from a plant controlled by the same parent company.

In their traditional reluctance to enter joint ventures, many international companies are mindful of such problems, which they anticipate will arise sooner or later. They are also conscious of the differing viewpoints often held by investors in underdeveloped countries, especially the possibility that they will demand an excessively large payout of profits when the strength and development of an enterprise may require that all or most of the earnings be retained. They are justifiably concerned that local partners in a joint venture may press for the employment of relatives or friends in positions for which they are not qualified. If the prospective joint venture partner is a government agency, the foreign partner may be worried over the prospect that a change of government may result in the enterprise's falling into disfavor with the new government.

In view of these valid fears which foreign investors often hold in regard to most proposed joint ventures, why are joint ventures becoming increasingly acceptable to companies considering foreign investments? The main reason is that joint ventures are so strongly preferred by the governments of many developing countries that it is often a question of accepting a joint venture arrangement or missing out on an attractive investment opportunity. While few governments go so far as to state flatly that only joint ventures will be permitted, it is clear that they usually create more favorable conditions for joint ventures. The positive advantages of joint ventures are also becoming more evident to foreign investors. In the increasingly nationalistic environment of most developing countries, a joint-venture arrangement amounts to nothing less than insurance for a foreign investor. The joint nature of the venture makes the foreign firm a partner in national development rather than a target for antiforeign attacks. The local associates in the venture provide the new enterprise with a ready-made local image and with local spokesmen who are likely to be influential in advancing the company's interests and protecting it when problems arise. On the strictly financial side, the joint venture enables the foreign company to set up a project with less of its own money and thus with less risk than would be possible in a wholly owned investment.

In most joint ventures, the foreign partner will be a private investor, almost always a private company or sometimes more than one. There is nothing in the idea to prevent a foreign government or an international agency from being the foreign partner, but this is a rare situation. On the developing country side of the arrangement, however, the local partner may be either private or government, or a combination. Most foreign companies would have some good reasons for preferring private investors as their local partners in the joint venture. Private associates would be more likely than government officials to bring practical local business experience to the new enterprise, and there would be reason to expect that they would be more likely to look at business questions from a purely business viewpoint. Changes of government would be less likely to upset the continuity of the joint-venture arrangements if the local partner were a private businessman or private company.

The participation of the local government, usually through the intermediary form of a development corporation or some such institution, is an alternative which has both advantages and disadvantages. On the plus side, the active involvement of the government is a significant assurance of official recognition and support, something which may be valuable to the new enterprise when it is in need of special help such as a change in tariffs, a tax exemption, or assurance of a large government purchase of its product. Moreover, nothing will serve as well to give a foreign-sponsored enterprise a good national image as the participation of the government in its ownership. The government may be a good partner because it is likely to have a somewhat different view on company policy than a private local investor. A government is not likely to be in as much of a hurry to draw dividends as a private individual; in fact, it may well prefer to see a company reinvest its earnings to provide funds for expansion. Offsetting these advantages of having the government as a venture partner are several negative points. Most serious is the possibility that a change of government might upset the harmonious relations between the foreign partners and their local associates. While an incoming government would inherit its predecessor's legal connection with the venture, the personnel would probably change and the danger of conflicts would increase. Political partners, even with continuity, have another disadvantage: they may attempt to use the enterprise for partisan political purposes including the finding of jobs for the party's faithful.

Reluctance on the part of a foreign company to accept a government as an investment partner may be natural, for in its home country the company would not think of entering into such an arrangement. But it should be remembered that in an underdeveloped country sources of private capital and methods of private capital accumulation and investment may not have been developed. In many countries the only means by which any large amount of capital is accumulated is through the government marketing boards which buy agricultural produce from the farmers and sell it on export markets. The margin between the buying and selling price for the produce is sometimes sufficiently great and the volume involved so large that hundreds of millions of dollars of capital are accumulated. Capital accumulation on such a scale would be impossible in a primitive society if the full proceeds from the sale of the agricultural crops were distributed to the peasant farmers. In many countries the best way to make the capital accumulated in this way productive is through government investment of the funds in joint ventures with private foreign companies having the technical and management experience to ensure that the investments are wisely used.

Government Policy in Industrial Financing

As has been pointed out throughout this book, leaving industry to the private sector does not imply that a government eager for rapid industrial growth can afford to adopt a do-nothing policy. There is much to be done in the preinvestment phases of any industrial project, and there is also a vital role which government financing should play in regard to private industry. It is important that this role, which includes participation in joint ventures as well as other forms, should be clearly defined on the basis of principles which are well understood.

The best basis for government participation in industrial financing is the catalyst principle, that is, the use of a limited amount of government funds to bring forth a larger amount of private investment. This is called the catalyst principle because of its similarity to the use of a catalyst in chemical reactions. The catalytic element may be small in size and in cost compared with the other ingredients, but it is of great importance for it can set off the reaction which otherwise would not take place.

The catalyst principle applies to industrial financing in an underdeveloped country for a number of reasons:

1. Reduction of risk. By providing a part of the financing for an industrial project, government reduces the amount which the private sponsors need to supply. This reduces their risk, and in many cases may be sufficient to attract private investment.

2. *Assurance of official approval and support.* When a government participates in the financing of an industrial project, it demonstrates in the clearest and most tangible manner that it approves of the project. This is an assurance of great importance to a private investor, especially a foreign investor, for it goes far in convincing him that the project will enjoy whatever concessions or support it needs from the government.

3. *Improved public image.* A project which has some government financing is in a much better position to secure public approval than one which is purely private. This is of great importance in any country where private business has had a poor reputation in the past and where there is antagonism between the public and private business. Instead of being regarded as something which is used by the wealthy class to exploit the people, a project which has government participation can become a symbol of national development. For a project with foreign financing and management this is even more important than for a purely local private industry. Instead of being a target of antiforeign attacks by nationalistic extremists, a jointly financed project may be viewed as a partnership in which foreign funds and know-how are associated with national development.

4. *Improvement of rate of return.* If some or all of the government participation in a project's financing is in the form of loans rather than ownership of equity, the financial structure of the project will have more leverage and thus higher profitability to its owners. This occurs when the shares are a smaller amount of the total project financing than would otherwise be the case, and the rate of return on the shares is higher as a given amount of profits will be distributed among a smaller number of shares.

A government's objective in using the catalyst principle in project financing should be to obtain as much private investment in industry as possible with a minimum investment of government funds. This is another form of "leverage." By investing a relatively small amount, a government obtains benefits through a multiplication factor which justifies the use of scarce government funds for industrial projects which would not warrant government investment on a wholly owned basis. The aim should be to make the multiplication factor as large as possible. It is not possible to state what percentage of a project's total investment should be supplied by a government. The percentage varies from one project to another—some will require a substantial government investment, others little or none. It will vary from one country to another, and it will vary from one stage of development to another in a country. Generally speaking, however, the catalyst principle implies that the catalytic element, the government investment, will be small in relation to the private investment it generates. In a joint venture the government participation will usually be a minority one in relation to the total share capital of a company. Occasionally it may be equal to the private investment in shares to give a 50-50 basis of ownership, or it may even exceed the private ownership. The percentage is not as important as the principle that the responsibility for management should rest with the private owners, for their skill in management is the main thing which needs to be obtained from the private participants.

In emphasizing that the objective of government should be to attract as much private capital as possible with a minimum investment of its own resources, it is equally important to stress what a government's objective should not be. A government should not make its investment in industry in order to get the highest possible rate of return on its funds. Appropriate though this basis may be for private investors, it is contrary to the whole idea of catalyst-type investments. The government, on this principle, is not investing in industry to make money. It is investing to generate a higher rate of private industrial investment than would otherwise take place. If the projects are primarily selected and financed by private investors risking substantial amounts of their own funds, there is a built-in assurance that the projects will have commercial profitability in which the government will share if it owns stock. There will also be assurance that risks will be reasonable and that the capital invested by the government, whether in shares or in loans, will be fairly safe. It will be hard for any government to do better than the private investors in estimating the returns and risks on a project. What the government must do is to base its investment decisions on a careful evaluation of how little it needs to invest in order to attract the largest possible amount of private investment.

This is not to suggest that a government should ignore other factors, such as relative priorities of various projects, in making catalyst-type investments in industry. Even if it operates exclusively on the catalyst principle in financing industry, the government's funds for the purpose will be limited because of competing demands for funds for other development purposes. The rationing of the limited funds for industrial financing will require that careful consideration be given to the way in which the funds will be used. The choice of alternatives may be wide. The funds available in any year might be used as a catalyst investment in only one large project deemed to be of high national economic priority. At the other extreme, they might be used as catalysts for hundreds of small private projects. The decision should rest on thorough study of the probable value to the national economy of the alternative projects. This does not mean that all investing has to be deferred until all possible projects are analyzed, but it does mean that value judgments have to be made as to priorities at least by kinds of industry.

Methods for Government Investment in Industry

A decision to invest on the catalyst principle in projects which are managed and mainly financed by the private sector still leaves open a number of questions as to how the policy should be put into operation. A primary question is whether the government financial participation should be in the form of equity, that is, shares of joint-venture industrial companies, or in the form of debt, that is, loans to companies which are wholly privately owned. Each approach has its advantages and disadvantages, and generally a government should be flexible and use both financing forms as required. Investment in shares in a joint venture makes the government a part owner of the enterprise and thus entitles it to share proportionately with the private investors in whatever profits are made. This has distinct advantages: it makes the enterprise a true partnership and provides a way for the people of the country as a whole to share in the returns of the industry. This can be regarded as being similar to the "patronage refund" which a cooperative distributes to its members who make its surplus possible. It can even be looked upon as a form of social ownership in which the public share in the ownership of industry. A sharing of ownership by this means is a way to "make the best of both worlds," public ownership and private ownership. The sharing of the profits of the enterprise between the private participants, who supply the management and part of the capital, and the public, who supply the remainder of the capital and who pay the company's way through being purchasers of its products, may represent the fusion of two ways of life which best meets the needs and aspirations of the people of many developing countries. The alternative method of financing—loans—is, by comparison, a way of aloofness. By giving a loan to a company, the government has first claim on the company's finances for payment of interest and repayment of the loan on the terms agreed upon. The government's position, however, is that of an outsider and not of a partner. Normally it will have no say in the conduct of the company's affairs and not even the right to have an observer listening in on the discussions of the company's business. Such an arrangement will do little to make the enterprise a national venture or to answer criticisms aimed at the project's private or foreign ownership.

A government should be flexible in its policy as to how it will stand ready to participate in project financing. The primary objective, it must be remembered, is to attract a maximum amount of private investment, especially foreign investment. This means that the wishes of the private partners are all-important. If giving a loan to a project can make it attractive to the private investors because it will make the venture more profitable for them (through providing greater leverage), this may be what should be done. If, on the other hand, an equity investment in a full joint venture will attract more private investment because of the greater assurance of official support, this may be what is required.

When a government participates in financing a project by granting loans, the question of loan limits and terms becomes important. When a government assumes the position of a lender to an industrial company, it gains no right to share in profits, but it does have the protection of having a mortgage on the assets of the enterprise and thus a first claim on assets in case the enterprise becomes unable to maintain service on its debt. Prudence suggests that the loan should only be for a part of the original value of the assets which are mortgaged as security. This is because the assets would rarely bring their original value if they had to be sold in case of bankruptcy. Normally a loan which is greater than half the original value of the assets would be hazardous and should be avoided. Loans of 90 per cent or more of the total cost of a project, which have been made by some governments (such as the corrupt regime of Batista in Cuba), serve only to allow the government to assume practically all the risks while the owners have a fantastic leverage to profit unreasonably with almost no investment of their own funds.

Regardless of whether a government participates in the financing of new industry through sharing in ownership in joint ventures or through making loans to completely privately held companies, it is important that the government's participation be made as nonpolitical as possible. As previously noted, a major objection to having a government as a joint-venture partner lies in the danger that changes of government may upset a relationship with private partners. Another risk is that attempts will be made to use the enterprise for partisan political purposes. These dangers may be lessened if the government's financial participation is insulated from partisan politics (and even from the ordinary work of government) by channeling the government's industrial financing through a semi-independent agency such as a development bank or a development corporation. If the agency involved is only partly government-owned, the insulation will be even greater. The national interest in the economic success of the enterprises financed is so great that the government investments in them should be regarded as being above politics, even though the party in office at the time successful projects were started may naturally expect to claim credit for having done something worthwhile for the development of the country by supporting the ventures.

For a government ready to help finance the development of private industry, an alternative to investing in joint ventures or granting loans to private companies is to grant government guarantees for financing arranged from other sources. This is a method which, if cautiously and wisely employed, may never require the use of a government's scarce resources. Under this system a government, usually through some inter-mediary institution such as a central bank, a development bank, or a development corporation, offers to guarantee the repayment of loans granted by local or foreign lenders to local companies for approved in-vestment projects. The availability of a government guarantee may open up sources of financing not otherwise available and may serve to reduce the cost of borrowing by reducing the risk to the lender. Any such re-duction in cost is important not only to strengthen the enterprise, but also to conserve the nation's foreign exchange, which would be needed to service the debt. A leading example of this form of support for private companies may be found in the World Bank loans, which are made to private companies only if the government issues its guarantee.

The Naturalization of Industry

The unacceptability in most developing countries of perpetual foreign control of the industrial sector was mentioned earlier in this chapter. The temporary foreign domination of industry may be acceptable in coun-tries where the advantages of a massive inflow of industrial know-how are understood. In these countries industrialization may proceed rapidly with most of the capital in the early years coming from foreign sources. Many of the new factories will be wholly owned by the foreign com-panies which set them up. Most of the others will be joint ventures in which the foreign interests have control. In the field of medium- and larger-sized enterprises, foreign control is bound to predominate in a country which seeks rapid industrial development by methods advo-cated in this book. I recognize that few of today's developing nations would be content to accept this situation as permanent, nor do I sug-gest they should. As more and more people in any country become suf-ficiently trained and experienced to move into the top management posi-tions in industry, and as a local capital market is developed to provide a basis for financing industry, it is only right that industry should grad-ually cease to be foreign-controlled. This process of moving from foreign ownership and control of industry to local ownership and control can be referred to as the "naturalization of industry."

There is, of course, one way to naturalize industry which is quicker and more direct than any other, that is, to nationalize it—a method used by many countries too impatient to seek more practical ways to reach the legitimate goal of local control of industry. Nationalization of in-dustry which has been established by foreign investors has all the dis-advantages of state-initiated industry. Furthermore, if it is done on much of a scale and without the niceties of generous and rapid compen-sation, the country can suddenly end all prospects of further inflow of industrial capital and know-how for many years to come. Getting rid of foreign control of industry by this method is like throwing out the baby with the bath water.

Short of such drastic methods, how can industry which is predominately foreign-owned and controlled be naturalized so that it will be subject to the control of local nationals, who, in turn, will be subject to the control of both the formal and the informal pressures which reflect national interest? The natural process is that there will be a gradual and voluntary conversion to local management control as more and more local citizens become qualified and move into higher positions in the companies. This is a transition which most of the most farsighted international companies promote through training and advancement programs. Admittedly, this process will stop short of real control in most cases as long as majority ownership is foreign. The other side of the process is that the company will voluntarily make shares available for purchase by local citizens and that the percentage of the ownership which is national will steadily increase. This part of the process happens less surely than the progression of locals into management positions because some foreign companies are simply not prepared to accept a minority position in company ownership and control.

There are gradual ways to naturalize industry which offer the prospect of making the best of both worlds. There are two broad areas—the financial and the personnel—which are at the root of reasons for naturalizing industry, and the approaches to solving the problem can be divided into these two classes. The financial naturalization of industry which originally came in wholly or at least majority-owned by foreign interests can be encouraged in various ways. To start with, a government may insist upon provision for some degree of local participation in the financing of an industry as a condition of allowing the industry to be set up or as a prerequisite to qualify for new industry incentives. Instead of making the conditions absolute, a government might be wiser to offer special incentives, such as longer tax exemption or more tariff protection, if a new industry is set up with local financial participation right from the beginning. Usually it is better that the local participation required or encouraged should be a minority share of ownership. Few legitimate foreign investors will want to risk large amounts of capital in foreign projects which are controlled by people in whom they do not yet have absolute confidence in regard to their business, technical, and personal acceptability as partners. This kind of confidence rarely exists in the minds of foreign investors venturing into a strange country. It should be recognized that they will often welcome local minority participation, but that rarely will they accept local financial control, especially at the beginning. A practical way to get a new foreign-sponsored industry on the road to financial naturalization is to require that 20 per cent or 25 per cent or even up to 40 per cent of the initial capital shall be open to subscription locally. If private local investment is not forthcoming to take up the allotted shares, the government, directly or indirectly, should consider participating in the financing by buying the shares. Government shares thus acquired should usually be kept available for sale to local private investors who may become interested when the project's success is assured. Through this device of selling its shares, the government can revolve its development funds and reinvest the money in shares of new companies which are not yet able to sell their shares to the public. The acquisition of a minority financial interest in a new industry by local investors or the local government has a double advantage: it represents a good start at naturalizing the industry, and at the same time it helps attract foreign investment and know-how by reducing the risk and giving assurance of local support for the industry.

If local ownership of the industry does not progress beyond the original minority participation, it will not bring about the desired financial naturalization of the industry, even though it has been good as far as it has gone. The gradual increase in the portion of local ownership of an industrial enterprise may be encouraged by tax and other incentives which are based on making substantial parts of new share issues available for local subscription. The critical point comes when, as a result of such requirements, the majority ownership is about to become local rather than foreign. At that point the operation may be so well established and successful that the foreign firm will be happy to remain on as a minority shareholder, especially if the local shareholdings are widely held and not concentrated in a block which would take over control. If it chooses not to accept a minority position, the alternative is for the company to sell its interest to local investors who may by then be prepared to invest fully in a going concern. The means by which local investment may be diverted to industry and by which funds may be channeled into the acquisition of shares in companies which were originally almost entirely foreign may include local stock exchanges, mutual funds, investment companies, and development banks. These institutions may provide means by which investments in industry can be diversified to reduce risks. The existence of these institutions will make it more likely that the soundness of investments will be determined by independent and capable investment authorities.

The other aspect of an industry's naturalization in a developing country—the transfer of the key managerial and technical positions from expatriates to local nationals—may be even more important politically than its financial naturalization, but sometimes more difficult to accomplish. The supply of industrial managers and technicians sufficiently experienced to operate sizable industries is shorter than the supply of capital in many countries. Until the important positions in an enterprise are occupied by local people, however, the industry will be regarded as foreign even if a significant part of the capital has come from local sources. The fact that it takes longer to develop a good supply of senior industrial personnel in a country which has not had industry than it does to raise capital should not be surprising. In the most industrialized countries people rarely reach the higher levels of technical or business management, that is, positions above the foreman level, with less than ten to fifteen years of experience in the industry after appropriate technical and other training. We cannot expect faster results in developing countries, nor can we expect the supply of well-qualified industrial management personnel to catch up with the demand for such people in a rapidly advancing industrial sector. No matter how many constructive measures are taken to speed up the supply and to open doors so that those who are ready may occupy key positions, most countries will find they must rely on foreign industrial staffing in key positions for much longer than either the local nationalists or most foreign investors would wish.

Much can and should be done, however, to ensure that the training and development of nationals for industrial management positions is accelerated as much as possible and that their skills are properly utilized as soon as they are developed. Action along these lines is important to solve the acute shortage of local nationals capable of filling key positions and to show those who are critical of foreign control that everything possible is being done to hasten the transfer of industrial control from foreigners to local nationals. The problem can be approached in many ways. The provision of more and better training facilities is, of course, basic. There is a need not only for technical education at the high-school level, but also for engineering colleges and business administration colleges which will give advanced training in all aspects of management including financial management. Most countries need, but many lack, the kind of university typified in the United States by the Harvard Business School, where advanced but practical training is given in the solution of business problems. Foreign assistance in establishing the facilities to train personnel for industrial management is quite readily obtainable.

Assuming there is a reasonably large and growing supply of people who are ready to advance into industrial management positions, governments can do various things to make sure they are given the work opportunities they need to progress further. The government may make its grants of various incentive benefits conditional upon the new industry's undertaking organized training programs to develop personnel from within their organizations so they can be advanced to higher positions. The continuation of some of the incentive benefits can be made to depend on evidence that worthwhile efforts are being made to train and advance local personnel. To avoid the danger of arbitrary decisions on whether a company is doing what it should do, the evaluation of in-service training and promotion programs could be made the responsibility of an independent board on which both government and private industry are represented. Some special incentive could be devised to reward those companies which did an outstanding job in the field of training local personnel for key positions.

In their natural desire to hasten a process which is bound to be slow at best, many governments make the error of establishing rules which are so rigid that they defeat the objective of maximizing both the rate of industrial development and the rate of naturalization of the key positions. Some governments require that a specified percentage of the employees should be locals or that a certain percentage of the payroll should be paid to local employees. Others try to get the same results by limiting the number of foreign personnel who are granted visas even for temporary assignments. Rigid restrictions such as these are self-defeating. At best, they can accomplish no more than the incentive approach outlined above; at worst, they may discourage the entry of industries which are important to the country. Foreign investors often will not come in unless they feel certain they can bring in and retain the foreign personnel they need until local substitutes are ready for the positions. No foreign investor in his right mind will risk his capital unless he is satisfied that his project can be staffed with people, either foreigners or local, who are capable of making it successful. This attitude is not really in conflict with the desire of a developing country's government that locals be trained and put into key positions as rapidly as possible. This is also the objective of any intelligent foreign investor who cannot afford for public relations reasons to have any other policy and who should be able to gain financially by reducing the number of foreign personnel as quickly as possible, if for no other reason than because they are costly in terms of the high salaries and special benefits which are necessary to attract highly qualified American or European industrial personnel to assignments in developing countries.

A government has another way open to it in carrying out a policy of encouraging naturalization of key positions in industrial firms. In those joint-venture companies in which it has invested, either directly or through development banks or similar agencies, the government through its representation on the boards of the companies concerned can keep up the pressure for the training of locals and their advancement to key positions. This is the inside approach which is likely to meet with cooperation from the directors who represent the foreign shareholders, for they will welcome the opportunity to show how well they are doing in training and developing local talent within the company.

The replacement of foreign personnel with locals is sometimes discouraged by pressures on foreign-controlled industrial companies to give locals who are advanced to higher technical and management positions the same pay and the same benefits as were given to the expatriate staff they replace. In some countries this has even gone to the ridiculous extreme of giving locals "home leave" to the foreign country from which the expatriates previously came. It should be recognized that a company may be willing to appoint a local to a key position even if his experience and qualifications are somewhat less than the position really requires. This willingness should be encouraged, for nothing will make people develop more than having responsibility thrust on them. If the company is nevertheless forced to give the local man who has less than the desired qualifications the same salary and perquisites which were necessary to attract an experienced foreigner to a location far from his home and interests, then it may conclude that it will delay replacing him with a local until the local man is every bit as good. The foreign company needs a financial incentive to encourage it to substitute untried nationals for the expatriates in whom it has confidence. The incentive should be the opportunity to make substantial savings. This is not to suggest that the local men who are moving up should be poorly paid. On the contrary, their salaries should be high compared with alternative opportunities in the country so that industry can attract the best men the country can offer and so that the most qualified people are attracted to careers in industry. On the other hand, it is not reasonable for relatively inexperienced local men, already being advanced faster than their qualifications justify, to be paid as if they were sought-after industrialists in countries where salary levels are high, where people with their skills are scarce and heavily in demand, and where such personnel will only go abroad if offered special inducements.

Will this process of gradual naturalization accomplish the objective of bringing the industrial sector predominately under local ownership and management? In some countries with higher levels of education and rapid development of local capital markets, there is reason to think it will. There is much that a government can do to hasten the process without "killing the goose that lays the golden eggs." In general, persuasion through positive incentives rather than penalization for failure to meet naturalization in both the financial area and the personnel field is likely to bring better results while keeping the investment climate attractive to additional foreign investment.

While I believe the path of gradual naturalization is the ideal one for most developing countries, I recognize that it does not meet the popular demand for more rapid naturalization of industry which exists in many of the developing nations. Does this mean that the only answer to public clamor for a rapid naturalization of industry is nationalization with the concomitant loss of the priceless input of individual initiative and foreign know-how? An alternative could be developed in an attempt to make the best of both worlds. It would be based on a frank recognition that while the foreign industrialist is needed desperately by the developing countries, he is needed only temporarily. This implies that in order to secure the advantages of the foreign industrial capital and know-how, the developing countries would have to pay a price which would be attractive to the foreign industrialists to the point of being irresistible. It also implies that foreign ownership and control of the new industries would be accepted by the developing countries only for a temporary period. A plan to meet these conditions would have to be based on a schedule of naturalization to be agreed upon in advance by both the foreign investor and the developing country's government.

How would a plan of industrial development through foreign investment coupled with a prearranged schedule of naturalization work in practice? The foundation for the plan would have to be investment incentives, such as those described in this book, which are sufficiently attractive that they would virtually assure the foreign investor of a high rate of return on his investment for the period of the arrangement. The period would have to be long enough—ten to twenty years—to permit the foreign investor to repatriate his original investment plus a fairly high return on his investment. During this period the foreigner would be assured of a continuation of the incentives which would assure the planned levels of profitability. In return for a situation in which his profits are practically guaranteed, the foreign investor would agree to the preplanned schedule of naturalization. This would specify the rate at which the foreign investors would agree to divest themselves of their ownership of the enterprise by making shares available for local purchase. It might also specify or at least regulate in some way the price basis on which shares would be placed for local sale. A typical schedule for divesting ownership might provide that 5 per cent of the shares would be made available for local sale each year for ten years. At that point, when 50 per cent of the shares were scheduled to pass into local ownership, the foreign company would have the option to continue with the schedule and be a minority shareholder or to place the entire balance of its shares on the local market. For the scheme to have any appeal to the foreign investor, he would need assurance that the full amount of shares made available to local purchasers each year would be purchased and that he would be given preference, or better yet, a guarantee of convertibility of the local currency received for the shares. If the private capital market of the country has developed well, and if the enterprise is a successful one (as it should be with the incentives offered and the foreign management provided), it is probable that all or most of the industrial shares made available under the plan would be purchased by local private or institutional investors. The key to the plan, however, would have to be assurance by the government that it would stand ready to purchase, at the price based on the prearranged formula, all shares which are not purchased by private investors.

As far as I know, this idea, whose originator is not known to me, has not been developed in any detail, much less tried in any country. It appears to offer various important attractions to both parties. To the prospective foreign investor it would remove the great uncertainty which now stands in the way of most industrial investments in developing countries—the uncertainty as to whether the investment may be naturalized or even nationalized without compensation before it has provided the investors with a return of their capital plus an appropriate reward. While no government can positively guarantee that the contracts it has made will not be repudiated by another government, the existence of an agreement involving prescheduled naturalization should go far to discourage naturalization of industry by shortcut methods. The preplanned naturalization system should appeal to foreign investors as a way to get an attractive return for their know-how and the temporary use of their capital in a situation in which much of the present uncertainty is removed. From the point of view of the developing country the system would have distinct advantages. It would offer the prospect of faster industrial development through a more rapid inflow of capital and technology than occurs in the present situation of uncertainty which surrounds foreign investments in nationalistic countries. It would make the foreign exchange costs of industrial development more predictable. Above all, it would enable advocates of industrial development through the importation of industry to secure acceptance of their policy when the prospect of indefinite foreign ownership and control of industry would otherwise result in irresistible political pressures for the immediate nationalization of industry despite its inevitable effect on stifling the future inflow of industrial capital and experience.

The main weakness of a plan of this kind is that local investors might not come forth to buy the shares as they were made available, and thus the naturalization schedule would fall apart unless the government stepped in to buy the shares as offered. If the enterprise had turned out to be highly successful, private investors would come forward in most instances; even if they failed to do so, the acquisition by the government of shares in a successful enterprise might not be a bad alternative. The problem would arise in the case of enterprises which were not doing well, although these should be in the minority among enterprises set up with foreign majority control and with the full technical and managerial support of leading foreign firms. Projects which were doing poorly might be exempted temporarily or permanently from the scheduled sale of shares to local investors. This would leave the problems in the hands of the foreign owners who, after all, took on the projects as business risks and who would have a much stronger incentive to solve the problems involved than if they were assured that the local government would "bail them out" of projects if they failed.

To work out the practical details of a system of industrial importation based on prearranged and guaranteed naturalization of the investment requires some experimentation. To embark on some experiments along the lines suggested does not require commitment to the use of the proposed system on any large scale. In fact, it would be only reasonable for a country to work its way gradually into a system of this kind. Even when it became fully developed, there is no reason to think that a country's inflow of foreign investment would all have to come under the plan. It might be found that the suggested system would be useful in relation to some kinds of industries or some kinds of investors, and not others. A country might well offer a prearranged scheduled naturalization system as one basis on which foreign investment in industry would be welcomed, while permitting and encouraging foreign investment in industry to continue as before for those foreign investors who preferred the old system.

11

Industrial Planning
and Progress Reporting

What Is Industrial Planning?

Just as a corporation needs to do budgeting to organize its future plans, to maintain accounting and statistical records for the proper control and operation of its business, and to publish reports for the information of its shareholders, a comprehensive industrial development program needs planning, operating statistics, accounting, and progress reporting. The purpose is similar—to establish future plans on the basis of an analysis of past experience, to provide information essential for efficient operation, to inform those interested in what results have been achieved, and to attract the funds needed for future operations.

Industrial planning in its most comprehensive form naturally exists in those economies which are centrally planned in regard to all sectors, including the industrial. If an entire economy is state-owned and operated, each sector must be allocated its share of new investment funds, and presumably this is done on the basis of the relative value to the whole economy of investment in each sector. This becomes a comprehensive problem of input-output analysis. To be done properly, planning of this kind must rest on a complex and accurate statistical basis. This is not the kind of industrial planning being discussed in this chapter, for it is assumed throughout this book that we are dealing with economies in which the industrial sector is largely under private ownership and management, even though subject to considerable government influence.

What is the function of industrial planning in a private industrial sector? It consists of three important elements: (1) the collection, analysis, and presentation of industrial sector information needed as input for national economic planning work which must include and relate all sectors of the economy, whether private or public; (2) the collection, analysis, and utilization of industrial project information which is useful operating data for actual or potential industrial investors; and (3) the collection, analysis, and presentation of aggregative data relating to the progress of the industrial development program.

The national economic planning agency of a country normally has the responsibility for the preparation of the nation's over-all economic development plan. The plan must cover all sectors of the economy, for one of its purposes is to bring together in one place the essential present and estimated future data on economic inputs and outputs of each sector in order to arrive at totals for the economy as a whole. Even though the plan deals in estimates which may be subject to a margin of error, it is of great importance that the plan be essentially complete; the omission of information on any sector would make the totals seriously inaccurate. The national economic plan has several important uses. First, it constitutes an advance budgeting of the government's planned investments over a period of years for capital purposes, that is, for investments in assets of long-term value such as roads, educational facilities, public buildings, and industrial projects. Second, it includes estimates of private investment, from both local and foreign sources, even though these are not subject to government decision as are the government's direct investments. Third, it contains estimates of the country's over-all availability of funds for investment and shows whether the resources, government plus private, equal the estimated needs, government investment plus private investments. The gap between available funds and total requirements will show how much more is needed to realize the investment targets. And fourth, it will show the estimated foreign exchange receipts and requirements for each year and the shortage, if any, which has to be met by drawing down reserves or by obtaining foreign loans, grants, or investments.

The preparation of a national economic plan is important for many reasons. If properly based on adequate studies, it should result in an optimum distribution of government investments among the many competing needs which exist. It should be a help in avoiding major unplanned deficits which could have a serious inflationary effect. It encourages long-term planning in regard to projects needing government capital funds, thus increasing the prospects of getting good value for the resources spent. By revealing an orderly approach to capital projects and their relative value to the economy, it makes it easier to secure favorable long-term financing for infrastructure projects from international financing agencies. By showing the anticipated gap between resources and needs, especially in foreign exchange, the plan may help to attract foreign grants and other assistance and to emphasize the need to attract as much private foreign investment as possible.

In a mixed economy such as most developing countries have, in which all or most of the infrastructure is in the government part of the economy and in which manufacturing industry is mainly in the private part, the industrial sector is not as directly involved in national economic planning as are the sectors in which government investment predominates. However, there may be significant government investments in the industrial sector, such as the development of industrial parks, and government investments in industrial projects. These all become part of the advance capital budget in the plan. The industrial sector is also in the plan in regard to anticipated inflow of foreign exchange through private investment and the sale of industrial products exported. It is also represented in the expected outflow of foreign exchange for servicing foreign industrial loans; for paying for imported materials and parts, royalty and licensing fees, and foreign exchange costs relevant to foreign personnel; and for paying out profits and repatriating capital. All of these need to be forecast for several years ahead on the basis of existing and anticipated new industry. Projections as to the size and nature of the future industrial sector are also important for anticipating needs in other sectors. For example, industrial power and transport needs must be forecast to plan investments to develop power and transportation facilities. Industrial growth prospects have to be known to determine trained manpower needs as this will require investment in technical schools. The expected development of industries based on expanded production of local raw materials may require investment in the agricultural sector to open up new land to grow the materials that will be needed. To determine these and dozens of other interrelationships, much needs to be known about the industrial sector as it exists and as it is expected to develop year by year during the life of the plan.

Planning for an industrial sector in which the investment decisions are almost all made by private investors is by nature very different from planning for the development of the infrastructure where most of the investment decisions are governmental. The difference is so great that it is almost misleading to refer to both processes by the same name. Industrial planning of the kind I am talking about consists mainly in estimating what private investors will do and then in calculating the consequences of their investment decisions in terms of foreign exchange effects, labor force demand, power needs, etc. In making estimates of the amount and nature of industrial investment which will take place year by year for five or ten years into the future, we are setting targets for industrial promotion. Whether the goals set will be reached will depend on the ambitiousness of the targets and the effectiveness of the industrial development program.

Information Requirements

In a country in which industry is left mainly to private investment, information needed for industrial planning and for the industrial program itself is often lacking, incomplete, or unreliable. One of the basic tasks in establishing a comprehensive industrial development program is to set up a practical industrial information system. Such a system must be designed to meet the information requirements for all purposes at the same time. What information is really required to serve all the needs?

The best way to determine what industrial information should be collected is to try to visualize what use will be made of the system when it is operating and when it contains information on each industrial establishment and on the industrial sector in total. The users of the system will include the central economic planning agency; the various agencies whose programs depend in part on industry as customers (for example, power, technical education, railways); the industrial development agency itself; and private and prospective industrialists. The needs of these various users of the system will differ considerably. For each year the national economic planning people will want information on such matters as estimated output, foreign exchange inflow and outflow from the industrial sector, targets for private investment both local and foreign, import requirements of industry, and export targets. Officials of other government agencies will need information on estimated industrial power requirements by geographical areas, expected railway freight growth, estimated water needs of new industry, and estimated numbers of each kind of skilled worker needed. The industrial development agency itself and existing or prospective private industrial investors will use the system in connection with industrial feasibility studies; it will show much in regard to the capability of existing industry to meet needs, about existing industries as a market for projects which can make items of industrial input now being imported, and about the availability of inputs for new projects from existing industries. The industrial agency will also use the aggregative data in publicizing industrial growth targets and in reporting on industrial progress. The evidence which can be shown of industrial development success may well determine whether an adequate budget will be appropriated to continue and expand the program.

For every manufacturing establishment, that is, every factory of a certain minimum size or larger, a number of facts must be collected in one central industrial information center for the country. Opinion differs from country to country as to what the minimum size for inclusion in "industry" should be. Many countries include only manufacturing establishments with ten or more employees, frequently collecting information on smaller establishments separately. The following facts are usually collected for every factory included in the system:

1. Name of enterprise
2. Street address
3. Mail address
4. Form of ownership
5. Date established
6. Name of owner or company president
7. Name of manager
8. Total investment
9. Source of capital
10. Any foreign connections?
11. Pioneer status?
12. Principal products
13. SIC code numbers of principal products
14. Number of employees
15. Principal materials used
16. Sources of principal materials
17. Value of annual sales, by product
18. Any product exported?
19. Size of plant (floor area)
20. Electric power consumption
21. Water consumption
22. Fuel type and consumption

Much more information could be obtained on every establishment, and in some industrial information systems it is obtained. It is important, however, to avoid being overly ambitious in setting up a new system. Systems frequently are too elaborate, and the result is failure to get the information which is really vital. It is usually better to start with a minimum system and seek only basic information and then expand the system later when it is operating on a reasonably complete basis. By then more will be known about what information is really needed; there is no point in collecting data which will never be used.

The central industrial information system should contain not only the basic data on every existing industrial establishment in the country, but also as much information as possible on every project under construction and on every project which appears to be definitely committed, even though construction has not started. The information on the new projects is especially important in connection with feasibility studies, for those doing the studies need to know what is going on in the industry in question, or they may jump to conclusions which are already out of date because of projects already being constructed. Those concerned with promotion also need to know of projects already committed. The information on new projects is also important in evaluating industrial progress.

Some of the industrial information is directly usable in the form of data on individual projects. Some of it is only useful if totals are prepared which combine the data on a large number of separate projects. Once the information system contains reasonably complete data on all or practically all industrial establishments, it is only a matter of clerical work and analysis to prepare the aggregative data needed.

How to Develop an Industrial Information System

A good starting point in setting up an industrial information system is to design a basic card on which the essential information on each industrial establishment can be recorded. Under sophisticated conditions in advanced countries with many thousands of industrial enterprises, the information might be kept on computer tapes or punched cards; but as long as the number of industrial plants is not more than a few thousand, manual methods will be adequate. The card should contain the twenty-two points listed above, with plenty of space for filling in the information on each point.

In every country some information on industrial establishments exists in several different places within the government and sometimes outside of it. One approach is to set up a card on each establishment which is listed in various places, adding whatever information is available. The sources may include the agency which registers firms for incorporation, the ministry of labor registration for factories, tax records, applications for incentives, and industrial census records. By cross checking information from one source to another, it may be possible to build up a fairly complete system which can be used as a starting point pending the use of other methods such as taking a new industrial census.

The more comprehensive approach, and probably the best one in most situations, is to make a clean start by undertaking a complete industrial census. Ideally, this would involve sending a census taker in person to every industrial establishment where the required information would be obtained. Penalties would exist for companies which failed to supply complete and accurate information. An alternative method is to send out questionnaire forms by mail, again with a penalty for failure to respond. The mail method, though apparently cheaper and quicker, is not likely to result in a satisfactory census unless a good industrial mailing list is available in the first place and unless considerable followup checking is done by field men afterwards. An industrial information system which falls seriously short of covering all industrial establishments may be worse than useless, for people may depend on the information it contains without recognizing its incompleteness. A reasonable target for a new system would be 90 per cent coverage of industrial establishments by the end of the first year, even though some details of basic information would very likely be missing from many of the cards. After the system has been set up on a fairly complete basis, it must be kept up-to-date by annual revisions. Even though it is desirable that the original system be based on a direct visitation basis, the revisions may be done by mailing out questionnaires, provided sample checks are made for visits and care is taken to incorporate in the system all new project information which comes to the attention of the industrial development agency during the year.

Some Uses of Industrial Information

Much of the use made of industrial statistics is internal within the industrial development agency. Cards and groups of cards will be referred to in connection with feasibility studies, market surveys, etc. They will also be used in answering questions from private industrialists or prospective investors or from staffs of other government agencies. It is desirable that some of the information also be available to the public in convenient form. A basic reference source in any country is the industrial directory, which is compiled from the official information system. Some of the information on the cards, such as that relating to investment and sales, is of a confidential nature and should not be published or revealed outside the agency except when it is consolidated into totals for groups of companies. For each industrial establishment the following items of information should be published in the official industrial directory:

Name of company
Street address
Mail address
Company president
Company manager
Date established
Principal products and SIC code numbers
Numbers of employees, by size group
Total investment, by group
Annual sales, by group

As part of the industrial directory, or separately, information on industrial progress should be published at least once a year. Evidence of industrial growth is an important part of the publicity campaign which is needed to support the industrial development program. Nothing succeeds like success, and nothing attracts more investment to industry, or budgets for industrial promotion, as much as the news that industrial development is progressing rapidly. Important as such publicity is outside the country to attract the interest of potential investors, it is equally necessary inside most countries to generate public support for the industrial program.

PART 3

Incentives for Industrial Development

12

Tax Incentives

Income Tax Exemption

Other than tariff protection, the most widespread incentive used to attract investment to industry is income tax exemption. The majority of the developing countries which are eager to attract foreign capital offer it as one of their major incentives. The income tax exemption is often referred to as a "tax holiday." The period of exemption is almost always five years or more, and some countries offer as much as ten years.

The popularity of income tax exemption as an industrial investment attraction device is not surprising. Many of the factors affecting a country's desirability as an industrial location are outside of the country's control or are subject to change only slowly as a country develops. In this class are the size of the local market, the industrial skills of the people, the availability of local capital for industry, the distance from world markets, and the availability and cost of services needed to support industry. Even the important factor of economic and political stability is often a difficult thing to change constructively, especially in the initial stages of an industrial development program. One major incentive, income tax exemption, stands out as something which can be offered immediately and with no apparent cost. For a country searching for ways to improve its industrial investment climate, the adoption of an income tax exemption program is often thought of as a natural first step.

A period of income tax exemption is a way to attract new investment to industry in a country by dramatically improving the prospects of commercial profitability compared with what would be possible in the country without tax exemption and compared with what would be possible in other countries which are competing for the same capital. It is therefore an investment attraction device. It also recognizes the truth in the infant industry argument that new industries need to be assisted in improving their profitability in the early years when their costs are higher and their revenues may be lower than normal. While tariff protection is the traditional way to help infant industries producing for the domestic market, it is of no help to export industries, which are the industries which make the most sense in many developing countries. Income tax exemption is an incentive which is appropriate for export industries, for which location may well hinge on tax factors; it is equally well suited for meeting the needs of domestic market industries.

The world-wide popularity of tax holidays for attracting new industry is due largely to the experience of Puerto Rico, whose remarkable success in attracting more than one thousand industries mostly financed by outside capital in twenty-two years is regarded as being primarily the result of its ten-year income tax holiday. The former chief economist of Puerto Rico's Economic Development Administration, H. C. Barton, Jr., stated: [1]

> There is considerable evidence, however, that tax exemption is much the most important single factor influencing firms which do decide to invest. In the five year period prior to the enactment of the first effective law, only 13 firms were promoted and, in many instances, this was in expectation that they would, as most of them did, receive tax exemption grants after the law was passed. In response to a recent survey among U.S. firms that now have factories in Puerto Rico, 83% of the respondents cited tax exemption as being a major reason for their decision. Beyond this, and in a sense more reliable, is the unanimous opinion of all Fomento staff members coming in frequent contact with prospective investors. They are convinced that tax exemption is the main motivation, often the only one, for considering Puerto Rico in the first instance and that it is an important factor in almost all the positive decisions that are made.

Income tax exemption became an important part of the Puerto Rican industrial development program in 1948 when it became evident that private capital from the mainland United States had to be attracted on a large scale because this approach offered the prospect of far more industrial growth than could be obtained by the state-owned industry approach which had been tried first. An important milestone in the Puerto Rican program was the report on the Ten-Year Industrial Plan for Puerto Rico which was prepared in 1950 by the Arthur D. Little

[1] H. C. Barton, Jr., "Puerto Rico's Industrial Development Program, 1942–1960," paper presented at the Center for International Affairs, Harvard University, Cambridge, Mass., Oct. 29, 1959.

Company, consultants to the island government. The report endorsed the tax exemption plan in this way: [2]

> The question of whether tax exemption is a practicable and efficient means of attracting industries to certain areas has been much discussed. Some students of public finance scorn it, claiming it causes maladjustment in the location of industries and is a tool whose competitive use endangers sound finance on the community level. Practical experience in industrial promotion, however, clearly indicates that tax exemption is a very effective incentive. Although income tax exemption for manufacturers is of no value until the manufacturer has made a profit, it is nonetheless psychologically the greatest advantage which a manufacturer sees in Puerto Rico. It has been the possibility of higher net gain, because of the tax exemption, which has caused many manufacturers to decide to try to make a go of an operation in Puerto Rico despite the obstacles. . . . It is recommended that Puerto Rico continue its program of industrial tax exemption. . . . The Insular Government should not weaken an incentive whose cost, for practical purposes, consists only of foregone revenues that might not otherwise exist, as contrasted with out-of-pocket expenditures.

Teodoro Moscoso, the administrator of the Economic Development Administration of Puerto Rico, made the following remarks on the tax exemption device in 1958: [3]

> Our experience has shown us that the tax exemption program constitutes the most effective means of awakening interest on the part of industrialists. . . . The most important tool they [Puerto Rico's 50 industrial promotion representatives] carry in their sample cases is tax exemption for industry. . . . Tax exemption can be considered somewhat in the nature of a government subsidy, but it has various advantages over other types of subsidies such as direct cash payments or protective customs duties. The most important advantage is that when exemption is granted to a firm that obtains no profits and finally fails, the government loses nothing. . . . Further, tax exemption requires a minimum of administration and expense: the entire budget of our Tax Exemption Office amounts to some $60,000 yearly. Tax exemption provides a solid incentive for an industrial firm to increase production and productivity, thus enabling it to pay higher wages. For their part, subsidies and protective tariffs tend to protect the inefficient and encourage restrictive and monopolistic practices. Another point in favor of tax exemption is that it provides for the highly-successful ventures a very considerable reserve of earnings that can be reinvested in rapid expansion, as is indeed the case

[2] Arthur D. Little, Inc., Report on Ten-Year Industrial Plan for Puerto Rico, 1951, reprinted 1961, available from AID, Washington, p. 43.

[3] Teodoro Moscoso, lecture given at the University of Puerto Rico, November, 1958, published in *Proceedings of the Economic Planning Seminar of the Commonwealth of Puerto Rico, 1958*, Regional Technical Aids Center, ICA, Mexico, 1960.

of many of the factories sponsored by the Economic Development Administration. . . . In my personal opinion, a well-thought-out and scrupulously administered tax exemption program is essential in attracting investment capital to a country under development.

On another occasion, Mr. Moscoso made these comments: [4]

Most governments have at their disposal, in addition to the various powers of regulatory agencies, a most powerful tool in the management of fiscal policy. Puerto Rico's experience with tax exemption has demonstrated that tax incentives can be a powerful inducement to investors, like those in the United States who would otherwise be subject to heavy taxation. We believe also, that tax incentives can help break down local traditional preference for investment in real estate and trade. It is clear, however, that tax exemption, even for a limited period, is destructive of equity and progressivity in the tax structure per se, but that this effect may be more than offset by higher income for the economy as a whole.

The experience of Puerto Rico in the use of income tax exemption has been thoroughly analyzed in a study which should be required reading for anyone concerned with industrial investment incentives.[5] My conclusion is that the income tax holiday was the incentive which got the Puerto Rican industrial program moving and made its success possible. Much can be learned by other countries from Puerto Rico's experience in using tax exemption as a "triggering device" to start the inflow of outside industrial capital, especially for export industries. At the same time, it must be recognized that the tax holiday would not have been such an effective incentive if Puerto Rico had not been able to offer other favorable investment factors such as duty-free access to a major market (mainland United States), low-cost labor, good government, and stable currency. This indicates that as part of a "package," a tax holiday may be the crucial element to add if the other elements are right; but it does not suggest that tax exemption can attract investment to a country where the other investment climate factors are unfavorable.

The overwhelming importance of tax exemption as an incentive in the Puerto Rican program and its later adoption as a feature of many other industrial development plans has led many development workers to place great reliance on it as a standard incentive which should be a part of every industrial development program. At the same time, advisers in taxation for underdeveloped countries have come forward to point out many undesirable features in tax exemption, and some have con-

[4] Teodoro Moscoso, "Industrial Development in Puerto Rico," *The Annals of the American Academy of Political and Social Science,* Philadelphia, January, 1953.

[5] Milton C. Taylor, *Industrial Tax-exemption in Puerto Rico,* University of Wisconsin Press, Madison, Wis., 1957.

cluded that the device is a dangerous one which can do developing countries more harm than good.[6] Clearly it is time to take a more critical look at tax exemption as an investment attraction device. Is it an incentive which should be used by a country seeking to attract capital to industry, always, never, or only under certain circumstances? If it is used, can its advantages be retained while avoiding the disadvantages? Are there alternative ways to attract capital and make new industries more profitable which avoid the disadvantages of tax exemption systems?

Before exploring the pros and cons of tax exemption as an incentive, it is appropriate to comment on one of the main arguments of the critics of the tax exemption incentive—that other factors are more important to prospective investors than taxes. Those who oppose tax exemption sometimes go to great lengths to show that investors are more concerned about the political and economic stability of a country, about the size of its market or the markets it has free access to, and about factors affecting manufacturing costs, than they are about tax exemption. I would be the first to say this statement is true; but it is irrelevant to the real question, which is, "Should a country add tax exemption to whatever other favorable features its investment climate may have?" No advocate of the tax exemption incentive would suggest that this incentive is an alternative for other positive elements in an investment climate or that a tax holiday system can offset seriously negative features. It must be assumed that any country which really wants to attract investment to industry will do all that it can to remove or minimize the bad features in its investment climate and to improve its good features. The question then remains, "Should tax incentives be added, and if so, in what form?" This is the question to which this chapter is devoted.

Another irrelevant argument sometimes advanced by those who oppose tax exemption by developing countries is that many investors would prefer tax reform to tax exemption. They point out that the tax systems in most developing countries are outdated, inefficient, inequitable, and often corrupt. Sometimes the tax rates on corporation profits are so high they discourage investment. A company which will have to live with a bad tax system indefinitely after an exempt period may be more interested in seeing the whole system reformed than in merely being able to ignore it for a few years. All this is very true. Poor tax systems are common, and their reform is of high priority for many reasons, including improving the industrial investment climate. To grant tax exemption as a temporary incentive for new industries is not to condone the faults of the tax system or to stand in the way of its reform. The questions of tax reform and tax exemption are separate and should not

[6] Jack Heller and Kenneth M. Kauffman, *Tax Incentives for Industry in Less Developed Countries*, Law School of Harvard University, Cambridge, Mass., 1963.

be confused. Although some developing countries may need only one or the other, most may benefit from having both tax reform and tax exemption.

The Case for Income Tax Exemption

The primary argument for income tax exemption is that it is a simple, direct, and effective way of improving the commercial profitability of most investments which fit the terms of eligibility. The improvement in the rate of return is a matter of simple arithmetic. If a country has a corporation income tax rate of 50 per cent, exemption will double the rate of return on investment. A project which would give a return of 10 per cent on total investment if taxable, and which would thus be regarded as unattractive by most investors, suddenly can provide a return of 20 per cent if there is tax exemption. The increase in profitability is not only dramatic in size, but also calculable at the time when the investment decision is made, which is particularly important since investment decisions usually depend in part on profitability calculations. For an export industry, the increase in estimated profitability due to tax exemption would be adequate basis for selecting one country as a location rather than another with no exemption, all other things being roughly equal. In fact, the increase in prospective earnings would probably be sufficient reason to choose a location with slightly greater risks or other disadvantages, provided they were not regarded as really serious. For a local market industry, the estimated profitability of a project would be satisfactory in many instances with exemption and unsatisfactory without it. For either kind of industry a manufacturer would be inclined to look upon tax exemption as a kind of subsidy to make up for some or all of the extra costs involved in setting up a new industry in a country where industrial skills are scarce and markets undeveloped. To be granted tax exemption would be like receiving a subsidy for the costs of getting established in a nonindustrialized place. Looking at the exemption in another way, an industrialist might feel that it is only right that he should not pay normal taxes during the period when he is paying the cost of training workers and doing other things necessary for industry from which the country and future industry will benefit as much as he will. Tax exemption is a way in which the economy can share with him the extraordinary costs which arise for the pioneer industries. Taking the tax principle of ability to pay as his theme, the new investor might argue that he is entitled to tax exemption in the early years of his project when profitability has not reached normal levels because of the costs of operating in an economy which has not yet been made ready for industry.

Most of these arguments which might be cited by the investor make sense from the viewpoint of the developing economy also. Tax exemption is a way for the country to pay the pioneer industrialist for his expense in doing many of the things which must be done to create the conditions for further economic growth. Moreover, it is a simple and direct way to subsidize the costs of pioneering. In giving tax exemption to industries which would otherwise not be established, a country loses no revenue, nor does it have to draw on the public treasury as it would have to do to pay cash subsidies or to pay the costs of training workers and doing other foundation work for industry.

Tax exemption also appeals powerfully to a prospective investor because it reduces his risks by providing a means of getting a faster payout of the investment. It is only natural that many potential investors in underdeveloped countries are extremely nervous about the possibilities of loss due to political or economic troubles which might arise in the future. While an investor might have some confidence in the safety of his investment for a few years, his degree of nervousness will increase sharply the further off the day is when he will have recovered and repatriated his original investment. The exemption of earnings from taxation during this critical period will dramatically shorten the payout period. This alone may be enough to reassure an investor and bring him to a favorable investment decision.

While the typical investor wants to be confident that he will be able to get out his investment without loss if things turn bad in a few years, he is usually hopeful that his investment will be for the long run. This is the viewpoint which a country wants investors to have. Tax exemption for the first five or ten years can serve as a strong investment incentive for the investor who wants to invest for the long pull, for it provides him with a way to build up his capital quickly by reinvesting all or most of his tax-free earnings. With a tax-exempt profit of 20 per cent on total investment all reinvested, an investor can double his capital in less than five years. As Puerto Rico found, this is especially appealing to investors of moderate means—for instance, those prepared to start projects requiring initial investments in the range of $50,000 to $200,000. The fact that profits which are tax-free in the country where they are earned are often taxable when repatriated to the home country of the investor provides a strong reason for reinvesting such earnings. As capital accumulation is of such importance to countries which are industrializing, the combined effect of tax exemption in the developing country and nonexemption in the capital-exporting country can be highly desirable.

However important the calculable effects of tax exemption may be on rate of return, risk, and accumulation of capital, this is only half the story. Investment decisions are only partly arithmetical. Emotion unquestionably plays a major part in the decisions of most investors. This is the real key to understanding why Puerto Rico's tax holiday was

so successful in attracting investors. American investors, and businessmen generally, have worked themselves into an emotional state about
the high level of income taxes. The 52 per cent income tax rate on corporation profits which existed during most of the twenty postwar years
(until the reduction to 48 per cent effective in gradual steps through
1964, 1965, and 1966) became a symbol of the increased role of the
government in controlling as well as taxing business. The deeply felt
animosity of a large percentage of American businessmen toward the
New Deal and later governments which pursued policies widely thought
to be hostile to private business was expressed in an emotional resent-
ment of the income tax rates. To investors with a psychological complex of this kind, the prospect of locating a project in a place which
would provide a ten-year exemption from all taxes seemed like an
offer of heaven. It was almost too good to be true. Release from taxes
was not regarded merely as a calculable financial advantage; it was
almost a reaffirmation of a long-held belief which had seemed to be lost
forever. Through its tax holiday, Puerto Rico quickly became famous
and almost irresistible as a place to do business. While the novelty
of a tax holiday and the psychological pull which it has exerted on
American investors have worn off a little over the years as more and
more places have adopted it as an investment incentive, there is no
doubt that it still has an emotional content which makes it valuable
as a publicity device for promoting investment. Quite apart from what
a tax holiday may mean to the rate of return on a project, it is strong
evidence that a country really wants foreign investment. A country
which talks about wanting foreign investment but fails to take the obvious step of showing its intent by granting tax exemption is hardly
likely to be taken seriously by investors who are besieged by generous
tax holiday offers from other countries. To offer tax exemption to foreign investors is the equivalent of saying that they are wanted, that
they are welcome, and that they will be well-treated. This psychological
reassurance from the government is what many investors need, and it
will mean more in many instances than the possibility of earning a
slightly higher return in an environment where there is no evidence that
the foreign investor is really wanted.

The critics of tax exemption rightly deplore the danger of developing
countries' becoming involved in a competitive race in which each tries
to outdo the others in offering more and more incentives to attract
the same foreign investors. Nevertheless, there is no doubt that any
one country may improve its position by offering more or better incentives than others, and no country can afford to lag far behind in what
it offers to prospective investors unless it has other features which make
up for its poorer incentives. In the scramble to attract foreign investment, there is great competition between developing countries, for the

supply of investment capital in the hands of internationally minded investors is not limitless. It is not correct to say, however, that the competition is generally direct. Occasionally, a company may debate whether to put a plant in country X or in country Y to serve export market A. In such a situation, the competition is direct, and any major difference in investment climate features or incentives may swing the decision to one country or another. Even less often, a company may decide to put a local market plant in country X or country Y, but in only one for the time being. Again, this is direct competition. More often, a company considers setting up a plant in a country for other reasons, such as the amount of product it already sells there or the pressures put on it to manufacture locally rather than import its product. In this situation, good incentives may help bring about an affirmative decision, or the lack of them, a negative decision. But this does not imply direct competition with the incentive level of other countries. It is reasonable to conclude that unless a country is in a very strong position to attract the investment it needs without giving incentives, it should give incentives, at least to the level given by other countries similarly situated. Whether tax exemption should be one of the incentives depends on an evaluation of the disadvantages of this particular incentive compared with other incentives the country might offer.

A country can hardly afford to offer a package of investment climate features and incentives which on balance is less valuable and attractive to propective investors than those offered by similar countries which also seek foreign capital. It is a mistake to think of all countries which need foreign capital for industrial development as being equally conscious of their need or as being equally aggressive. Most countries which profess to want industry do little or no investment promotion work and have done little to make the best of their situation by real efforts to improve their investment climate. Any country which has investment opportunities and a reasonably favorable industrial investment climate can get far ahead of most of its competition for capital by offering incentives which are not merely equal but superior to those offered by other countries in a similar position. Tax exemption is one of the incentives which should be considered in any attempt to attract capital by making a significant change in the investment situation.

The Case against Income Tax Exemption

Despite its attractive features, tax exemption does have some disadvantages to a developing country. These deserve serious consideration in deciding whether to offer tax exemption and in settling some of the details of a system if it is decided to have this incentive. A basic objection is that exemption from profits taxes gives the greatest benefit to the companies which need it the least, that is, to those whose profits are the highest. Those who are exempted from the largest amounts of tax will be those whose profits are sufficiently high that it may well be questioned whether the additional incentive is really needed to bring forth the capital required. If the purpose of tax exemption is to make the marginal project investible, that is, to improve the rate of return so the projects whose profit expectation is low if taxable will still justify investment, its benefits can be said to be given to the wrong projects. In terms of need, the projects which deserve subsidy most are those which will be unprofitable, at least for a time, because of the high costs of getting established. Such projects receive no benefit from a tax exemption system, and it must be recognized that this is a weakness of this type of incentive. A defender of tax exemption would reply to this argument that it is the prospect of high profitability plus tax exemption which will bring forth the most investment and that a country should not design its incentive system to attract marginal and unprofitable projects which can survive only if subsidized.

A major objection often advanced against exemption systems is that they are likely to involve a loss of revenue to governments of developing countries which are desperately short of public revenue to finance development efforts. If this is true, the objection is a valid one, for public revenue is crucial in a development program. There is no point in attracting private capital if its benefits are offset by a reduction in resources to build infrastructure on which the whole development plan must rest. A tax exemption program may or may not involve revenue loss. This depends on how the exemption plan is defined and whether one looks only at the short run or at both the short-run and the long-run effects. If a tax exemption program is narrowly defined to apply only to new industries or even to apply only to the first plant in any new industry, its revenue loss effects will be minimal even in the short run. If the program has any significance whatsoever, it must be assumed that it will result in the attraction of investments which would not otherwise take place and that the new enterprises, even if tax-exempt themselves, will generate tax revenue through secondary means, such as taxes paid by workers who would otherwise be unemployed. To grant tax exemption to projects which would not exist without the exemption incentive can involve no revenue loss in the short run and may add to the tax revenue in the long run when the projects become taxable after the end of the exempt period. The short-run revenue loss arises only if exemption is granted to projects which would be established anyway and which would be taxable if the exemption plan did not exist. As will be explained later in this chapter, this argument may have validity in a country like Mexico, where much industrial investment is taking place on the basis of the size of the market and the stage of development of the country. It has less validity in a country which has little industry and no prospect of attracting much unless it makes a drastic change in its investment climate.

The Puerto Rican Economic Development Administration attempted to calculate the balance between revenue lost through tax exemption and increased revenue gained through industrial development. Mr. Barton summarized the picture in 1959 as follows: [7]

> Taxes "foregone" by the Treasury now amount to roughly $15 million a year. . . . Everyone, Treasury officials included, realizes that very few plants of U.S. origin would actually have been established in the absence of tax exemption. For this reason, the direct loss of Treasury revenue is small. It has been estimated, however, that about 14% of the net income [equivalent to national income] directly and indirectly generated by a new export industry is taken by the Treasury in personal income, property, and excise taxes on successive turnovers. Actual revenue yield to the Treasury from all Fomento programs is now about $40 million a year compared to a theoretical revenue loss of about $15 million. Moreover, the Treasury "foregoes" the corporate income tax for only ten years. Thereafter, the surviving and therefore presumably profitable firms will begin to pay.

A third objection to tax exemption as an incentive is that an exemption system is hard to administer well, especially in a country short of experienced administrative personnel. If administered poorly, an exemption system may lose much of its value as an incentive, for the delays and costs of getting exemption approvals may become so great that the value of the benefits is nullified. In some countries it has become so difficult to get exemption approvals that some investors have concluded that the benefits are not worth seeking, so they invest or decide not to invest as if the exemption system did not exist. A tax exemption system is a kind of vicious circle: To be equitable and to avoid serious revenue loss, it must be fairly complex; to administer a complex system efficiently, it needs skilled personnel; but the skilled personnel are scarce and are urgently needed for other work. Ways around this dilemma will be outlined presently, but they are not a complete answer to the problem.

A fourth criticism of exemption systems is that they generate pressures which tend to make temporary exemptions either permanent or of longer duration than intended and pressures which tend to broaden the area of exemption so much that real revenue losses will occur. While it may be easier to end tax exemption than tariff protection, it is not easy; and governments may give in to the pressure to continue exemption when it should be ended. Pressures for broadened coverage of exemption are bound to come up from old industries hurt by new competition and

[7] H. C. Barton, Jr., op. cit., p. 26.

from local investors hurt by new foreign investors. Both are hard to refuse once a country has a tax exemption system. The more success which comes to those who press for longer and broader exemption, the more a country's tax system will be distorted and the more difficult it will be to get adequate revenue from a narrowing tax base.

A final objection which is often raised is that the value of tax exemptions as an incentive for foreign investment is largely cancelled out by the fact that a company usually keeps the benefit only so long as the untaxed profit is kept in the country where it was earned. Most capital-exporting countries, including the United States, will tax the profit once it is repatriated, so the exemption is not so much an exemption as a delay in paying the tax. When it is finally paid, it goes to the government of the capital-exporting country, which presumably is in much less need of it than the government of the developing country where it was earned. Because of a number of special legal provisions, earnings of a company in Puerto Rico may be partially exempt from United States tax when repatriated to the mainland. While the tax rules of the capital-exporting countries do partially cancel the benefits which a company can retain by getting tax exemption on their overseas operations, there are some benefits which can be retained in most instances. One of these is that the tax-free income can be reinvested abroad and thus used as a free loan until repatriated.

Conclusions on Income Tax Exemption

1. The advisability of income tax exemption depends on the stage of development. A United Nations report on the promotion of the international flow of private capital stated the following conclusion: [8]

> Broad tax concession schemes may therefore be more appropriate for an early state of industrialization. At this point, industry is not yet a major factor in the tax structure. The investor for his part may be expected to view a defective or burdensome tax system with more equanimity if he will not become fully subject to it until after he has had a chance substantially to recover his initial investment under the protection of special tax concessions—more so, if there is reasonable expectation of tangible progress in the improvement of the tax system during that period. Tax concessions may be particularly useful in contributing an initial impetus to the industrialization process, which should become self-generating at later stages.

At the early stage of industrial development to which the United Nations report refers, some of the most valid objections to tax exemption are of less significance than they are in a country which has al-

---

[8] United Nations Economic and Social Council, *The Promotion of the International Flow of Private Capital,* New York, 1960, p. 55.

ready acquired a substantial amount of industry. If a country has almost
no industry, and if it is getting very little industrial investment, the
real revenue loss due to a tax exemption system, even in the short run,
will be at a minimum. There will be every likelihood that a comprehensive industrial development and investment attraction program
will generate a capital inflow of sufficient size that personal income
tax on the new industrial personnel will be more than enough to compen-
sate for any revenue loss, even in the short run. The more industry a
country has, the more the revenue gains will be offset by the loss of
tax revenue on existing industries which have to be granted exemption to
avoid inequities and on new industries which would be established
even in the absence of an exemption system. In brief, it can be said that
a country with little industry and little prospect of industrial investment under existing conditions has practically nothing to lose by tax
exemption and much to gain. Granting tax exemptions does not assure
industrial investment; but it certainly improves a country's prospects
of getting new industrial capital if it has opportunities and a reasonably good investment climate. Starting an exemption program is a good
way to dramatize the beginning of an aggressive industrial development
program. A spectacular splash of this kind is clearly more needed by
a country which no one has ever thought of as a location for industry
than a country which is already widely known as being well on the
road to industrialization.

   2. *Tax exemption should be part of a comprehensive program.* Tax
exemption should never be instituted alone. It should always be incorporated as a part of an integrated and comprehensive industrial development program which involves all or most of the main features discussed
in this book. As a publicity device, tax exemption must be a part of a
broader program designed to stir up interest in the country and in
specific industrial investment opportunities. As a device to reduce
risks for investors and improve the prospective rate of return on projects,
it must be coordinated with other measures into a package whose total
effect is startling in terms of the size of the change produced. As an
evidence of the favorable attitude of government toward new investors
in industry, especially foreign investors, it must be supported by other
forms of assistance and cooperation. As a means to improve the investment climate, it must be accompanied by other changes which will
give credence to the seriousness of the country's intent to go as far as
possible in making the country a good location for industrial investment.

   3. *Tax exemption should be selective and limited.* In the interests
of easier administration it is tempting to suggest that tax exemption
should be so broad and sweeping that almost any kind of investment will
be allowed to share the benefits. The argument in favor of such an approach is that while the inequities and revenue loss would be great under

such a system, the total amount of investment generated might be correspondingly greater, and the losses might be more than offset by large gains. In some situations this might be true, especially in places where there is little governmental planning or control or direct involvement in the development process. Such a situation might have its roots in political preference for a laissez-faire environment or in an absence of administrative capability. In developing countries we are more likely to find an environment in which the government plays a more deeply involved part in development because of political acceptance of the active role for government. In such a situation, an incentive can and should be more limited and more selective, provided this can be accomplished within the bounds of administrative capability. In a mixed and partially controlled economy in the process of growth, it is usually possible to get the benefits of an exemption system while limiting the offsetting revenue losses. This can be done first by measures designed to grant the exemption only to investments which would not otherwise take place. Attempts along this line cannot be completely effective, but partial restriction of benefits can be achieved if exemption is allowed only for projects to make products not being made in the country or only for the first company which produces the new product. Revenue losses which are not offset by substantial benefits may be limited by granting exemption only to projects which will employ a fairly large labor force or which can show a significant amount of value added through the use of local labor or materials. This will prevent benefits from going to firms which import all materials and do little to upgrade them locally.

4. *Tax exemption should be as automatic as possible.* The problem of the administration of a tax exemption system is a serious one for countries which lack skilled administrators, as most developing countries do. In most countries it can be avoided partially, and I believe to a satisfactory degree, by making the exemption system as automatic as possible. The key to eliminating administrative delays, costs, and opportunities for malpractices lies in making the terms of eligibility for exemption clear and definite, leaving as little room as possible for value judgments by government officials. It should be recognized that highly specific written rules, applied mechanically, will not have the finer elements of discrimination inherent in a system involving the value judgments of highly skilled administrators. A system of written rules becomes increasingly essential the scarcer qualified and honest administrators are. The published rules as to eligibility for tax exemption should be so clear that anyone could determine whether a proposed project is entitled to benefits or not. A system of this kind will result in some inequities: Some projects which really deserve benefits may be

excluded, and some which should not get exemption may get it. But by and large, in most countries the more automatic the system is, the better it will be.

Mechanics of an Income Tax Exemption Program

In designing an income tax exemption program, policy decisions have to be made on many points which will determine the scope and nature of the scheme and thus its effects on the fiscal system as well as its value in attracting industrial investment. One of the first questions is whether the exemption should be allowed for manufacturing projects only or for other businesses as well. Since the purpose of the scheme is usually to foster industrial growth and not merely economic growth in general, the scheme most often applies only to manufacturing enterprises. Sometimes tourism is included in view of its importance as an opportunity in many countries. The growing of agricultural crops is usually excluded, but their processing should be included as it is manufacturing. Mining and petroleum development should generally be excluded because these are specialized operations which need special legislative treatment.

Industries which start by assembling imported parts are important to many countries as a steppingstone to later stages in which more and more of the parts may be manufactured locally. The definition of manufacturing should therefore be broad enough to include assembly, provided there is a reasonable amount of value added. Some arbitrary rule is needed as to what constitutes a reasonable amount of value added. The limit should be low enough, probably as low as 10 per cent in many cases, to encourage the start of industries which must use nothing but imported parts at first. At the same time, it should be high enough to avoid abuse by those who would import an almost completely assembled product and merely add one or two final parts to enable the operation to be called assembly and make it eligible for tax benefits.

The income tax exemption systems in many countries allow benefits only for enterprises producing products which are not already being made in the country. In most situations this is an appropriate restriction. It avoids the problem of giving exemption to a new firm which will compete with an existing one or of having to give exemption to the existing firm, with consequent revenue loss, in order to avoid causing unfair competition. In the countries where tax exemption is most needed—those with little existing industry—the restriction rarely causes rejection of many applications for tax exemption. Countries in which the new industry rule would impair the effective use of an exemption system are those which have existing local manufacture of a wide range of products and which thus have less need of a tax exemption incentive.

In setting up an exemption system, the question always arises, Should there be a list of products whose manufacture would qualify for tax exemption? If the list is a very long and comprehensive one, it may have value in attracting attention to the wide range of opportunities for making new products in the country. The disadvantage is that there are bound to be omissions, no matter how carefully the list has been prepared. Desirable projects may be excluded if the system is an automatic one, or else a place might have to be provided for value judgments in adding new products to the list. A published list has the disadvantage that it will almost always be out of date, as new projects are set up and products have to be deleted. A product list which is short and obviously incomplete is undesirable because it will not attract favorable attention, nor will it permit the system to be automatic. An alternative to a detailed product list is a list which shows either included or excluded products by broad groups such as "metal products," "leather goods," etc. My inclination is to favor a listing by broad categories. Such a list does not get out of date. It attracts attention to the kinds of industry wanted, while providing a way to omit sectors of industry regarded as being of low priority. With a list of this kind, it should be stated that tax exemption will be granted for projects to manufacture any product of the listed categories not already being made in the country in commercial quantities. "Commercial quantities" could be defined as being sufficient to meet one-quarter or one-half of the apparent local consumption averaged for the past three years on the basis of imports plus local production.

Another question which must be decided is whether to grant the tax exemption only to the first plant to make a product or to other projects which come later. Limiting the benefit to the first project does much to encourage diversification of industry, and it rewards the pioneer firm, which usually needs the benefits more than firms which come later. The disadvantage of giving benefits only to the first firm is that this rule encourages monopoly with all its harmful features. However, in a country which has little industry and in which there will only be room for one plant for each product for many years anyway, I would favor limiting the exemption to the first firm to make each product.

Some exemption systems allow benefits only to new industries; others include expansions of existing industries. Expansion projects are often highly desirable, for they involve less risk than new ventures yet may meet an economic need and provide high benefits to the economy. Despite these advantages, I feel that generally they should not get the benefit of tax exemption, for a successful firm will normally expand even without special incentives. If an existing firm will expand only if granted tax exemption, the operation may not be as economic as it should be to warrant official support.

In all these alternatives, those designing the exemption system must keep in mind that the purpose of the scheme is not to subsidize industry in general, but to get new industries which would not be established without the extra incentive of tax exemption. Only in this way is the revenue loss kept within reasonable limits which can be more than offset by new revenue generated through industrial expansion. Once a country starts giving tax exemption to projects which compete directly with existing industries, the owners of the old plants will press for subsidies, whether needed or not, in the name of preventing unfair competition.

As the purpose of a tax exemption system—indeed, the purpose of the whole industrial development program—is to attract sound industries which are economic from the viewpoints of both the economy and the private investor, the question arises, Should the benefits be restricted to industries which have been examined in detail and found to be feasible and of high value to the country? In theory, one would think that a screening to separate the good projects from the bad would be justified. Obviously, no government would want to offer special tax incentives to projects which are so unsound or uneconomic that they are not desirable anyway. In practice, however, experience indicates that a detailed screening of projects should not be a part of the process of granting tax exemptions. The screening process would mean a time-consuming delay even under the best circumstances when a government has an adequate staff of capable project analysts. Most developing countries lack the personnel to do such work well. Even if the people are available, they can be employed more productively elsewhere in the development program's work. The tax incentive program is for private investment projects, and it must be assumed that the investors who are putting up most of the financing for a project have examined its feasibility very thoroughly, at least from the viewpoint of its probable commercial profitability. There is no need for government officials to recheck this analysis. If the country has avoided excessively high protective tariffs and has avoided subsidizing a project through granting foreign exchange at an unrealistically low rate for importing machinery, it is probable that the national economic profitability will be high, or at least positive, for any project which the investors consider investible.

The duration of tax exemption is another question which must be settled. Few of the income tax exemption plans grant exemption for less than five years. Even fewer grant exemption for more than ten years unless, as in Puerto Rico and Peru, they are used as a device to attract investment to locations which are regarded by investors as being less desirable but which the country wishes to have developed. Whether exemption should be for five, seven, or ten years, the most popular periods, depends on the competitive situation in which a country finds itself in regard to incentives being offered by other countries. Exemption for less than five years seems hardly worth offering. The fact that ten-year ex-

emption is widely available suggests that if it is justified to have a tax
exemption scheme, it is best to give the maximum period which is generally granted.

In some countries, Nigeria being one, the length of the exempt period
depends on the amount of investment. This is hardly a logical basis for
determining the period of exemption. While it is reasonable to require
a minimum of investment for eligibility for any exemption, to avoid encouraging a multitude of industries so small as to be uneconomic and
to avoid the administrative burden of processing large numbers of applications from very small companies, the period of exemption should have
no relation to the amount invested.

The tax exemption device is used in Peru and in some other places as
a means to attract industry to remote or depressed areas of the country.
The method in Peru is to offer longer periods of exemption to industries
in places which are thought to be less desirable than other locations.
Puerto Rico in recent years has also used a similar system in an attempt
to get industry out of the San Juan area and into smaller towns which
need employment opportunities. In Puerto Rico the exemption period
ranges from ten years in industrialized areas to seventeen years in areas
with few employment opportunities. To the extent that incentives are
at the appropriate level to attract industries to the locations which investors prefer, I see no harm in offering something more to those who
are prepared to accept what they may consider to be less desirable locations. However, it must not be thought that extending a tax holiday
from say five to ten or fifteen years will be very effective in getting industries in remote locations unless they are reasonably attractive on all
other points.

The starting date for a period of tax exemption is a detail which needs
careful consideration in setting up a tax incentive system. There are
three main alternatives to choose from: the period of exemption can start
from the date the application is approved; it can start from the date the
plant starts operating; or it can start from the date the company reaches
profitability. The argument for starting the exemption period from the
date of approval is that the project's sponsors are thus placed under
strong pressure to get the project constructed and into operation as
quickly as possible to avoid losing valuable tax-holiday time. Presumably,
the investors will have sufficient other incentives to accomplish this objective. The second alternative, exemption starting from the date production starts, is the one most commonly used. Usually, it is defined to
mean the date when production on a commercial scale starts, to avoid
counting time used for testing machinery and getting into full operation.
The third method, exemption starting from the time profitability is
reached, has much to recommend it, for it allows the full benefit to accrue to a project which, because of the nature of its business or because

of unfortunate problems, does not reach the breakeven point quickly. This alternative in effect guarantees the full exemption period to every firm which starts and stays in business. It strengthens the appeal of the tax exemption, which would lose much of its incentive value if a good part of the exemption period for a project were likely to be lost through the expected delays in building the plant and reaching the breakeven point.

One good way around the problem of giving appropriate tax-free benefits to a company which might have some years of losses after its period of tax exemption started is to provide that an eligible new industrial enterprise would be given income tax exemption for its first five or ten profitable years, regardless of when they might occur.

Another way around the problem is to allow a carry-forward of losses. The tax exemption rules can allow a company to carry forward the amount of losses in its early years, before it has any profits to be declared exempt, to the years after the tax holiday when the company would otherwise be subject to regular income tax.

For most countries for which an income tax exemption system is warranted, the rules which would be appropriate to qualify new projects for exemption can be summarized as follows:

1. Projects must involve manufacturing—that is, processing or assembly—or tourist facility operation.

2. In the case of assembly projects, the value added locally by the use of local labor and/or materials must add at least 10 per cent to the c.i.f. cost of the imported parts and materials.

3. Projects must manufacture products falling within the broad industrial categories listed.

4. Projects must involve manufacture of a product not already being made in the country in commercial quantities, that is, in quantities sufficient to meet one-quarter or more of apparent local consumption.

5. Projects must involve new manufacturing activities, not expansions of existing operations.

6. Investment must amount to $25,000 or more, and projects must employ ten workers or more.

An income tax exemption system based upon eligibility rules such as those listed above can be made almost entirely automatic to avoid the delays and other problems involved in evaluating applications in systems requiring value judgments before approval is given. Automaticity in the exemption system can be secured by rules prescribing that the applicant must submit reasonable proof that his project will meet all relevant conditions listed and that once having done so, his application for "pioneer status" (or whatever approved status is called) will be effective automatically, say one month from the filing of his application, unless the officer in charge rejects the application with written reasons within that time. Some countries require that notice of applications for tax-exempt status be published and in some cases that public hearings be held to give anyone an opportunity to object if he feels that the application is invalid for any reason or contrary to the public interest. This is a democratic safeguard which is worth having. Within a one-month schedule there should be time to publish a notice of the application and invite objections. The minister in charge should have the right to refuse any application on the grounds that it is contrary to the public interest, provided the reasons for rejection are made public.

The value of having a tax exemption system which is automatic and thus not subject to the delays and malpractices which are inherent in a screening system is so great that consideration should be given to making the system even more automatic than the procedure just described. The ultimate in automaticity in a tax incentive system would be to avoid entirely the requirement of advance approval—the granting of pioneer status. This could be done by amending the income tax laws to provide that any firm which met certain conditions in any year would be exempted from income tax at the time it filed its income tax returns, without advance approval as to tax-exempt status. The conditions would have to be very clear and specific to avoid the danger of a company's being refused exemption to which it considered itself entitled. The specified conditions might prescribe that to be eligible for exemption a company must (1) produce only products falling within a category on the pioneer list, (2) produce a product or products not manufactured in the country at the time the company started operation, and (3) not have claimed tax exemption in more than four previous years. A company which met these simple conditions would not be required to apply for pioneer status and wait for approval to be granted. It would simply start operating, knowing that it could have exemption from income tax when the date for paying the tax arrived just by filing evidence that it had complied with the stated conditions. This would take care of the majority of cases which, under these simple rules, either would qualify for exemption or would not. There would, however, be a minority of cases in which some doubt might exist in the minds of the project sponsors as to whether their claim for exemption would be acceptable. To take care of such cases, any company should have the right, if it wished, to submit its evidence in advance, even before making a financial commitment to the project, in order to obtain a tax ruling as to eligibility for exemption. While this might involve some delay, as would all cases requiring analysis of evidence and judgments of tax authorities, it is better to have a system which delays a few applications than one which delays all. I know of no country which has gone this far in making a tax incentive system automatic, but it is clear that something along these lines is well worth trying.

Exemption from Import Duties

Import duty relief, commonly referred to in some countries as IDR, is second only to income tax exemption as the tax incentive which is commonly offered to encourage industrial development. The relief from import duties may involve complete or only partial exemption. It may apply only to capital goods imported for a new industry, or it may apply to materials and parts to be used by the industry. Potentially, IDR is one of the most important incentives which a country can offer, and it has a place in almost every comprehensive industrial development program, in one form or another.

It is surprising that some countries which want to industrialize continue to levy customs duties on machinery which must be imported for new industry. The duty levied in most countries is not as high as the duty on consumer goods, but it is often as high as 20 per cent. The result is that the cost of industrial machinery is increased by that amount, thus raising the total investment requirements of the project. Anything which adds 20 per cent or even a smaller amount to the cost of establishing a new project has several seriously adverse effects. The additional investment needed may in itself be a barrier which prevents the project from being financed at all. The larger amount of capital which must be committed adds to the investor's risk and thus increases the possibility that he will decide not to make the investment. If the project is financed anyway, its operating costs will be increased by the amount of additional financing charges, and the cost of the product will be increased by added depreciation charges to write off the higher cost of the capital equipment. If the enterprise makes goods for the general public, the increased price reduces the market. If it produces parts or materials for other industries, the higher price makes the purchasing industries less feasible, for the cost of their inputs has been raised. Either result is contrary to the needs of industrial development. While the effect of customs duties on capital goods is bad enough on industries producing for the home market, it is even worse on export industries: It may make their products uncompetitive on the world market, thus depriving the country of the foreign exchange earnings and other important benefits of export industries.

Any tax on equipment for new industry is bound to lessen the amount of industrial equipment imported, just as a tax on a luxury product reduces the amount imported. There is no logic in taxing new industry by charging import duties on new equipment while at the same time professing a desire to encourage the maximum amount of industrial development. One taxes something which is to be discouraged, not something which is to be encouraged. Some countries—Nigeria, for one—have a general policy of listing industrial equipment on the duty-free import list.

This is clearly the best policy for any country at an early stage of industrial development. If it is logical to allow industrial equipment to enter duty-free, it is also logical to give the same privilege to spare parts for the equipment, whether brought in originally or later. One thing that a developing country cannot afford to do at any time is to discourage the import of spare parts needed to keep industry operating. Duty-free entry for industrial machinery should be permanent and automatic.

The situation becomes less clear-cut for a country in which there is a significant amount of local manufacturing of industrial equipment. If the industrial machinery of local manufacture can meet world standards of quality and price, or if it can come reasonably close, it is only right that its use should be encouraged. At the same time, care must be taken not to force new industries to use unsuitable, seriously inferior, or unreasonably high-priced equipment just because it is made locally. There are plenty of examples of whole industries, for example, the textile industry of Argentina, being held back from modernization through being required to use the machinery made locally. It is easy to do serious harm to dozens of important industrial enterprises by protecting one small and inefficient capital goods manufacturing plant. A reasonable policy would be to permit duty-free entry of all industrial machinery unless the specific item required is available of local manufacture and of equivalent quality, at say not more than a 20 per cent higher price. Rather than an outright exclusion of imports of equipment which is regarded as being competitive with locally made capital goods, it may be a better policy to levy duty on imports at a moderate rate which is sufficiently high to encourage use of the local product but to allow a firm to import the item if it considers the difference in quality worthwhile.

Whether to grant duty relief on the import of material and parts for industry is a more difficult question. In the long run, the advantage to an enterprise which could arise from IDR on materials and parts may be even greater than exemption on industrial equipment. The likelihood of revenue loss will be greater on materials, however, even if materials or parts which are available of local manufacture are excluded from the exemption. This is because the country, in all probability, collects duty, often at a fairly high rate, on the finished product if imported. When local production of the item starts as a substitute for importing the product, the country collects no duty on finished goods; and if IDR exists for materials and parts, there is no duty on the things which go into the finished product. How far a country can afford to go in granting this and other incentives which involve a real cost to the economy will be examined in Chapter 15. For now, it is sufficient to state as a general principle that some degree of IDR is usually needed if a country is to get industries which will upgrade imported materials or assemble imported parts. If the rate of duty is the same on the materials or parts as on the finished product, it is unlikely that anyone would wish to manufacture the product locally rather than in larger and more efficient plants where production is already taking place in advanced industrial countries. This is the basis for arguing that what is often needed is a differential between the duty on parts and the duty on the finished product. If the duty on automobiles is 25 per cent, the duty on parts to be locally assembled into automobiles can hardly exceed 10 per cent or 15 per cent if an assembly industry is to be attracted. The same principle applies to most assembly and many processing industries, which initially must depend almost entirely on using imported ingredients.

Some countries give IDR on materials and parts only to companies which are already in operation and only if they can show that they would be unprofitable if they had to pay the duty on the imported items. This may be a useful device to prevent existing industries from going out of business, thus wasting the capital which has been sunk in them. However, it is not useful in promoting industrial development. If IDR is to be used as an incentive to attract new industries, its availability must be guaranteed in advance to prospective investors who meet the required conditions. It can then be taken into the calculations of profitability. It should be used as a means of increasing the profitability of projects to the point where investment will take place. The revenue loss involved in attracting industries to process imported material or assemble imported parts for the local market is such that one cannot recommend an automatic exemption of all such imports from duties. On the other hand, it is important to go as far as possible in making incentives automatic to avoid delays, uncertainty, and malpractices in granting approvals. An answer to this dilemma may lie in establishing and publicizing various levels of IDR which might be available. For example, it might be determined after calculating the costs and benefits to the economy involved in typical cases that it is worthwhile to establish the rule that material and parts which are not available locally of appropriate price and quality may be imported at half the duty which applies to the finished product. With such a rule, there might be instances in which a project is given more IDR than is really justified, in other cases, less. But the errors of one kind would tend to offset the other, and there would be great advantages in having an established principle rather than in having to decide on each application separately.

Import duty relief has a great advantage which distinguishes it from income tax exemption and which may justify its use even when income tax exemption is not warranted. IDR reduces costs and risks for all enterprises, which should be the objective of a good incentive. Income tax exemption, in contrast, gives benefits only to a firm which is already profitable and which thus is in less need of subsidy than one which is struggling to reach the breakeven point.

Tax Incentives for Export Industries

The advantages to a developing country in fostering export industries have been mentioned at various points in this book. Export industries are important, above all, for two reasons: First, their market is virtually unlimited if they can be competitive, and thus their growth may lead the rest of the economy instead of following it, as import substitution industries must do. Second, they earn foreign exchange, which is almost always the most precious element in a country's resources for development. Despite the obvious need to do all that is possible to speed up the growth of export industries, many countries do exactly the opposite. They tax export industries to the point where capital is diverted to local market industries or to nonindustrial uses where its contribution to the country's development will be smaller in most instances. While there may be situations in which an export industry has such a competitive advantage in the world market that an export tax will not impede its development, I believe these cases are rare. Normally, an export tax is a bad thing for a country's development and should be avoided.

The need for fostering exports is so great for most countries that some kind of tax advantage for export industries is often called for. If analysis shows that the value of an export industry to the economy exceeds its commercial profitability (and this is generally the case), a subsidy to accelerate the growth of the export industry may be a sound expedient. This might be the situation in which an export industry uses local materials or labor which have no alternative use and which thus would be wasted if the export industry were not expanded. The purpose of the export subsidy is to improve the commercial profitability to the point where more capital and skills are attracted to the industry than would otherwise occur.

If an export subsidy is to be granted, there are various ways it can be done. Often a good way is to devise a special tax incentive. This may be in the form of import duty relief if the industry must depend to any great extent on imported materials or parts. Free ports and free zones in various parts of the world are based on the principle of allowing materials and parts to enter without payment of duty, for manufacture into finished products which are exported or which pay normal duty if imported into the country from the free zone. This requires the physical separation of the free zone from the rest of the country, and police supervision to ensure that smuggling across the fence does not take place. An alternative to the free zone is to allow a refund of customs duties which have been paid on material or parts which are used in the manufacture of goods which are exported. This is referred to as a "customs drawback." It serves the purpose of not taxing the materials and parts which are processed for export, but it does so in a rather cumbersome way. The manufacturer must tie up substantial amounts of working capital in the payment of duties which will be refunded later. In some countries, the system has involved awkward administrative procedures and long delays which are costly as well as bothersome to the manufacturer.

The subsidization of export industries is being accomplished in Colombia by an imaginative tax device which could well be adopted by other countries. In Colombia, industries operating under a special plan for export industries are allowed to assume for tax purposes that the profit on export sales is 40 per cent of the export sales revenue. This assumed profit is entirely income-tax-free as far as the export side of the business is concerned. The law also permits any remaining part of the tax-free assumed profit which has not been used in canceling the profits on the export business to be applied against the tax which would be payable on the domestic sales of the same company. Thus, a company whose business was equally divided between domestic and export sales, both of which were equally profitable, would be able, if that rate of profit were 20 per cent on sales, to achieve full exemption from income tax. Whether the 40 per cent rate used in Colombia is appropriate or unnecessarily high is a question which should be examined by countries which are thinking of following this example. However, the principle of giving a special tax incentive for export industries is sound, and the device of reducing taxes on the profits of domestic sales on the basis of the volume of export sales is a good way to accomplish this objective.

Another way to give an additional incentive for the development of export industries is to allow them a greater income tax exemption than that granted to local market industries. If a five-year exemption is allowed for local market industries, export industries could be given a ten-year exempt period. The economic advantages of export industries are such that their claim for special treatment goes far beyond the infant industry argument on which the temporary exemption from income tax is based for industry in general. This suggests that what is most suitable may be a permanently lower income tax rate for export industries than for local market industries. If a country has a 40 per cent income tax rate on corporation profits, it might be appropriate to encourage export industries by levying only a 20 per cent rate on their profits. The foreign exchange earnings and the benefits the export industries can bring as leaders of the industrial sector may amply justify a revenue reduction of this magnitude. As in the case of revenue losses in general due to exemption of new industry, the loss will be less than it appears because it must be assumed that the exemption will cause a more rapid growth of the export industries than would otherwise occur. Thus as much or more revenue may be generated at a lower than at a regular rate of taxation.

Tax Incentives to Attract Industrial Personnel

To return to a theme mentioned a number of times before in this book, industrial technical and management personnel may be even more scarce in a developing country than capital. The import of such people, on a temporary basis, to serve as transferers of industrial skills to local personnel is the most urgent need of many countries. It is frequently found, however, that the personal income tax structures in developing countries serve as a barrier to the inflow of the needed industrial staff from abroad. This is because the personal income tax rates are usually graduated rather steeply, and the industrial personnel, especially at their overseas rates of pay, are in the higher brackets. A man who would be in a moderate tax bracket of say 25 per cent (on marginal income) in his home country may find himself in a 50 per cent to 70 per cent tax bracket if he moves for a few years to an underdeveloped country where he is needed as a manager of a new factory. In one country seeking new industry, it was found that a man earning a typical United States industrial management salary of $15,000 a year would have had to pay an income tax of 44 per cent of his total salary, compared with 17 per cent in the United States. Increasing the individual's salary is not a satisfactory answer to this problem. In order to take care of the additional tax and leave the American technician with his base salary and a tax-free 25 per cent overseas bonus, he would have to be paid about $60,000, because the company would have to pay tax on tax. A salary cost of this size might well be prohibitive and might discourage the bringing in of the technician who would be essential for setting up the new business and training local staff. The proper solution to the problem is to allow temporary foreign industrial personnel exemption from personal income tax. Since most technicians working outside their own countries for extended periods can also obtain exemption from the personal income tax of their own countries, a tax-free situation is created which is a powerful incentive for them to take overseas assignments, despite the personal inconvenience and career disadvantages which are usually involved. In view of the world-wide difficulty in attracting high-quality industrial personnel for overseas assignments, an exemption of this kind, which costs the developing country nothing, is a highly desirable means to help solve a difficult industrial development problem.

India has recognized the importance of lessening the tax burden on foreign technical personnel by granting exemption from tax on their salary for one year without prior approval. Technicians whose employment contracts have been approved in advance by the government are exempt from tax for three years from date of arrival. For a further two years the employer of the technician may pay his tax, and such tax is not regarded by the tax authorities as income of the technician. Thus a technician may be personally freed from Indian tax on his salary for five years, without serious burden on his employer. This is the kind of policy which should exist in almost every country which needs more foreign technicians to help develop industry.

13

Tariff Incentives

No incentive for industrial development has been used as long or as universally as the protective tariff. It is the classic way to improve the commercial profitability prospects of an industrial project sufficiently to attract investment. It is popular with those who are most directly concerned—the government officials who want to get industrial development without spending scarce government funds on incentives which cost money, and the investor who can benefit from protection immediately his project starts producing. Tariff protection always has its advocates, those who can improve the profitability of their enterprises, and usually these advocates are influential. Those who stand to lose when tariffs are raised —the consuming public—are rarely represented in the discussion. In this chapter the advantages and disadvantages of the protective tariff as an industrial development incentive will be discussed, and suggestions will be made as to how this potentially powerful incentive can be used in controlled ways to lessen its many harmful features.

Few developing countries have tariffs which are suited to their needs. Most of them have protective tariffs mixed in with an antiquated system of revenue tariffs inherited from earlier times. The structures in most countries are still basically revenue tariff systems, which is not surprising for they were developed at a time when customs duties provided almost all revenue for most governments. The extent to which a country still depends on customs duties for public revenue is a measure of its stage of development. Few countries have made serious efforts to develop a tariff policy appropriate to their present stage of development, one really suitable to the needs of economic development and particularly industrial development. Until a country establishes a suitable tariff structure, it must expect its development to be distorted seriously.

There are many reasons which combine to make it difficult for a country to replace an archaic tariff structure with a modern one based on sound economic development principles. Most developing countries still have to depend on customs duties for a large part of their government revenue through lack of other revenue sources. Unfortunately, it must be said that all too often customs duties are not replaced by more modern taxes because the better taxes, such as income and inheritance taxes, would fall more heavily on the wealthy class. Dependence on customs duties for revenues tends to discourage the development of markets because the duties often raise the price of goods to such a degree that most of the people can afford to buy even less than they otherwise could. This is one of the serious limiting factors on the growth of local market industry. Through failure to develop alternatives to customs duties as rapidly as possible for financing the government, the industrial development of many countries is being unnecessarily delayed. While this may serve the short-run interests of a few people, it is contrary to the interest of the great majority.

Revenue tariff systems are also a reflection of the colonial type of public administration which still lingers on in many countries which are now independent. When these countries were colonies, the colonial rulers set up revenue-type tariff structures, for this kind of system was easiest to administer and was an effective way to make the residents of the colony pay directly for the costs of ruling them. In many ex-colonies, the revenue administration still consists largely of a customs duty collection agency operated with surprisingly little change from colonial days. Newer tax agencies such as income tax collection departments have grown up, but these rarely enjoy the prestige or support which is still accorded to the customs service. In a redress of this imbalance there is a great opportunity for many countries to move away from colonial-type revenue administration to a public revenue system more appropriate for independent nations entering an early stage of industrialization.

As long as a country is in a purely colonial situation—exporting raw materials and importing practically all manufactured goods—the tariff structure may consist entirely of revenue tariffs. It is a simple and straightforward system which achieves its objective and which is free from serious internal conflicts or contradictions. Once manufacturing starts, however, the difficulties arise. Capital will not flow naturally to manufacturing various products in which there is a natural economic advantage. It will be attracted to making products which happen to have a high rate of duty, regardless of the inherent economy or diseconomy of producing them in the country. In itself, this artificial pulling of capital to projects simply on the basis of their tariff rates is harmful to the development of the economy, because the same capital could be used more profitably for the economy if it were used to develop production along strictly economic lines. This is an example of how the power of government is often misused to make the things which are uneconomic from the country's viewpoint more commercially profitable than those which are economic. If the situation stopped at that point, it would be harmful enough; but it inevitably gets worse rapidly. The new manufacturers will never be content with existing levels of tariffs. They will always demand and usually get higher rates of protection on the products they are starting to make. Justified as this may be on the basis of the infant industry argument (which will be discussed shortly), the effect is to shut off imports of the product. This does three things: it forces the consuming public to subsidize the new industry; it reduces the size of the market; and it reduces the revenue on which the government has been depending. The latter makes it necessary for alternative tax revenues to be found, usually by raising the revenue tariffs on items which are still being imported. Natural though this process may be, it is hardly beneficial to the public or to the country's development. The consumer will end up paying higher prices on both the products to be made locally and the products still being imported. The effect is not merely one of hardship for the public: It means a reduction of the size of the market and its growth prospects for both kinds of products, thus pushing further into the future the time when the local manufacture of either one can be done on an economic basis.

A country which has made a fair amount of progress in developing new local market industries will find, if it stops to examine its tariff structure, that it has a mixed-up mess of a system. There may be protective tariffs on some products that are being made locally for the domestic market and revenue tariffs on many items still being imported. On many products there will probably be high rates which have been imposed in the name of industrial development but which serve as import barriers because they limit the import of items not yet being made locally. In such a situation there is bound to be much confusion as to the purpose of the tariff system if anyone stops to consider whether it is helping or hindering the sound industrial development of the country. The purpose of this chapter is to present the arguments both for and against protective tariffs as an industrial development incentive and to suggest ways in which tariffs may be used effectively while minimizing the economically harmful effects which commonly occur. Before appraising the pros and cons of tariffs, it is appropriate to glance at the historic role which protection has played in some countries which are now highly industrialized to see if there is any basis for the claim that, in adopting protection as the main device for industrial development, the countries industrializing today are only following the successful example of those who developed industry in the past.

The Experience of the Industrialized Countries in Using Protection

In many underdeveloped countries advocates of a policy of high tariff protection to encourage industrial development often base their case upon references to the use of protection in countries which today are highly industrialized. They argue that industrialization requires protection and that protection was the major factor in causing such countries as the United States, Canada, and Japan to become industrialized. The authorities on the economic history of these countries give little support to such sweeping generalizations. The following quotations from three leading economic histories of the United States are revealing:

> The influence of the tariff on the development of manufacturers in the United States is complicated by so many other factors that it is difficult to establish causal relationships. . . . The negative conclusion seems justified that the protective tariff was not an important cause in the growth of manufacturers, as a whole, though some of them profited greatly by the protection granted them during the difficult years of infancy. It should not be overlooked, however, that the consumers paid a price, and in some cases a high one, for the benefits conferred on the protected industries. . . . Protection to particular industries stimulated their growth, but as a single explanation of the phenomenal industrial growth and present preeminence of the United States, protection alone is inadequate.[1]

> The United States became a great manufacturing nation first of all because of her unsurpassed natural resources. . . . Labor was secured by the natural rapid increase of population in an undeveloped country and by millions of immigrants, many of whom were unfitted by training and environment for other than factory work. American manufacturers could not look to the older countries for a large market, but had to build one at home in competition with foreign markets. Such a market was partially supplied by the continued growth of the population, but particularly by the needs of the great agricultural South and West. During the three decades 1900–1930 the domestic market was increasingly supplemented by a growing export trade as the United States embarked aggressively upon a program of extending her foreign commerce and investment. . . . The high tariffs which the Civil War inaugurated have become a fixture in our system and have undoubtedly stimulated manufacturing, both by the large profits allowed to well-established industries and by the protection given to infant enterprises. That the United States would have experienced a marvelous development of manufacture without a protective tariff there is no reason to doubt, but it is equally evident that high tariff walls have considerably speeded the growth of certain industries.[2]

[1] Ernest L. Bogart and Donald L. Kemmerer, *Economic History of the American People*, David McKay Company, Inc., New York, 1947, pp. 360 and 474.

[2] Harold V. Faulkner, *American Economic History*, 5th ed., Harper & Row, Publishers, Incorporated, New York, 1943, p. 407.

Most students of the problem would agree that the policy of high protection accelerated the process of industrialization and, in particular cases, aided the establishment of branches of manufactures that subsequently were able to stand on their own feet. It would be wrong to conclude from such cases, however, that the policy of protection was a necessary prerequisite to the development of manufactures in the United States, or that a net increase in real national wealth and income was the result.[3]

Japan may be rightly regarded as the country which has made the most remarkable strides in industrial development in the past century, considering its lack of industrial resources and its previous isolation. It is an especially appropriate example for many of today's developing nations to study since it is the only country of non-European origin which has so far succeeded in becoming industrialized. The place of protection in Japan's industrial development has been analyzed in William Lockwood's book, *The Economic Development of Japan:* [4]

Early Japanese progress along the road of industrialization was made with little tariff protection from foreign competition. . . . Until 1899 Japan's import tariff was limited to 5% by treaties with the Western powers. Only thereafter was it raised selectively on numerous products. . . . Rates were generally no higher than 10 to 15% until the general tariff revision of 1911. . . . After World War I tariff policy became decidedly protectionist. . . . Industrial tariff now invited comparison to that of nations ordinarily regarded as highly protectionist. . . . [However] . . . the main structure of Japanese industry as it developed after 1900 did not depend on governmental protection to a large degree. Tariffs on consumer goods helped to reserve the home market largely for both the Japanese industrialist and the Japanese farmer, freeing foreign exchange resources for the purchase of machinery and industrial materials. In both fields tariffs on consumer goods weighed most directly on real wage rates in the cities. However, they probably hastened industrial capital formation in the process. They made it that much easier for Japan to industrialize rapidly with little resort to foreign borrowing, despite her heavy dependence on machinery and materials from abroad. . . . On balance there can be little doubt that protection in home and colonial markets helped to extend the range and diversity of Japanese manufacturing. . . . The older industries needed little shelter from foreign competition over and above that provided by cultural differences and transport costs. But many newer industries requiring radical departures from traditional techniques and a large market for economical operation certainly benefited from tariff assistance, at least for a period of years. . . . In short, the classic "infant industry" argument found its justifications. . . . Whether the aggregate scale of industrial

[3] Harold F. Williamson, *The Growth of the American Economy,* 2d ed., Prentice-Hall, Inc., Englewood Cliffs, N.J., 1951, p. 537.
[4] William H. Lockwood, *The Economic Development of Japan,* Princeton University Press, Princeton, N.J., 1954, pp. 539–544.

output was enlarged by the tariff is more problematical. In some degree it probably was, for the reason just mentioned. But industrial protection served in part merely to shift resources from one group of industries, especially the export industries, to fields which would otherwise have been supplied by imports.

Canada is another country which is interesting to look at to see the role which tariff protection has played in industrial policies during the past century. The subject has been analyzed well by John Young in *Canadian Commercial Policy*, one of the reports prepared in 1957 for the Royal Commission on Canada's Economic Prospects.[5] This study points out that three factors have favored protectionism in Canada: the importance of customs duties as a revenue source until World War II, the pressure to protect infant industry, and the desire to avoid excessive economic dependence on the United States in order to maintain political independence from the big neighbor to the south. In regard to the latter point it has often been said that the tariff is the price which Canadians pay for having an independent country. The Canadian tariff was purely a revenue system in its early years, but pressures for protection started around the middle of the nineteenth century. By 1887 a protective system was established which had minimum rates of 17½ per cent. It remained the national policy despite occasional and minor reciprocal arrangements with British Commonwealth nations and with the United States. While nobody would dispute the fact that protection accounts for the existence of many of Canada's industries, the analysis for the Royal Commission estimated that as of 1956, Canada was spending about $1 billion a year (3½ per cent of Gross National Product) more for the products of its protected industries than the price the same goods could have been purchased for in the United States. The study also pointed out that there is an unseen other half to the burden—the economic cost to a country of having its export products discriminated against in markets where they have a natural advantage. Canada's protectionist tariffs meant higher American tariffs against Canadian goods and thus a diversion of Canadian production away from those areas—export production —which had the greatest potential value to the country.

A Canadian economist, Harry Johnson, answered those who advocated still higher protection for Canada with these comments: [6]

> The arguments that have been trotted out for protectionism are the customary old fallacies: the nation will become richer by subsidizing inefficient high-cost production of goods that could be purchased more cheaply by exports; Canadian production will become large scale and

[5] John H. Young, *Canadian Commercial Policy*, The Queen's Printer, Ottawa, Ontario, 1957.

[6] Harry G. Johnson, *The International Journal*, Toronto, vol. 16, no. 3, pp. 238–250.

efficient if only the market it serves is made small enough and oligopolistic enough by high tariffs; inability to compete in free competition with foreigners demonstrates superior potential efficiency justifying a concealed public subsidy; without protection Canadian industry would disappear completely and everyone would be out of work. . . . The most predictable effect of higher protection is that Canadians in the protected industries will have higher incomes, or be able to get away with less efficient performance, than they otherwise would, and this at the expense of the general Canadian community. . . . There is a serious danger that by concentrating their case on the emotionally appealing but economically unsubstantiated arguments for protection the nationalists will persuade the public into accepting policies which yield profits to some Canadians but at a loss to the country. . . . I know of no evidence which supports the view that the development of industry behind the tariff, rather than the export of resource products, has been the foundation of Canadian prosperity and growth in either the distant or the recent past.

Even a brief group of illustrations of how tariffs have been used by countries which have achieved a considerable amount of industrial development would not be complete without an example of a country which has carried the policy of protection to an extreme. Probably no country has gone further in this direction than Argentina, which is a classic example of how the economy of a rich country can be harmed by an industrialization policy based on high tariffs and neglect of exports. The Arthur D. Little report on industrial development in Argentina contained these comments: [7]

> We regard protection as it exists in Argentina today to be one of the major causes of the blight of high costs, low productivity, and lack of market growth, which characterizes much of Argentine industry. . . . In recent years protection has been at a level of 150% for a large part of industry. . . . The height of protection is such that, in many industries, it has removed any pressure for efficiency. The enterprises can be profitable without making a reasonable effort to control costs. The general level of protection is so high that it also removes pressure for quality improvement or control. . . . Market growth is severely restricted. In cases, which are common, of locally made goods selling for two or three times what the imported goods would sell for without duty, it is not surprising that the size of the market is often only a fraction of what would be at reasonable price levels. . . . The net result of protection is therefore much uneconomic industry, excessively high price levels, and the exclusion from the market of a large percentage of potential customers. . . . The high level of prices for manufactured goods, a result in part of overprotectionism, is undoubtedly a major factor in the continual

[7] Arthur D. Little, Inc., *Industrial Development in Argentina*, Cambridge, Mass., 1961, pp. 83–84.

pressure of workers for higher wages. We saw many evidences of a justified feeling that although much of industry is highly profitable to its
owners, labor does not benefit proportionately in wages or as members of
the consuming public, which is being victimized by having to pay excessive prices for goods made in the country. Through its policy of high
protection, the Government has given industrialists the opportunity to
act in a way which seriously weakened the confidence of the public in
the whole system of private industry.

The Basic Arguments for Protective Tariffs

The theoretical basis for protective tariffs was summarized in the
Arthur D. Little report on an industrial development program for Peru: [8]

> The great traditional argument for tariff protection for industrial de-
> velopment is the "infant industry argument." In a simple way this argu-
> ment may be described as follows: a country may be well suited to pro-
> duce economically a certain article which is presently being imported.
> It is difficult, however, for a producer in the country to make the item
> economically at first because of lack of experience, lack of trained work-
> ers, and the underdeveloped nature of the market. It is argued that under
> these circumstances a government interested in developing local manu-
> facturing should grant tariff protection so that the new local industry can
> be established and be profitable during the first few years while it solves
> its problems, trains its workers, and develops its market. It is implied in
> this argument that the need for the tariff will be temporary and that it will
> be withdrawn as soon as the new industry reaches normal levels of effi-
> ciency. It will then be able to stand on its own feet and meet foreign com-
> petition without tariff protection.
>
> The infant-industry argument makes a great deal of sense under cer-
> tain conditions. Even under the most favorable circumstances it is rare
> for an industry which is new to a developing country to be able to achieve
> normal levels of efficiency, productivity, and profitability during the first
> few years. This is true even of many new industrial enterprises in well
> developed countries. It is therefore important and economically necessary
> for new industries which have a clear prospect of being economic for
> the country to be assisted over the difficult first few years.
>
> The infant industry argument assumes, naturally, that the particular in-
> dustry to be protected has the basis to become economic within a reason-
> able length of time. This means that it must have the potential ability to
> produce competitively with imported goods at the cost for which they can
> be landed in the country before any taxes. The cost of transport of the for-
> eign goods imported presents a certain natural level of protection which
> requires no legislation. Whether a proposed new industry would have a
> reasonable prospect of becoming efficient and economic in a reasonable

[8] Arthur D. Little, Inc., *A Program for the Industrial and Regional Development of Peru*, Cambridge, Mass., 1960, pp. 21–22.

length of time is something which can usually be calculated fairly accurately. An analysis of the elements of production required and the cost of those elements compared with their cost in other countries is an important part of the calculation. If it can be shown that the important items of raw materials and labor, power, and other factors can be made available in the country at about the same cost and quality as in other countries, then it may be supposed that eventually competitive production costs should exist providing the same scale of operations is possible.

The infant industry argument makes the greatest sense in situations where a local manufacturer may have access to a very large market once he has achieved reasonable efficiency in production. He will then have the economies of scale. This was the situation in the United States. In smaller countries, where the infant industry argument is advanced most strongly, it generally has less validity, for the size of the domestic market is so limited that production costs will be high because of the necessarily small scale of operations. In producing some goods it is true that eventually a market can be developed which will be adequate to permit reasonable economies of scale, but in other lines the market will have no prospect of reaching an economic size in any reasonable length of time, and therefore the assumption of eventually reaching competitive costs may be completely unrealistic.

A somewhat related and perhaps more important argument for tariffs in a developing country is referred to as the "young economy argument." Described briefly this argument is that new industries in a developing economy find it difficult to be competitive at first, not because of inefficiencies within the particular plant but rather because of the underdeveloped nature of the economy itself. There is a general lack of a trained labor force. There are shortages of power and other common facilities. There is a general lack of purchasing power in the community which limits the possible market for most manufactured goods. There is an absence of supporting services and supply facilities which are necessary for the efficient operation of industry. There is a lack of a capital market and the cost of borrowed money is excessively high because of the mistrust of industry generally and the lack of available capital. The distribution system is inefficient and fails to merchandise the manufactured products economically. These and many similar obstacles are not related to any one industry, but they are conditions within the society which can be altered only by a simultaneous growth of a large number of manufacturing enterprises. The young-economy argument is that in this situation it is necessary to encourage and stimulate the establishment of a wide range of manufacturing enterprises, each of which by its own growth will contribute to solving the problems which stand in the way of all industrial development. It is argued that the price which must be paid to start the momentum of development is a tariff which will raise the profitability of manufacturing industries generally to the point where a significant number of new ventures will be started. This is therefore an argument for an increase in the general level of tariffs and not for tariffs which benefit only a few specific industries. Like the infant-industry argument it is of course not an argument for tariffs on items which would never be produced in the country, for such a tariff would be purely a revenue tariff and not a development protective tariff.

A third basic argument for protective tariffs to foster the establishment of industry which would otherwise not be commercially profitable is one which, as far as I know, has never been given a name, but which might well be called the "unused resources argument." A characteristic of most nonindustrialized countries is that many of their resources are idle. This applies particularly to labor, but sometimes also to land, forests, water power, and other natural resources. If not absolutely idle, much of the labor is used where it is not really needed. This is referred to as "disguised unemployment," for the excess labor could be removed without making any noticeable change in the output or the amount of work done. Since the idle resources are not adding anything to the country's gross national product, they can be thought of as being free resources—that is, resources which cost the economy nothing if it finds useful employment for them. The basis for saying the resources have no value lies in the opportunity cost line of reasoning which attributes to anything the value it would have if used in the best alternative use open to it. As unemployed labor has no alternative use, its real value to the economy is zero.

Once the assumption that idle resources are "free resources" is accepted, it is easy to see that protective tariffs may be justified as a way to bring into use, and get some value from, resources which are idle. If, through the device of a tariff (which is really a way to make the purchasers of a product subsidize its producers), it becomes commercially profitable to manufacture a certain product in a country, and if its manufacture draws into use a substantial amount of the free resources, something useful may have been accomplished. As long as the subsidy, that is, the difference between the c.i.f. cost of the item if imported and the cost if produced locally under protection, is not as great as the cost to the local manufacturer of bringing the idle resources into production, it can be said there is a net gain to the economy.

If a country has a large amount of idle labor and other unused resources, it can improve its national income by a program of subsidizing new industry to bring the idle resources into use, provided it does not go too far and pay such a large subsidy that the over-all effect is to reduce the national income. If a country wishes to subsidize industry on this basis, a protective tariff is one means which might be used to raise private commercial profitability to the point where capital will be made available to the new industries.

Looked at in another way, one might say that the unused resources argument is a variation of the law of comparative advantage. This law states that a country need not have an absolute advantage in order to make the production of an item economic: All that is required to justify local production is that were the article in question manufactured it be under less disadvantage than any alternative product which could be produced. Let us imagine a country in which it costs at least 20 per cent more to manufacture any article than in the country in which each article could be produced most cheaply. This does not mean that the country should import all the products; in fact, it would usually be impossible for it to do so, for it would probably have no way of earning the necessary foreign exchange. In this sad situation, which is reality for many countries, it will be economically sound to produce locally those items in which the country can come closest to the best international costs and import the others, even if it has to subsidize the export of some items it does make in order to earn enough foreign exchange for the imported items. Protective tariffs would be one way to bring about the local production of the items of least disadvantage.

The Practical Advantages of Protective Tariffs

The most compelling reason for making protective tariffs a part of an industrial development program is that they work. They are effective in getting industries established. Their application, of course, is limited to local market industries, for protective tariffs can do nothing to help industries which must compete on export markets. If import substitution is found to be an important area of industrial opportunity in a country, there is no doubt that protective tariffs will get results and get them quickly. As long as the local market for the product is inelastic—that is, not reduced proportionately if the price goes up—a tariff increase may be the simplest and quickest way to create a price level which will make local manufacture commercially profitable and thus investible.

In contrast to granting cash subsidies, as some countries are doing to attract new industries, giving tariff protection costs the government nothing. The subsidy is paid by those who purchase the products of the protected industry. In view of the budget problems of developing countries and the difficulty they have in raising funds for development purposes, this is an important feature. It may be easier for a government to "tax" the consumers by forcing them to pay the subsidy in the form of higher prices for what they buy than for it to raise money for cash subsidies by collecting more taxes.

The rapidity with which new industries can be attracted on the basis of tariff increases is another distinct advantage. If a developing country has an economic-sized market for a product, it is probable that several potential investors are already thinking of the possibility of local manufacture. The granting of a tariff increase on the product may be all that is necessary to make an investment attractive. Once the situation has been made potentially profitable enough, it is probable that someone will soon take advantage of the opportunity. At this point, prompt investment results can be expected. If for no other reason, some company will take the plunge to avoid the danger that its market will be taken away by a competitor who has been attracted by the tariff increase.

In attracting capital to early investment in industrial projects, a protective tariff serves an important use. It draws capital into industry from other uses which may be less productive; above all, it is likely to bring in foreign capital which otherwise would not come to the country. Accompanied as it will be by industrial know-how, the foreign capital is invaluable. Provided this process does not go too far and cause capital to be put into industry when it could be used to greater economic advantage in other sectors of the economy, this is all to the good.

As an effective industrial attraction device, tariff protection may serve to strengthen the foreign exchange position of a country. This comes about through the inflow of capital which would not come otherwise and also through import substitution, as the industries which tariff protection brings are those which will produce locally goods which formerly had to be imported. Normally, the foreign exchange component of the locally made goods will be less than the foreign exchange cost of importing the finished product, so a net foreign exchange saving should result. However, the gain may be accompanied by an increased rigidity in foreign exchange requirements. This will be discussed later.

There are many ways in which a country can get itself ready for industrialization. It can expand its educational facilities, especially its technical schools, and even set up practical training centers for specific industries. It can establish industrial estates which provide convenient services for industry along with good sites and buildings at low cost. It can provide power, water, and other utilities at reduced prices. Some of these aids have to be provided by government. Some can be provided by the new industries if the financial opportunities for them have been made sufficiently attractive that they can pay the costs of the pioneer industrial facilities and still have a level of profitability which will attract investment. While tax incentives are good for creating the prospect of high retainable profitability after a new industry is operating successfully, tariff protection is an even more direct incentive and a more certain assurance that the new enterprise will be profitable. Protection creates the immediate prospect of higher return by making possible a higher sales price for each unit of product. Nothing is more likely to induce an investor to undertake a local market project which will have substantial training and other pioneering expenses than the certainty which protection can give him of reimbursement from the start of his initially heavy operating costs.

From the viewpoint of the economy of the underdeveloped country, the most compelling argument for tariff protection for industry is that this is a means to bring into production resources which would otherwise be idle or which would be used in less productive ways indefinitely. For local market industries, there is no doubt that tariff protection can do much to accomplish this important economic development objective. For example, as long as import duties are low, it may be more attractive to import furniture; but if the duties are high, an immediate incentive will exist to use the country's unused forests and its unemployed labor to make furniture locally for the national market. Even if higher prices for the consumer and some reduction in quality result, there is likely to be a net gain for the country.

The Case against Protection

The idea of trying to develop a country's economy by seeking self-sufficiency and the substitution of locally made products for imports has fascinated economists ever since people started studying economic questions. Modern economists have rarely explained the basic truth about the advantages of international trade over self-sufficiency as well as Adam Smith did in 1776: [9]

> To give the monopoly of the home-market to the produce of domestic industry, in any particular art or manufacture, is in some measure to direct private people in what manner they ought to employ their capitals, and must, in almost all cases, be either a useless or a hurtful regulation. If the produce of domestic can be bought as cheap as that of foreign industry, the regulation is evidently useless. If it cannot, it must generally be hurtful. It is the maxim of every prudent master of a family, never to attempt to make at home what it will cost him more to make than to buy. The taylor does not attempt to make his own shoes, but buys them of the shoemaker. The shoemaker does not attempt to make his own clothes, but employs a taylor. The farmer attempts to make neither the one nor the other, but employs those different artificers. All of them find it for their interest to employ their whole industry in a way in which they have some advantage over their neighbours, and to purchase with a part of its produce, or what is the same thing, with the price of a part of it, whatever else they have occasion for. What is prudence in the conduct of every private family, can scarce be folly in that of a great kingdom. If a foreign country can supply us with a commodity cheaper than we ourselves can make it, better buy it of them with some part of the produce of our own industry, employed in a way in which we have some advantage.

[9] Adam Smith, *Wealth of Nations*, quoted by Seymour E. Harris in *International and Interregional Economics*, McGraw-Hill Book Company, New York, 1957, p. 9.

Adam Smith's elementary argument for international trade instead of protection and economic isolation was a starting point, and the theory has gone through many elaborations and refinements. But few economists have ever disagreed with its basic point that a country will be richer if it concentrates on producing those things for which it has an economic advantage. The major clarification of the original theory came from Ricardo about 1817, when he showed that trade could be carried on between two countries on a sound and mutually advantageous basis, even when one of them produced both of the commodities traded with less labor than the other, provided that its advantage was greater in making one product than the other. John Stuart Mill, another great pioneer in this field of economic analysis, summarized the matter in this way in 1877: [10]

> To render the importation of an article more advantageous than its production, it is not necessary that the foreign country should be able to produce it with less labour and capital than ourselves. We may even have a positive advantage in its production; but, if we are so far favoured by circumstances as to have a still greater positive advantage in the production of some other article which is in demand in the foreign country, we may be able to obtain a greater return to our labour and capital by employing none of it in producing the article in which our advantage is least, but devoting it all to the production of that in which our advantage is greatest, and giving this to the foreign country in exchange for the other. It is not a difference in the absolute cost of production, which determines the interchange, but a difference in the comparative cost.

These arguments on the economic advantage of trade over narrow isolationism are basic to a consideration of the protective tariff issue because the tariff is a major impediment governments place in the way of the international exchange of goods. The tariff can be regarded as the leading device to encourage the manufacture of goods locally which would otherwise be imported from places where they could be made more economically.

There are many aspects of the economists' case against tariffs. One of the most fundamental is that protection diverts resources—capital, management, and labor—from uses to which they would be applied in the absence of the protection system to use in protected industries which would otherwise not be established. It is not necessary to assume that other uses would be ideal to realize that a large-scale transfer of resources from one type of use to another should only be brought about by a government when it is clearly established that the economy as a whole will gain by such a transfer. In some situations, which will be

[10] John Stuart Mill, *Essay on Some Unsettled Questions of Political Economy*, quoted by Seymour E. Harris in *ibid.*, p. 18.

discussed below, a diversion of resources may be justified economically. But it often happens that in adopting more protectionist policies in the name of fostering industrial development, no attention is paid to the economic loss involved in taking resources away from other sectors of the economy where the resources may have greater economic value to the country. The price for using resources in a less economic way is simply that the country will be poorer—the national income will be reduced.

A classic example of a country which systematically ruined its economy by overprotecting industry and thus diverting its resources to uneconomic manufacturing from an economically profitable export sector is Argentina. One of the world's richest countries in terms of agricultural resources, Argentina has few of the real problems which explain the underdevelopment of many nations. Argentina at one time had a higher gross national product than Canada; now it is less than one-third. The basic factor in causing the economic disaster in Argentina was that local industry was overdeveloped, through protection and other means, to such a degree that capital and labor were drawn away from the agricultural sector on a large scale. Agriculture was Argentina's strength in exports, for the country could produce high-quality meat and grain at low cost because of remarkably favorable conditions of soil, terrain, and climate. The more success the country had in its drive for industrialization, the poorer it became, for it built industry at the expense of the sector in which it had both a relative and an absolute advantage in world terms. Through export taxes and other means, agricultural exports were burdened with much of the cost of subsidizing uneconomic industry. The subsidizing of uneconomic activities by economic ones goes on in most countries, mainly through protection which diverts resources into uneconomic uses. Usually the process is not carried as far as in Argentina, where it ruined a rich country; but even when used more sparingly, the protection device tends to reduce an economy's earning power and thus its standard of living. It is ironic that while the GNP is being reduced, the advocates of protection proclaim how the country will prosper through having still more industrial development and how national stature can be acquired by ceasing to be exporters of primary products.

It must be admitted that many new industries do require some kind of subsidy in their early years; otherwise, private investment cannot be attracted to them. This is true for many projects which are basically sound and which represent the creation of facilities to produce products in which a country will have a strong competitive advantage in world terms, once the new industry has reached normal levels of efficiency. A major disadvantage of tariff protection as a means to give a needed subsidy is that tariff protection is an indiscriminate kind of subsidy. Once established, it is likely to be received by many industries which do not need it. A subsidy may be needed, for example, to help a country's first textile mill get established. Once the country has a protective tariff on cloth, however, future textile mills will be subsidized as much as the first one.

More serious is the fact that protective tariffs, once established, tend to be permanent. While the tariff might originally have been justified on a temporary basis to attract capital to sound industrial projects, those who benefit from the subsidy have every reason to do their utmost to see that it continues forever. Usually they are politically influential and can accomplish this objective. While I shall suggest later in this chapter a device of temporary tariffs, I recognize that in most countries the political pressures of selfish interests are such that tariffs will tend to be permanent, regardless of the harm they do to the country.

From the over-all view of industrial development, protection exerts an extremely bad influence through its harmful effect on the growth of the local market. A tariff, if it is used at all by a local manufacturer in pricing his product, results in raising the price over levels which prevailed when the item was imported. For almost any product raising the price reduces the quantity that can be sold, although the amount by which sales are cut because of a given amount of price increase depends on the price elasticity of demand. A 50 per cent increase in retail price for a product such as salt, which a consumer buys in small quantities and which represents a very small part of his total expenditures, may cause only a slight reduction in the quantity that can be sold. This is referred to as an "inelastic demand." The same price increase for radios may cut the market in half by eliminating large numbers of potential customers who cannot afford the higher prices for a purchase in the non-necessity category. This is called an "elastic demand." It is only reasonable to believe that most products are in this class, especially in a developing country where income levels are low for the great majority of people. If a tariff by raising prices of a product reduces the market for the product directly, as happens in most cases, it will usually make the production of the item less economic, for the scale of operations is likely to be minimal anyway. As production volume is reduced, the costs of making most things goes up sharply. Many manufacturing possibilities which represented an opportunity to produce at a fairly economic cost with the size of the market which existed at pre-tariff prices will be marginal or worse at higher price levels which reduce the marketable volume and thus increase the production cost. A country which has sought to encourage industrial growth by a high tariff policy may well find that it has made many of its potential projects unfeasible. If a particular project goes ahead anyway, either because the market is big enough even if reduced somewhat or because it has an inelastic kind of market which will not suffer, the harm to industrial growth generally will still exist. The consuming public which pays more for the locally made item will have that much less money to spend on other things. This is bound to reduce the market for other products, eliminating still more industrial possibilities which might otherwise have had a large enough market to be feasible.

When a country embarks on a policy of tariff protection, it generally puts the tariff on a large number of products, irrespective of whether they are being produced in the country. This gives protection (probably not needed) to old local industries and also a strong incentive for some new ones to be established. Generally it will also raise prices on many products whose local manufacture is not likely for some time because of the limited size of the market. This is especially harmful to industrial development prospects, for the higher prices will discourage imports and delay indefinitely the time when the local market will be large enough to justify a manufacturing plant of minimum economic size. A developing country needs market growth above all, for it is the smallness of most local markets which limits the amount of local industry which can be economic. Tariff protection, whether on products which are being or could be produced in the country or on products which are still years away from feasible local manufacture, operates to reduce the market. It also tends to limit the range of things which can be made at reasonable costs for the local market, both in the short run and in the long run.

The artificial fostering of local market industries by means of a protective tariff policy may do its greatest harm in discouraging the development of export industries which, for many countries, offer the means to generate economic growth rather than to follow it. As protection is a device which affects only local market industries, it tends to make this kind of industry more profitable than export industries. Capital, management, and labor will be drawn away from developing export industries. The harm done does not stop at that, however. Because of lack of competitive pressure for efficiency, protected local market industries tend to have low productivity. Acceptance of low efficiency is a blight which spreads through the entire industrial community, affecting management and labor alike. Once this disease has thoroughly infiltrated, the difficulties of building highly efficient and productive export industries may be so great as to be unsurmountable. The problem is partly one of attitudes and partly one of costs. With the assurance of high margins, the owner of a protected local market industry may be able to pay higher wages to his workers than the owner of an export industry, which has to absorb transport costs (and sometimes tariffs in the country where the product is to be sold) and still meet international competition from the world's largest and most efficient plants. The establishment of high levels of wages and other employee benefits by protected local market industries may make it impossible to set up export industries which can compete internationally. The creation of an industry sector composed mainly of highly protected local market industries may eliminate a larger industrial development opportunity in the export sector. In a country's industrial economy, one can see a force at work which is similar to Gresham's law in the monetary field, "bad money drives out good money." In industry it can be said that "overly protected industry drives out export industry."

Anything which discourages building up export industries is seriously out of keeping with the trend of the times. Finally, after generations of high protection by most countries, the world seems ready to start accepting what the economists have always said, that all will gain most by a free international exchange of goods in which each country concentrates on making those things in which it has the greatest comparative advantage. The success of the European Common Market has stimulated the development of the Latin American Free Trade Area and the more rapidly advancing Central American Common Market. The Latin American trend toward freer trade represents a remarkable change of direction by a group of countries which has had some of the highest protective tariff systems in the world. Finally, it is coming to be realized that the industrial development future of Latin America would be dim indeed if it were to be limited by the small size of most of the national markets. In this rapidly changing environment, a country has the choice of adapting its policies to future needs or clinging to the past. The future opportunity lies in creating internationally oriented industrial sectors in which there is considerable emphasis on larger-scale plants able to compete in regional or world markets. This kind of industry can be had only if the right conditions for it are brought about. A country which maintains the old policies of high protection and emphasis on local market industries will find itself left behind by countries whose governments see the international trend in industrial opportunities and adopt policies which meet the new needs.

The foreign exchange aspect of fostering local market industries through tariff protection needs further consideration, especially as one of the motives for encouraging import-substitution industries by protection is to save foreign exchange. It is true that a country may need less foreign exchange to import the necessary parts or materials for local manufacturing or assembly than to import the finished products. But the gain is often less than expected. Foreign exchange may also be needed for payments under licensing or royalty arrangements, for costs of management assistance and foreign personnel, and for repatriating earnings of the local market industries if they have foreign-ownership participation. The most serious foreign exchange problem which arises when a country starts local manufacture or assembly of products formerly imported may lie in the rigidity which this change introduces into the country's foreign exchange budget. As Argentina and many other countries have found, it is much harder in times of foreign exchange shortage to reduce foreign exchange allocations for imported parts and materials than for the finished product, especially if the product is of a luxury or semiluxury type. For example, if a country imports radios, it can simply cut off imports of radios when foreign exchange is short. Doing so will have no serious effect on the local economy; in fact, the local economy may benefit from the spending of funds which otherwise would have gone for imported goods. But if the country has a radio assembly industry, set up because of tariff protection, a cutting off of imported parts would have the serious effect of putting out of work the workers of the radio assembly industry. Politically as well as economically and socially, this may be difficult to do. The seriousness of this problem depends, of course, on how much of a country's industry is dependent on imported material or parts.

One of the worst aspects of protection is that it encourages, shields, and perpetuates inefficiency in industry. The protected industry does not have to be efficient to survive, unless it has efficient local competitors. It is shielded from the competition of efficient firms which compete on the world market. The production costs of the local firm may be out of line, and the quality of its product may be poor. However, it will have little incentive to improve for it does not have to compete with world standards of price or quality. Moreover, this unfortunate situation is not temporary but tends to be permanent, giving local industry, and even private business in general, a bad name.

Private industry in a developing country can hardly afford to encourage the creation of any situation which will hurt its public image. In most of the developing countries, most of the industries which do exist and which are not owned by foreign interests are owned by a small group of wealthy people. Often, they are the same minority who dominate the ownership of land, urban real estate, mines, and other productive resources. A high protective tariff system is likely to make the small industrial ownership group more wealthy, within the limits of the industrial sector which can prosper in a small domestic market. The industrial owners, recognizing that their high profits depend on artificial price levels sheltered by the tariffs, are almost certain to be very conservative. They will be fearful of changes such as common markets which might encourage more industrial development but which might hurt the old, protected industries. They will resist the granting of incentives to encourage competition, for they benefit in many instances from monopoly positions. They will usually oppose efforts to attract more foreign investment, for the inflow of capital and new ideas may mean upsetting the old and profitable patterns. A country which adopts a highly protective tariff system may well find itself with some new industry but also with an extremely conservative industrial group which will be a barrier to dynamic industrial growth on a competitive and international basis.

The political and economic implications of a highly protective tariff policy are worth contemplating. The customers of the protected industries, and these may include most of the buying public of a country, can be expected to be dissatisfied if they have no alternative but to buy locally made goods which are more expensive and of lower quality than imported products. The fact that the owners of the highly protected local industries are prospering will not go unnoticed. In most countries, the elite who own the protected industries are already under attack by those who advocate more economic and social equality. By perpetuating or extending a high tariff system, local industrialists may be digging their own graves: The political changes which grow out of public dissatisfaction about prices and the other faults of local industry are hardly likely to stop with moderate reforms which might bring about sounder policies for private industrial development.

How to Control Protection while Using It as an Incentive

The debate over the advantages and disadvantages of tariff protection is as old as the study of economics, and it is not surprising that policy makers in many developing countries are thoroughly confused about what to do. On the one hand, they see the many seriously harmful effects of building an industrial development program on a high-protection basis. On the other hand, they are subject to the pressure of those who seek protection, and they recognize the considerable merit in the infant industry argument and some of the other justifications advanced for a protectionist policy. The governments of the developing countries cannot avoid the dilemma which the tariff question presents to them. Their countries do have tariff structures which cannot remain unchanged in view of the pressures which exist. In this situation, many governments adopt no clear policy. They let themselves be pushed and pulled by the conflicting forces at work. Their tariff structures remain confused, contributing little to the development of the country. An alternative is to accept the persuasive arguments for using tariffs as an industrial development incentive, but at the same time to establish limits and controls on protection which are designed to prevent it from getting out of hand to the point where its harmful features become serious. There are various ways of doing this.

The first principle that must be accepted if a country is to protect itself from the harmful effects of high tariffs is that no more than a moderate amount of protection should be available to any industry. No one can say exactly what the limit should be. Nobody would say that a

5 or a 10 per cent level is likely to cause a serious misallocation of resources or to give such a great advantage to local market industries that export industries would be discouraged. Most students of the problem would feel that a 40 or a 50 per cent tariff level would bring a host of serious problems. The level which might be sufficient to offer some needed support for infant industries and to do something to attract investment while avoiding most of the dangers would be somewhere in between. My feeling, and this cannot be substantiated with numbers, is that a tariff level of 15 or 20 per cent is one which offers incentive without serious adverse effects. A level above 25 per cent will offer stronger incentives; but on balance, in my opinion, such a level is likely to do more harm than good to an economy and to the industrial sector.

Avoiding too high a general level of protection is not the only way of controlling the tariff device. If we take the infant industry and the young economy arguments at face value, the need for protection is much greater when a new industry is set up. As the industry solves its problems and as the industrial sector in general grows larger and more diversified, the need for protection should diminish. Protection would clearly be much less harmful if a way could be found to prevent it from being permanent. A way to do this was suggested in the Arthur D. Little report to the Government of Peru: [11]

> We recommend that Peru establish a new system of temporary development tariffs to be granted on a highly selective basis, and only on the recommendation of the Development Corporation. Tariff increases to attract new industries should be made only through this system. The following conditions should apply:
>
> a. Temporary development tariffs should be granted only in order to secure the establishment in Peru of manufacturing projects expected to be of high value to the national economy.
>
> b. A temporary development tariff should be effective from the date the first major project to manufacture the product commences commercial operation.
>
> c. Temporary development tariffs should be strictly limited to a specific number of years and should not be renewable. We suggest five years should be the standard term, as this period would be enough for any sound project to reach normal profitability.
>
> d. Advance authorization of temporary development tariffs should be granted only for a specified time necessary to organize and construct the first project to manufacture the item in commercial quantities.
>
> e. Temporary development tariffs on any product should be in

[11] Arthur D. Little, Inc., *A Program for the Industrial and Regional Development of Peru,* p. 24.

addition to existing tariffs. They should not be more than the total of existing tariffs on the product (taking into account both specific and valorum). In any event, the total of the existing tariff and the temporary development tariff should not be more than 50%.

I recognize the difficulty in removing protection once it has been granted. Not only the owners of the affected industry, but also its workers will exert every possible pressure to have the protection made permanent, whether really needed or not. At the same time, I am hopeful that the government of some developing country will be sufficiently persuaded by the logic of a temporary development tariff system to try it as an industrial incentive with enough safeguards so that abuse of the device can be avoided.

A variation of the idea of a temporary development tariff in the form of a surcharge over the regular tariff, which could then be kept at a low level, would be to reduce the temporary development tariff gradually until it expires. The rule could be that 10 or 20 per cent of the temporary development tariff would be taken off each year. Thus, for a given product, we might have a regular tariff of 20 per cent which would be permanent and a temporary development tariff of 30 per cent which would be reduced each year for five years. The protection schedule would be as shown in Table 7. By reducing the temporary develop-

Table 7

	Regular tariff, %	Temporary development tariff, %	Total tariff, %
First year..................	20	30	50
Second year...............	20	24	44
Third year................	20	18	38
Fourth year...............	20	12	32
Fifth year.................	20	6	26
Later years...............	20	...	20

ment level of protection each year, the new industry would receive a substantial amount of subsidy when it needed it most to meet the extraordinary costs of getting started. As its infancy expenses gradually diminished and as its productivity improved, there would be a gradual reduction in the level of protection. It is possible that this system would be a way to avoid the shock a company would have if it lost all its temporary protection at one time. Reducing the shock may lessen the dangers of successful pressure for continued special protection.

Another approach to controlling protection is to make whatever protection is granted conditional on specified performance. In many developing countries the new industries which are established through protection to serve the local market are monopolies. This is inevitable, for in most cases the market is too small to be attractive to more than one establishment even with protection. The monopolistic protected industry poses a special threat to the community in which it operates for it may use its monopoly position to exploit the public by charging excessively high prices or selling inferior goods. One way to protect the public interest while still giving an incentive to get the industry established would be to make the continuation of high tariff protection conditional upon the product being priced at no more than a fixed percentage above the c.i.f. cost of imported goods of comparable quality. This percentage would be smaller than the rate of the tariff.

While the economy must have some safeguard against permanent high tariff levels on any product, the prospective investor will consider the tariff more valuable as an incentive if he also has some assurances. One assurance which is worth giving and which costs a government nothing is that whatever level of tariff protection is given for the new industry will remain in force for a specified period of time. If the protection is given in the form of a temporary development tariff, the period it is to last will be known. If the protection is to be in the form of a higher regular tariff and the duration is indefinite and unknown, it would be desirable for the government to give an assurance that the tariff would not be lowered for the specific product for a reasonable period of time, say five or ten years. Such a guarantee might well contain some conditions as to pricing if the industrialist seeks a higher level of tariff to exclude imports not merely to raise their price.

An important thing to remember in tariff setting for industrial development is that protective tariffs should never be established until there is a local industry to protect or unless one is immediately in prospect. As I mentioned previously, a tariff on an item which is still going to be imported will have the effect of reducing imports and thus slowing down the growth of the market for the product. This is bound to delay the day when the local market will be big enough to make local manufacture really economic. Anything which limits market growth limits the amount of industrial development. Provided foreign exchange is available, the policy from an industrial development viewpoint should be to permit duty-free entry of all products whose local manufacture is thought to be a possibility within the next five or ten years. The protective tariff should be put on only when the market has reached an economic size and local production appears feasible: Generally, it should be put on as an investment incentive as part of the incentive package offered to get a specific investment.

The Prohibition of Imports

Strictly speaking, the absolute exclusion of a product which otherwise might be imported is not a matter of tariff policy; but its effect is so similar to that of a high tariff that the device should be considered as an alternative to a tariff as an incentive for a new industry. Most investors who are contemplating setting up a local market industry in a developing country would probably prefer a prohibition on imports of the product they will be making to the granting of a protective tariff, however high. A prohibition on importing the product is absolute, while tariff protection is not. With a tariff, anyone who wishes to pay the duty may import the item, assuming that foreign exchange controls or import licensing do not stand in the way. A new manufacturer who wants to have all the market for his new industry would naturally prefer to avoid the danger that some of his potential customers might be able to choose to continue importing a competitive product. There are many examples of cases in which even a 100 per cent duty is not enough to prevent the importing of a popular foreign product in preference to a locally made item selling at a lower price.

From the viewpoint of the country and its consumers, prohibition of imports is a dangerous device, for it always creates the possibility of abuse by a new monopolist. Without some likelihood of competition from imports, the local manufacturer is under little pressure to produce goods of standard quality. Nor has he any incentive to keep prices down, especially if he is producing a product for which the demand is inelastic. The public must have the safeguard of being able to import a competitive product, even if the cost would be high because of the protective tariff granted.

It must be recognized, of course, that import prohibitions, like high levels of tariffs, may come about because of foreign exchange shortages and not because of their acceptance as industrial incentives. Regardless of why they are imposed, the harmful effects are going to be the same. Anything which makes local market industry artificially profitable will attract resources from more economic uses, discourage market growth, and put the development of export industries at a disadvantage.

14

Other Incentives

While tax and tariff incentives are the most common inducements offered by developing countries to encourage industrial growth, their prominence should not take attention away from the many other industrial incentives which also warrant consideration. Most comprehensive industrial development programs need tax and tariff incentives, but they also need many of the twelve other kinds of incentives and supports for new industry which will be described in this chapter. These have all been used successfully by countries or regions seeking to attract new industry. Some will fit certain situations better than others, but the possible usefulness of each should be carefully weighed in designing a program for maximum industrial development.

Factory Sites, Buildings, and Industrial Parks

For many new industries which a country may be trying to attract, the cost of land and buildings may be a substantial part of the total investment required. Any action which enables the prospective investor to avoid all or part of this cost will reduce his risk and may increase his estimated rate of return. Avoiding ownership of land and buildings is particularly important to some kinds of industries, for example, those which are labor-intensive and which prefer to preserve their mobility by not putting down deep roots in any location.

Sometimes the need is to provide land for factories: in other situations, the factory buildings. In many places, it is difficult to obtain suitable land for industry in good locations and at reasonable prices. This creates a problem which may result in a proposed factory's being located elsewhere or even in the prospective investor's becoming discouraged and giving up his project. An important incentive in such situations is the provision of good factory sites by the government or its industrial development agency. Sometimes all that is needed is for the government to acquire suitable land and reserve it for industrial purchasers, to whom it is made available at moderate prices for outright purchase. An alternative is to let the new industries have the sites on long-term leases. The price set for purchase or lease of land can be adjusted to reflect whatever degree of subsidy may be thought necessary to use the land as an incentive to attract new industry.

Land for new industry may be scattered in various locations wherever suitable sites are available, or it may be concentrated in one place. If new land for industry is developed on a fairly large scale as a unit, it is usually referred to as an "industrial estate" or an "industrial park." Any country should consider the industrial park as an important potential way to attract new industry. The industrial park is not a new idea, nor one confined to underdeveloped countries. The concept of an industrial park was described in a report for a community industrial development organization in the United States by the Arthur D. Little Company in this way:

> Shortly after the industrial revolution in Great Britain, industrial estates were established in many of the factory cities. These estates platted land around the industry for homes, recreation areas, roadways, and service facilities. The use of the land was controlled and related to the needs and convenience of the industry which it served. In the late 19th century, the concept of controlled industrial land was introduced in the United States in the form of a planned industrial district. The first district, called the Clearing Industrial District, was located—and is still functioning—in Chicago. The more restricted concept of an industrial park came into wide use only in the last 20 years. At the present time in the United States, depending on the rigor of definition, over 400 industrial parks involving approximately 150,000 acres of industrial land are in existence.
>
> Raw land zoned for industry is the basic ingredient of any industrial site. Add to this the availability of facilities and utilities and make the land available for immediate sale, and you have the requirements of planned industrial land. Such characteristics alone, however, do not constitute the minimum requirements that qualify a piece of industrial realty as an industrial park. An industrial park is a tract of land subdivided and developed according to a comprehensive plan for the use of a community of industries. Streets, railroad tracks, and utilities should be installed or ready to be installed before the sites are sold to prospective tenants. The plan must provide for continuing management and insure compatibility between the existing character and activities of the community and the industrial operations that locate there. An industrial development which contains some of these elements is a planned industrial district; one which contains very few of these elements is raw industrial land.

In India and in many other developing countries, industrial parks have become an important part of the industrial development program. Sometimes they are limited, as are many of the American ones, to the provision of industrial land which is serviced by water, power, sewers, roads, railways, and similar basic facilities. More often in developing countries, the industrial parks go a stage further and provide factory buildings, usually of a fairly standard type, for lease to new industries which do not wish to construct their own buildings. Enabling a new industry to rent suitable accommodation in an industrial park offers many advantages. The amount of investment needed for the project is reduced substantially; also, the risk is lowered, not only because a smaller amount of capital is being committed, but also because it is easier to give up the project with a minimum of loss in case of failure. An additional advantage is that a project may get into production much more quickly if it is not necessary to go through the long process of acquiring land and having buildings constructed. To the extent that the cost of the land and buildings is subsidized to provide an additional incentive for investment, the new industry benefits even more.

Buildings for new industries do not have to be located in an industrial park, although concentrating new industries does have distinct advantages since they can more easily serve each other as customers and suppliers if they are close together. The main thing is to ensure that buildings needed by new industries are available when needed at an attractive price. In 1950 the Arthur D. Little Ten-Year Industrial Plan for Puerto Rico contained the following comments, which served as the basis for a large program of building factories as industrial development incentives: [1]

> The lack of good factory space on an immediately available basis is frequently a major reason for prospective manufacturers to decide against locating in a particular community. Many of Puerto Rico's own prospects have lost enthusiasm on learning of the present shortage of first-class buildings. Time required to construct new buildings may seriously delay the venture's getting underway, and increase the cost of getting started. . . . Provision of factory building space under some type of favorable incentive terms has been a feature of many successful community industrialization plans. Entrepreneurs evaluating various locations have become accustomed to aid in this aspect of their investment and risk in establishing in a new area. . . . Construction of useful buildings represents a permanent addition to the industrial resources of the community, more or less regardless of the degree of success of the venture initially occupying the premises. It is necessary to consider adequate industrial buildings as a necessity in any broad industrialization program for Puerto

[1] Arthur D. Little, Inc., *Report on Ten-Year Industrial Plan for Puerto Rico,* 1951, reprinted 1961, available from AID, Washington, p. 29.

Rico, and as one of the most universally attractive aids which the Insular community can offer to industrial enterprise.

The construction of factory buildings for new industries quickly became one of the major features of Puerto Rico's industrial program. Up to 1957, an agency of the government had constructed 234 building projects, containing 4.8 million square feet of floor space for factories and commercial projects, at a total cost of $43 million. Of the 234 buildings, about three-quarters were leased to private enterprises, and most of the remainder were sold to new businesses.

Whether a country embarking on its first industrial development program should set up industrial parks, with or without buildings for sale or lease, or whether it should undertake the construction of factory buildings not on an industrial park depends on the circumstances of the situation. Important elements to consider are the present cost and availability of good industrial sites; the laws governing ownership of land by foreigners; the delays involved in getting title to land and in getting a building constructed; the availability and cost of good factory buildings for enterprises wanting to buy or lease accommodation; the kinds of industry which are thought to be likely prospects and their needs as to accommodation. A decision to make the provision of land or buildings for industry a part of the incentive package is one that should not be taken lightly, for the costs involved may be great. The question deserves a thorough examination by experts who are qualified to evaluate industrial needs for land and buildings and to determine whether the cost of a major program in this field, either subsidized or not, is justified.

Even if it is decided that sufficient factory buildings are available for leasing to new industries and that a construction program is therefore not needed, it may be worth considering whether an industrial accommodation subsidy should not be initiated anyway as a special incentive. If it is thought desirable to offer direct subsidies for new industries, a rental subsidy may be one of the best kinds. It should be in the form of one year's free rental for new industries or a portion, say one-half, of factory building rentals for a period of two or three years.

Transportation of Factory Equipment

If a country seeking industry is in a location which seems somewhat remote to the prospective investors, an incentive which may be worth offering is assistance in paying the cost of the inward shipment of industrial machinery. Without such aid, the investor may feel that a location is out of the question compared with others because of the high cost of moving the necessary factory equipment. The Arthur D. Little Plan for Puerto Rico advised that a subsidy of one-half the cost of shipment should be offered to new industries to take care of the additional cost of setting up in Puerto Rico rather than in a location on the mainland of North America. It was also suggested that a subsidy of this kind should not be limited to enterprises receiving other aid under the development program, but should be available to any enterprise bringing in new equipment which would add to industrial production capacity. This is a good way for a country which is remote from its potential investors to lessen the investment barrier created by distance.

Labor Training

One of the major burdens on a new industry in an underdeveloped country is that it must invest heavily in training its workers, whereas in an industrially developed country, it can find workers with industrial training and experience who can be productive with little additional training expense. While a government wanting to develop industry will do much by way of providing technical schools, this will not eliminate fully the need for on-the-job training in the factories. During the training period, the new enterprises will have to provide materials and expensive machinery and pay some wages. During this time usable production may be small. A new enterprise which provides training of this kind for workers entering industry is not just helping itself: it is making a long-run contribution to the industrial development of the country. It faces the probability that over a period of years, many of the workers it has trained will move on to better jobs in other industrial enterprises. For these reasons, one of the most logical expenses of new industry which can be subsidized as an additional incentive is the cost of training new workers. As part of the industrial incentive package, a new industry can be offered a cash subsidy of up to a specified amount for every worker who receives training over a stated period of several months. Some flexibility in the amount granted is desirable since the costs of materials and equipment required for training vary widely depending on the industry. Normally, the training subsidy should not cover all the training costs; rather, they should be shared by the new enterprise, say on a 50-50 basis.

Power and Other Services

In most developing countries, the utility services used by industry are provided by government agencies. These include electric power, water, telephone communications, sometimes natural gas, and usually railway transportation. The total cost of these services represents, for some industries, a substantial part of total manufacturing costs. A government which considers that a moderate amount of more or less permanent subsidy is justified for industry may well choose to provide it by supplying some or all of these essential services at lower-than-regular rates, even at lower-than-real total costs. By doing so, a government is avoiding the common mistake in developing countries of overcharging industrial users for public power and other infrastructure services, thus discouraging industrial growth by adding to its costs. A government which offers low rates for power and other services provided to industry acts directly to reduce costs and thus to improve the commercial profitability of industrial enterprises. It is also doing something which has publicity value in attracting industry.

It should not be thought that offering special rates for industry is a device which only a government would consider. In many of the more industrialized countries, it is customary for both public and private power companies to sell power to industries at rates considerably lower than those to residential customers. One reason is that industrial power demand is generally more stable than domestic demand, thus permitting a more economic load factor for the power system. Another reason is to encourage industrial development. While low rates for power and other basic services to industry are usually given on a permanent basis, there is no reason why a special discount could not be granted for a limited period of years as an extraordinary incentive for new industries.

The granting of special lower-than-normal rates for freight on government-owned railways also merits consideration. If low rates would improve the commercial profitability prospects of a major project sufficiently to make it investible, and if the project were to use mineral or forest raw materials which otherwise would not be used, a policy of subsidizing transport costs might be well justified from the national economic viewpoint. Likewise, a system of special freight rates on export products might make it commercially feasible to expand some industries located far from seaports which could not export successfully if they had to pay regular freight rates to get their products to shipping ports. The idea of specially low rates for transporting freight or providing electrical power as an inducement for new business is a well-established one among private suppliers of transportation and power service. They regard incentive rate structures as good business practice which should result in building larger loads, reducing costs, and thus in the long run providing its own means for offsetting the discounts offered. This justification for subsidized rates as an incentive is even more valid for governments providing a service to new industry.

Financing

Financing costs represent a large part of the budget of almost any industrial enterprise. This is true in the industrialized countries, but it is much truer in the developing countries where capital is scarce and interest rates are high. Some degree of subsidy to bring down interest costs for new industries is one of the most useful ways in which a government can give a worthwhile incentive for new industrial growth. Not only is the subsidy valuable in reducing the amounts which have to be found for interest charges, but also the provision of the loans is in itself an important incentive, for it helps solve the problem of getting sufficient financing which is an absolute obstacle to many good projects. The more financing which can be obtained by way of low-cost loans, the less must be found in the form of equity capital. For the investor, this reduces the problem of raising capital and the amount of risk, and it increases the profitability by providing leverage: the rate of return on equity will be increased because a given amount of profit will accrue to a smaller total amount of share capital.

Subsidized financing of new industries is a particularly good incentive for several reasons. Since each loan application is considered on its own merits, it is possible to be selective and give the subsidy only to those projects found to be of high priority and value to the economy. It is possible to insulate this incentive from politics and malpractices by making subsidized government financing for new projects available through a development bank or a private financial institution. It is an incentive which is not permanent: it is given once to get a new enterprise established, and it expires when the loan is repaid. Finally, it is an incentive in which the government has some protection against loss since it can obtain a mortgage on some of the project's machinery and other assets. In the event of the project's failing, some or all of the loss may be offset by taking over the assets which were mortgaged. The provision of equity capital instead of loans is another way of using financial participation as an incentive for new industry. It is often preferable for other reasons; but as a subsidy, it lacks the valuable feature of low-cost loans—the immediate reduction of costs and the improvement of profitability which result from giving the private investors leverage in the capital structure of the enterprise.

Cash Grants

Incentives may take dozens of forms; many are deviously indirect means by which a government can subsidize a new industrial enterprise sufficiently to make it attractive to private investors. No other way is as simple and as direct as the cash grant. This is a subsidy which is used by a few places seeking industry, notably both Ireland and Northern Ireland. It has much to recommend it, especially when compared with tariff protection and tax holidays, which have undesirable features to offset some of their advantages. The cash subsidy is simplicity exemplified. A government offers a cash grant of say one-third of the cost of a new project, the buildings, land, and equipment. By reducing the amount of private capital needed, the grant lowers the risk to the private investors and increases the probable rate of return. Financing problems are reduced, for a smaller amount of capital is needed. Operating costs of the project will be lower because the cost of the fixed assets has been reduced and thus depreciation charges are smaller. All these benefits are important for they improve profitability. Cash grants are a means of raising commercial profitability directly and quickly for projects considered to be of high value to the economy.

The psychological value of a cash grant cannot be overestimated. Anyone appreciates a gift, especially if it is cash and has no strings attached, other than the requirement to establish the project which the investors want to set up anyway. From the viewpoint of a government, the cash grant has advantages, too. It can be made selective through a tight screening process, or it can be made quite automatic as desired. While a government may feel it is giving away something if it gives a cash grant to a new industry, it should remember that its real objective in giving any kind of subsidy is to attract the new industry. Looking back on the experience of many countries which have made loans to new industries or which have taken shares in them or owned them outright, one might well conclude that in most cases the important objective of getting industry established and operating successfully with a minimum of government subsidy might have been realized better in most cases if outright one-time cash grants had been made to private projects which had the assurance of good management.

Consulting-type Assistance

The idea of a government development agency providing assistance to prospective investors in getting their projects established has been discussed in Chapter 9. What I propose here is the possible use of similar methods for assisting new industries after they have started operation. The assistance in either case can be described as being of a consulting type, that is, the provision of professional-level services directed to solving problems of the enterprise being served. In one instance, a company might want a market survey; in another, help in setting up a cost-accounting system. In a third, it might need assistance in training workers in more productive work methods. These are services which well-run industrial enterprises in the developed countries frequently obtain from private industrial consulting organizations. If they are available either free or at low cost from a development agency, they may represent an incentive which will be welcomed by new industries and which will be regarded by them as a valuable support. Perhaps even more important, the provision of such services may do much to improve industrial productivity, thus giving the economy the benefits of more industrial output for the capital used in industry. The consulting services may also lessen the danger of failures of new industries, which always represent a loss of capital to the economy and a discouragement to potential future investors.

The provision of assistance to industry need not be limited to consulting-type help provided within the enterprise. Assistance in developing export markets is an example of outside help which may be a valuable incentive to attract investment to a new export industry. A country which has trade representatives abroad who are able to do a competent job in developing export contacts and providing export market information to the interested firm may be able to provide a service of real worth. The readiness and capacity of a government through its development agency to provide free assistance to prospective investors and later to the operating industries is more than an incentive which helps attract industry. It is evidence of a country's desire to have new industry and of its concern for the continued success of industrial enterprises.

Guarantees

The reduction of risk in a project is one of the primary objectives of any potential investor. Since it is risk which discourages most foreign investors from making investments in developing countries, the reduction of risk by various kinds of guarantees is a form of incentive which should be considered. Guarantees may take many forms. As discussed in Chapter 5, guarantees against nationalization, guarantees of currency conversion privileges, guarantees that foreign technicians may be brought in, and guarantees against adverse changes in tariffs or taxes for a specified time may have value as measures to improve the investment climate. These should be thought of as incentives which can be offered to attract new industry. While no government can give positive assurance that its guarantees will be honored by later governments, written guarantees which constitute a contract between an investor and the government do have some value in almost any country and give some protection to the prospective investor. Another kind of guarantee which a government can give as an incentive is an assurance to an investor that he will be protected from competition for a specified time. This a government can do by not granting a manufacturing license to a second firm in the industry, if the country has an industrial licensing system. Alternatively, a government can assure the first firm of an advantage by guaranteeing that tax and other incentives granted to it will not be given to a competitor for a stated period. Guarantees of this kind have the serious disadvantage that they confer a monopoly or semimonopoly position on one company, at least for a time. They should be used with caution unless safeguards are built in to protect the public.

Assurances of Government Purchases

Since the government is a major purchaser of many manufactured products in any country, assurances by the government of substantial purchases from a new industry may often constitute one of the most powerful incentives which can be offered to attract the new industry. Normally, it is the small size of the market which makes a project marginal in a developing country. Even worse from the viewpoint of the potential manufacturer is the possibility that he may not be able to capture enough of the limited market to make his operation worthwhile. This may be because of continued competition from imports or from other local plants. If the product is one which the government uses in significant quantities, an assurance of a long-term contract to supply the product to the government may be enough to satisfy the investor that the market will be adequate to justify his investment. Of course, a government giving an advance assurance of purchase orders would need to safeguard itself with appropriate protective clauses concerning price and quality.

Official Approval of Product

In most developing countries, there is a strong preference on the part of the public for imported goods. In part, this is because of the poor quality which has been noted in many locally manufactured products. In any country which permits goods to be imported, even with fairly high duties, the problem of winning market acceptance after local manufacture has started by both the general public and governmental customers is one of the most serious difficulties a new industry may face. This problem has been approached quite successfully in some places through a system of granting approved status to locally made products which meet normal standards of quality. In some countries, Nigeria being one, the approval system is not a public thing but relates only to government purchasing. In this system, a manufacturer may apply for approved status which, if granted, gets his product on a list from which government purchases are to be made in preference to imported or unlisted products.

A broader use of the system has been tried elsewhere in which an official seal of approval has been placed on approved products or in advertising related to them to assure the general public of their quality.

This kind of approval system, if carefully operated, can do much to build up consumer confidence in locally made products. The idea of product approval by an official or semi-official agency is not limited to creating acceptance in the home market. In Japan, for example, many export products, such as cameras, must pass inspection for quality; if passed, they receive a label which certifies that they meet required quality standards. No doubt this system contributed to increased international acceptance of Japanese products at a time when many people had not yet realized Japan's capability to produce high-quality precision products. The use of central official inspection and quality review and labeling systems is a device which gives investors an incentive to start new industries: they know that once their enterprises are in operation, their marketing problems can be simplified through this mechanism.

Free Zones

For industries which plan to import materials or parts and export all or most of the finished products, a free zone may be an important incentive. This idea was discussed in Chapter 12, where it was pointed out that a free zone was a good way to avoid the costs and complications of a system of refunding duty previously paid on material or parts which were incorporated into products later exported. Industries of this kind are especially important in many places, and the creation of arrangements to facilitate this kind of operation can be well justified in such situations.

Development of Supporting Industrial Services

In a developed industrial economy, most individual business concerns need to perform only a small part of the total sequence of operations which result in a marketable product. They can buy many services from nearby specialty firms. Businesses which provide services to a number of finished-goods manufacturers can frequently do so at a substantially lower cost than would be incurred if each finished-goods manufacturer were completely self-sufficient. Firms which supply services to other businesses are often called industrial service industries. They are found in great variety in all highly developed industrial areas; their absence places a heavy burden (in both investment and operating costs) upon isolated industrial operations. Industrial service businesses in turn require, for their own profitable operation, the existence of a substantial industrial complex that can provide a market for their output. Because industrial services may be slow to develop in an area having little industry, and also because their own development can be a vital catalyst to other industries, they should be given special attention and aid.[2] Industrial services may include the following:

Industrial distributors carrying machinery, motors, tools, supplies, and
  spare parts
Electrical and mechanical maintenance and repair services
Catering services for in-plant feeding
Cleaning, janitorial, industrial laundry, and watchman services
Engineering services
Accounting and auditing services
Employee recruiting and training services
Testing-laboratory services
Credit-rating services
Market-survey services
Advertising services
Employee-transport services
Trucking services

The existence of these industrial services is so important to other industries and their absence is such a barrier to industrial development that special assistance to get this type of operation going should be classified as a valuable incentive to new industrial enterprises. A government which, through financial aids and other means, has a program to support the development of industrial service businesses should publicize this activity as one of its industrial incentives.

[2] *Ibid.*, pp. 94–97.

15

The Cost and Justification
of Incentives

In designing a comprehensive industrial development program in which incentives for private investment play a part, a government must weigh the costs and benefits of the incentives which it considers offering. The cost of subsidizing industrial development through incentives can be extremely high; but this is not to say that the price is not worth paying. Sometimes it is excessive; sometimes it is well justified. In view of the great amount which subsidies may cost over long periods in a nation's history, it is surprising how rarely the burden is calculated. It is even more surprising how little attention has been given to the cost of and justification for industrial incentives by development economists and advisers of both theoretical and practical varieties.

Why is it that the economic calculation of the real cost and benefits of industrial incentives is rarely made, let alone considered in planning for industrial development? Partly it is because some of the incentives, such as tariff protection, have gradually crept in through the back door in most countries. The change from a revenue tariff to a moderate, and then a high, protective tariff usually comes gradually through a combination of need for revenue, for conservation of foreign exchange, and for support of local market industries which have difficulty in being as profitable as their owners would like. Partly the cost of incentives is not calculated because it is paid out of many different purses, and the portion paid directly by an industrial development agency out of its own budget may be the smallest. More likely the burden of the subsidies is diffused in ways which defy accurate calculation.

Some is paid by the purchasers of the products of protected industries; some is paid by taxpayers who must pay higher taxes which are not identified as having any connection with the industrial incentives, but which make up revenues lost on goods formerly imported but now made locally. Some of the subsidies are paid out of the budgets of government agencies which are not directly a part of the industrial program, such as state railways or public power corporations, which provide service to industries at less than the real total cost. In some such instances, it might be said that the nonindustrial customers of the service corporations are subsidizing industry by paying more than their share of the total costs of the government corporations which serve both industry and the general public.

The fact that the real cost of industrial incentives may be hidden and diffused throughout a country is no reason to ignore the burden, for it may be very large. If its true magnitude were known, even in approximate terms, a government might well decide to change the amount of incentives or their kind in order to reach a more defensible balance between the costs and benefits involved.

This is not to suggest that incentives do not pay. On balance, I believe they do, at least over the long run. Some may pay much better than others. If the important calculations are made, a rational planning decision may be made as to what is an appropriate total package of subsidy for attracting industry, and a sensible selection may be made among various possible incentives to determine which ones are worth their cost and to allocate the burden where it may be placed most appropriately.

The subsidization of new industry, as has been pointed out many times in this book, is inevitable if private investment is to be attracted to industry on a large scale in most of the countries which are now in the early stages of industrialization. This is a fact which should be accepted willingly if not happily, even though it appears to run counter to the commonly held illusion that industrial growth and its advantages can come quickly and easily to an underdeveloped country. The subsidization of new industry is nothing more or less than a form of investment. The economy of a country is diverting resources from other uses, such as consumption or investment in the nonindustrial sectors of the economy, to the industrial sector. The diversion of resources to industry is made because it is thought, with or without calculation, that such a change will eventually bring economic and social benefits to make up for what is lost by not using the resources for other purposes.

The fact that subsidies for industrial development go into the private pockets of the new industrialists should not, in itself, cause particular worry, provided they are justified in size and the cost is recognized and is borne by an appropriate group in the economy. The alternatives to subsidizing private investors who invest in and manage new industries are for the government to do the investing and managing in industry, with the host of problems and the unsatisfactory results consequent upon this course of action, or for the country to forego the industrial growth it wants and needs.

The giving of subsidies to private industrial enterprises in order to make the projects investible, that is, sufficiently profitable to attract investment, can be described as an attempt to narrow a gap between the estimated value of the projects to the national economy, that is, their "national economic profitability," and their commercial profitability as estimated without or before any kind of subsidy. Those who have read my earlier book may recall that I defined national economic profitability as the value of a project to the country's economy. Even when the calculation of national economic profitability is made before any consideration of possible subsidies, there may be quite a difference between it and the estimated commercial profitability calculated according to usual accounting methods. A project may be worth more to the economy because it will use idle resources which are "free resources" from the national viewpoint, even though they carry normal costs to the private company which uses them. A project may also be worth more to the economy than to its private owners because it earns or saves foreign exchange, which may have a greater real value to the economy than the official rate may indicate. A project may also be worth more to the economy because of significant developmental benefits it brings, such as training or interindustry advantages which encourage other industrial growth. Added together, the calculable benefits a project might bring to the economy may exceed by a wide margin its anticipated profitability, without any subsidies, as a commercial proposition. The purpose of giving a package of subsidies to such a project is to raise the commercial profitability prospects to a level which will attract the needed capital and management so that the industry will be established. As long as the total amount of the subsidies given, directly or indirectly, secretly or openly, does not exceed the calculable value of the project to the economy, the subsidies can be justified on these grounds alone, without taking into account indirect and intangible benefits which may be impossible to estimate.

The questions which will be explored in this chapter are those which should be asked by any government which is reviewing its industrial incentives: What incentives are subsidies? How can the real economic costs of the various subsidies be calculated? What specific benefits of new industry contribute to providing a rational justification for subsidies? How can the benefits be estimated? What is the payoff period for investment in industry by means of subsidies? Who should pay the cost of the subsidies? How should the subsidies be apportioned in a country's industrial sector?

The Cost of Subsidies

Most incentives which may be offered to attract investment to industry involve some cost to the economy and can therefore be described properly as subsidies. Some of the things which can be done to improve the investment climate are exceptions: A policy decision on the part of a government to invite foreign investment and to assure foreign investors of a preferred position in the allocation of foreign exchange for the repatriation of earnings may be a strong incentive to encourage investment, but it is an exception to the generalization that incentives are subsidies and therefore cost something. Similarly, a decision to grant immigrant visas freely to foreign industrial technicians may be an important incentive for industrial investment, but it is not a subsidy. Apart from measures to improve the investment climate, most of the incentives described in this book do involve some cost to the government or to someone in a country and do therefore justify the term subsidy.

The nature of the subsidy and the allocation of its cost within a country vary greatly depending on the kind of incentive. A protective tariff is a means by which a government forces the purchasers of a product to pay a higher price for the item if imported. By raising the level of competitive prices, a protective tariff enables the local manufacturer to charge a higher price than he could otherwise. The customer who buys the locally made product is thus forced to pay a subsidy to the protected local manufacturer. A tax exemption incentive is quite different. It may or may not cause a revenue loss to the government. If it does, one can assume that the government must make up for the loss by raising an equivalent amount of additional taxes somewhere else in the economy. Whoever has to pay the additional tax to make up for the loss may be thought of as the one who is subsidizing the industrial company which is granted the exemption. The granting of import duty relief presents another quite different situation. If the IDR relates to the granting of exemption from duties on capital equipment which would otherwise not be imported, there is no revenue loss and no subsidization. If the goods would be imported anyway, the exemption represents a real revenue loss which, one must assume, will have to be made up by additional taxes, just as in the example of revenue loss due to income tax exemption. If the IDR is offered on the import of materials or parts for industry, the problem becomes more complicated. Local processing of imported materials or local assembly of imported parts usually represents, at least in part, substitution for goods previously imported in finished form. Here the revenue loss due to IDR would be the normal duties on the finished products, not the calculated cost of the duty foregone on materials or parts.

An example may be useful to illustrate the method of calculating the real cost to the economy of the granting of IDR on the import of materials for processing to make a product which would replace finished goods which would otherwise be imported. Let us assume that a country is considering granting an incentive for the establishment of a radio assembly factory to produce radios which would otherwise be imported. The revenue tariff on both radios and radio parts is 25 per cent. To encourage investment in a local assembly plant which would have the capacity to assemble 80,000 radios a year, the government is considering giving IDR on the parts which would be imported for local assembly. Assuming the radios assembled locally would take the place of radios with an average c.i.f. value of $50, the total c.i.f. value of imports of finished products which would no longer be imported would be $4 million. The customs duties foregone on these would be $1 million per year. The amount of revenue apparently lost through granting IDR on the parts for assembly does not represent real revenue loss due to the new local industry, for without the new assembly plant, the parts would not be imported as parts. What the assembly plant would do is eliminate the import of assembled radios. The amount of IDR granted on the parts, whether complete or partial, does not affect the amount of the real revenue loss directly. However, any revenue that can be obtained by retaining part of the duty on the parts will serve to offset the revenue loss due to not importing the assembled products. For example, if only partial IDR is granted on the parts, and a revenue from duty on the parts of say $200,000 can be obtained, then the net revenue loss would be the $1 million of duties foregone on the finished products no longer to be imported less the $200,000 of duties collectible on the parts at the reduced rate offered as an incentive for local assembly.

The amount of subsidy involved when a project is given income tax exemption is difficult to estimate for several reasons. First of all, there may be no revenue loss and therefore no subsidy. If the industry would not have been established without the tax holiday, and if its creation does not result in tax exemptions being granted to taxpayers who would have existed irrespective of the new project, the taxes foregone would never have been collected anyway. If it appears that this is not the situation and that taxes are not collected because exemptions are being granted from taxes which would otherwise have been collected, there is a revenue loss. Its cost to the economy can be considered to be the full amount of the revenue loss, on the theory that the government must impose sufficient additional taxes elsewhere in the economy to make up for the revenue loss.

The assumption that the whole amount of revenue loss arising through exempting a project from income tax, customs duties, or other taxes is a real measure of the amount of subsidy being given to a project needs further qualification. In Puerto Rico experience has shown that a new industrial project generates a considerable amount of new revenue for the government, even when the industrial company is exempt from all taxes. This is because workers, formerly unemployed or working at lower wages, will be paying personal income tax and because the company itself will be paying taxes which are not covered by the exemption. In Puerto Rico it has been estimated that about 14 per cent of the national income directly and indirectly generated by a new export industry is taken by the Treasury in personal income, property, and excise taxes on successive turnovers. Difficult though it may be to determine the tax revenues which will be generated by a tax-exempt project, there is no doubt that they are considerable and that an estimate must be made. The estimated amount of new revenues should then be deducted from the originally estimated revenue loss to arrive at a more realistic net revenue loss figure, which is the real amount of the subsidy.

How should we calculate the amount of subsidy which is given through imposing a tariff which protects a local market industry? The simple way is to multiply the difference between unit cost of the product on a c.i.f. basis and unit cost on a landed cost basis by the number of units which the local industry is to manufacture. This assumes, of course, that the local manufacturer will take full advantage of the protection and raise his price to the same level as imported goods with duty. In practice, this may tend to overstate the amount of subsidy somewhat, as the local manufacturer may have to sell a little below the landed price for the imported product in order to sell his output. This method of calculation does not take into account possible error due to incorrect valuation of the country's currency. If there is a large degree of difference between the official rate and the real value of foreign exchange, it should be taken into account.

An example will illustrate how to calculate the real subsidy cost of a protected product, with and without adjustment for currency valuation differences. A product which costs $1.00 c.i.f. will have a landed cost of $1.25 if there is a 25 per cent duty. If the foreign exchange has the value indicated by the official rate, the subsidy is $0.25 per unit of product. The selling price of the locally made product can be taken as $1.25. This price, multiplied by the number of units to be made, gives the amount of subsidy to be given to a project at the 25 per cent level of protection. However, if the foreign exchange is really worth twice the official rate to the economy, the real cost to the country of the product if imported is $2.00 c.i.f. If the locally made substitute for the imports sells for $1.25, it cannot be said that the country is subsidizing the local manufacturer. Assuming for simplicity of calculation that the local manufacturer has no foreign exchange costs in making his product, the saving of foreign exchange more than offsets the subsidy arising through the duty. In fact, in this illustration the economy would gain considerably through local manufacture, for by making the consumer subsidize the local manufacturer $0.25 per unit, the economy would gain $1.00 in value through saving foreign exchange.

The cost of most other incentives is easier to determine. The provision of land, buildings, capital, electric power, railway service, or other things made available to industry at less than their real total cost to the economy, usually through a government agency, represents a direct and calculable cost. The same is true for technical assistance and other services which may be provided free or at low cost to industry by an industrial development agency.

Economic Benefits Which May Offset Subsidy Costs

The cost to an economy of giving tariff protection or tax exemption or other incentives to attract new industrial investment may be substantial. The amount of the subsidy should be calculated, for even an approximate estimation gives a figure to compare with the estimated value of the economic benefits which the new industry should bring. Only by comparing the cost of the subsidies with the value of the expected benefits can an intelligent decision be made as to how far a country can afford to go in subsidizing new industry and still have a margin of national economic gain. The fact that the estimates on both sides are only order-of-magnitude approximations should not deter a government from making them. As long as the calculations take into account all the measurable factors and are carried out with a reasonable degree of accuracy, the results will be valuable inputs in the decision-making process in which the final evaluation of how far to go in offering incentives will be a value judgment and not a mathematical exercise.

There are many benefits which a new industry may bring to a country's economy. Some of the most important are the following:

Addition to national income
Use of unemployed or underemployed labor
Use of idle natural resources
Training for industry and business
Earning or conserving foreign exchange
Creation of markets or services which make other industries feasible
Creation or maintenance of economic and political order
Modernization of the economy
Attraction of capital from less productive uses
Strengthening of national security

Some of these benefits lend themselves to arithmetical calculation better than others. The first advantage on the list—addition to national income—is a benefit which should show in one figure the total of all the other measurable economic benefits which arise as a result of a new industrial project. A method of estimating the figure was described in detail in my previous book. The basis is to start from estimates of commercial profitability and make a series of accounting-type adjustments to reflect those points on which the cost or benefits of a project differ when regarded from the viewpoint of the economy rather than from that of a commercial enterprise. If this method of estimation is used, all the measurable benefits which a project may bring to the economy can be compared directly with the cost of the subsidies needed to attract the required investment. This approach does not take into account the unmeasurable economic benefits a project may bring, and in some cases they alone justify a substantial amount of subsidy. Only through value judgments can one combine the measurable and the unmeasurable elements of the equation.

As an alternative to using the national economic profitability approach to calculate a project's measurable economic benefits, many of the major economic benefits can be estimated separately to arrive at an approximation of what a project should be worth to the economy. If the project is to use idle labor or idle resources, the cost of these elements in the annual operation of the project may be estimated. If the resources would otherwise be completely idle, one can say that the amount the project can afford to pay for them represents a benefit the new industry is bringing to the economy. If the project will provide technical training and industrial experience for a substantial number of workers, this may be a great economic benefit. An estimate of the value of the training benefits may be arrived at by determining what it would cost the country to provide a roughly equivalent amount of training to the same number of people in technical schools. Admittedly, training in schools and training in factories are not exactly the same, the former probably being more theoretical and the latter more practical. A country needs both kinds of training; but it might well be argued that the training in skills and work habits in a modern factory may have as much value as the academic training given in a technical school, and the cost can be equated. The value to the economy of a saving or earning of foreign exchange can be estimated with sufficient accuracy by finding the net foreign exchange gain a project should bring about and placing a realistic value on the extra foreign exchange. If it is decided that the official rate understates the real value of foreign exchange to the country, a realistic rate should be estimated. The difference between the official and the real value rate multiplied by the net foreign exchange gain for the project will give a rough measure of the benefit to the economy of this aspect of the project's operation.

Some of the items on the list of potential benefits do not lend themselves to meaningful calculation. In this class are modernization of the economy, attraction of capital from less productive uses, and strengthening of national security. Setting a value on these benefits is a matter of informed value judgment, not of arithmetical calculation.

In attempting to find justifications for heavy subsidies to specific major projects, reference is often made to the multiplier effect which investment in new industry will have on the economy. There is no doubt that the increased spending in the economy which takes place when a new industry is being constructed and when it is operating does generate an increase in economic activity which goes far beyond the direct confines of the project. This is the multiplier effect. It is similar to what happens when a government spends a large amount of money on constructing highways and later in maintaining them. The sudden introduction of new spending into the economy, for whatever purpose, is expansionary. If, as in a deflationary situation in a developed country, there is idle production capacity which can be brought into use merely by increased spending, the effect is good. Economic activity increases and existing capacity is more fully used. If, as in most developing countries, there is a lack of productive capacity and little idleness in what does exist, an increase in spending may have only an inflationary effect unless it is offset by other forces. In one respect, however, the increased spending generated by a new industry can have a beneficial effect in an undeveloped country. Through increased spending many more jobs will be created than those on the direct factory payroll. Estimates of the size of this effect usually range from one to two new jobs being created outside the project for every new job inside the new industry. To the extent that the workers going into the new secondary jobs would otherwise be unemployed or employed less productively, this represents an important gain for the economy. In this sense, there is a multiplier effect resulting from the creation of a new industry, and it may constitute an economic benefit of some importance. Its size may be calculated by estimating how many secondary jobs are likely to be generated and what in total the earnings of the workers in those jobs should be. From this amount should be deducted what they could earn in alternative employment, if any, to arrive at the net gain which the economy receives.

Incentive Policy Questions

In addition to the cost of incentives and the offsetting economic benefits which a new industry may bring to a country, the giving of subsidies to attract new industry introduces a variety of other economic questions.

One of the most important is the incidence of the burden of subsidizing a new industry, that is, who pays the cost of the subsidy? If all subsidies were paid directly by the government, for instance, in giving cash subsidy grants or providing technical assistance services, the answer to the question would be fairly simple. The burden falls on the various elements of the national economy in exactly the same way as the burden of national taxation which is the source of the revenues used to pay the subsidies. In a country where the bulk of the revenue comes from taxes on the poor, it will be they who will pay most of the cost of the new industry subsidies. In a country with a progressive tax system, the wealthy pay proportionately more of the taxes, and they will be paying proportionately more of the cost of the subsidies. Where the burden of most industrial subsidies is placed is less easily determined. If the subsidy takes the form of tariff protection, the burden is on those who buy the protected product. If the item is a luxury one, the wealthy may be paying the subsidy. If it is a necessity bought mostly by lower-income people, they will pay the subsidy. If the subsidy arises through tax exemptions' causing net revenue loss, the subsidy will be borne by those on whom additional taxes are levied to make up for the revenue loss. In deciding on its incentive policy in general and on the specific subsidies which may be offered to a project, a government has considerable latitude in choosing the kind and amount of subsidy to be granted. In making the choice, due consideration should be given to where the burden will fall.

Another important issue in selecting which incentive to give is whether it is desirable or necessary to give a permanent subsidy in preference to a temporary one. My view leans heavily toward making major subsidies temporary—usually of not more than five to ten years' duration. Most of the main justifications for subsidies point in this direction. The infant industry and the infant economy arguments, the cost of training, the cost of market development, the lack of low-cost financing—all are persuasive reasons for making subsidies temporary. If a project is going to need permanent or indefinite subsidy, the whole case for subsidizing it becomes questionable. The project which has little prospect of becoming profitably self-sustaining without subsidy is probably not deserving of subsidy-type incentives in the first place. This can be interpreted as an argument for tax exemption and direct subsidies which are usually of short duration rather than tariff-protection-type subsidies which tend to be permanent.

In determining industrial incentive policy, consideration also should be given to whether the incentives should be greater during the early period of a country's industrialization than later, when industry has had substantial development. Such a policy makes sense. Subsidies for new industries are most needed when the economy is not ready for industry, when training costs are highest, when the capital market is not developed, when supporting services do not exist, and when the labor force is completely unfamiliar with industry. It is during this period that the strongest inducement must be offered if a country is to attract the industrial capital and know-how it needs. Once the industrialization process has gone on for ten or twenty years, industry will be much more favorably situated, and there should be little need for subsidies, except minor ones for some types of infant industries.

Should the subsidies be given only to the first project to make a particular product, or should they be given to anyone who wants to make it? If the subsidy is primarily a bait to attract the first investor to an industry, there is a strong argument for giving the reward only to the one who responds first. The second firm in an industry may be highly desirable to avoid monopoly, but it is likely to have fewer risks than the first firm. In all probability, it is the success of the first firm and the market growth it encouraged which have created the safer opportunity for the second firm. It is only when the subsidies are justified on grounds other than the attraction of a pioneer investment that they should be given to later arrivals. The subsidizing of additional firms may be well justified if they are export industries.

It must be recognized that there is a lag between the time the economy pays a subsidy to a new industry and the time when the economy will receive the return for the investment it has made to get the new manufacturing enterprise. This is scarcely different from the time lag experienced in any kind of investment. For many years, a country may be subsidizing its new industries as they are started, year by year. It may be a long time before the total value of the benefits from the new industries will more than offset the cost of the subsidies still being offered to more new industries. This is the period when a country is investing in its future. How much a country can afford to invest in its future by subsidizing industry is another question. The length of time and the amount it can invest will be determined in many cases by how well the basic strength of the economy is maintained in the nonindustrial sectors, and especially in the export area.

Appendix 1

THE 150 MOST LABOR-INTENSIVE INDUSTRIES IN THE UNITED STATES

Standard industry class. no.	Industry	Production workers per million United States dollars of product*
2443	Veneer and plywood containers.....................	169
3263	Earthenware food utensils.........................	159
3262	Vitreous china food utensils......................	123
2252	Seamless hosiery mills............................	108
2789	Bookbinding and related work.....................	107
2381	Fabric dress and work gloves......................	106
2327	Separate trousers................................	104
3151	Leather gloves...................................	102
3987	Lamp shades.....................................	101
2321	Men's dress shirts and nightwear..................	98
3269	Pottery products (n.e.c.)†........................	98
3141	Footwear, except rubber..........................	95
3251	Brick and structural tile..........................	94
2259	Knitting mills (n.e.c.)............................	92
2292	Lace goods......................................	92
2331	Women's blouses................................	92
2442	Wirebound boxes and crates......................	92
2322	Men's and boys' underwear.......................	91
2652	Set-up paperboard boxes.........................	91
3142	House slippers...................................	91
3962	Artificial flowers................................	91
2352	Hats and caps...................................	90
2361	Children's dresses...............................	90
2369	Children's outerwear (n.e.c.)......................	87
3259	Structural clay products (n.e.c.)..................	87
2328	Work clothing...................................	86
2387	Apparel belts....................................	86
2426	Hardwood dimension and flooring.................	86
1922	Ammunition loading..............................	85
3471	Plating and polishing............................	85

The 150 Most Labor-Intensive Industries in the United States
(*Continued*)

Standard industry class. no.	Industry	Production workers per million United States dollars of product*
2254	Knit underwear mills	84
3171	Handbags and purses	84
3961	Costume jewelry	84
2211	Cotton weaving mills	83
2311	Men's and boys' suits and coats	83
2753	Engraving and plate printing	83
3172	Small leather goods	83
3281	Cut stone and stone products	83
2351	Millinery	81
2791	Typesetting	81
3253	Ceramic wall and floor tile	81
3671	Electron tubes, receiving type	81
2341	Women's and children's underwear	80
3963	Buttons	80
2335	Women's dresses	79
2511	Wood furniture, not upholstered	79
3851	Ophthalmic goods	79
2329	Men's and boys' clothing (n.e.c.)	78
2385	Waterproof outer garments	78
2441	Nailed wooden boxes and shooks	78
3322	Malleable iron foundries	78
3565	Industrial patterns	78
3992	Furs, dressed and dyed	78
3021	Rubber footwear	77
3199	Leather goods	77
3264	Porcelain electrical supplies	77
2121	Cigars	76
2281	Yarn mills, except wool	75
3496	Collapsible tubes	75
3942	Dolls	75
1951	Small arms, 30-mm and under	74
2339	Women's outerwear (n.e.c.)	74
2421	Sawmills and planing mills	74
3161	Luggage	74
3995	Umbrellas, parasols, and canes	74

The 150 Most Labor-Intensive Industries in the United States (*Continued*)

Standard industry class. no.	Industry	Production workers per million United States dollars of product*
2429	Special product sawmills (n.e.c.)	73
2521	Wood office furniture	73
2241	Narrow fabric mills	72
2411	Logging camps and contractors	72
3679	Electronic components (n.e.c.)	71
2384	Robes and dressing gowns	70
2397	Schiffli machine embroideries	69
3572	Typewriters	69
2342	Corsets and allied garments	68
3229	Pressed and blown glass (n.e.c.)	68
3552	Textile machinery	68
2363	Children's coats	67
3321	Gray-iron foundries	67
3323	Steel foundries	67
2512	Wood furniture, upholstered	66
2732	Book printing	66
3479	Metal coating, engraving, etc.	66
3941	Games and toys (n.e.c.)	66
2253	Knit outerwear mills	65
2262	Synthetics, finishing plants	65
2389	Apparel (n.e.c.)	65
2391	Curtains and draperies	65
3544	Special dies and tools	65
3953	Marketing devices	65
3983	Matches	65
2279	Carpets and rugs (n.e.c.)	64
2398	Trimming and stitching	64
3636	Sewing machines	64
3732	Boat building and repairing	64
3872	Watchcases	64
3964	Needles, pins, and fasteners	64
2782	Blankbooks, loose-leaf binders	63
2224	Yarn mills, cotton system	62
3599	Machine shops	62
3255	Clay refractories	62

The 150 Most Labor-Intensive Industries in the United States (*Continued*)

Standard industry class. no.	Industry	Production workers per million United States dollars of product*
3731	Shipbuilding and repairing......................	62
3841	Surgical and medical instruments.................	62
2221	Synthetics, weaving mills.......................	61
2261	Cotton, finishing plants........................	61
2297	Scouring and combing plants....................	61
2323	Men's and boys' neckwear......................	61
2386	Leather and sheep-lined clothing.................	61
2432	Veneer and plywood plants.....................	61
2531	Public building furniture.......................	61
2794	Electrotyping and stereotyping..................	61
3451	Screw machine products........................	61
3993	Signs and advertising displays...................	61
3999	Miscellaneous products (n.e.c.).................	61
2097	Manufactured ice..............................	60
2519	Household furniture (n.e.c.)...................	60
3131	Footwear cut stock............................	60
2282	Throwing and winding mills.....................	59
2394	Canvas products...............................	59
2399	Textile products (n.e.c.)......................	59
2599	Furniture and fixtures (n.e.c.).................	59
2751	Printing, letterpress..........................	59
2793	Photoengraving................................	59
2284	Thread mills..................................	58
2298	Cordage and twine.............................	58
3299	Nonmetallic minerals (n.e.c.)..................	58
3361	Aluminum castings.............................	58
3369	Nonferrous foundries..........................	58
3988	Morticians' goods.............................	58
2337	Women's suits, coats, and skirts................	57
3261	Vitreous plumbing fixtures.....................	57
3545	Machine tool accessories.......................	57
3912	Jewelers' findings and materials................	57
3914	Silverware and plated ware.....................	57
3951	Pens and mechanical pencils....................	57
2655	Fiber cans, tubes, etc.........................	56

The 150 Most Labor-Intensive Industries in the United States (*Continued*)

Standard industry class. no.	Industry	Production workers per million United States dollars of product*
3221	Glass containers...................................	56
3362	Brass, bronze, copper castings......................	56
3673	Electron tubes, transmitting........................	56
3943	Children's vehicles................................	56
3562	Ball and roller bearings............................	55
3871	Watches and clocks................................	55
3984	Candles...	55
2283	Wool yarn, mills...................................	54
2541	Partitions and fixtures............................	54
3423	Hand and edge tools...............................	54

* Production workers per million United States dollars of product calculated from the *1958 Census of Manufactures of the United States* by dividing the number of production workers in each industry grouping by the number of million dollars of product manufactured. The industries listed represent about one-third of all industry groupings. The number of production workers per million dollars of product in the remainder of United States industry varied from 53 to 5.

† n.e.c. signifies "not elsewhere classified."

Appendix 2

ENERGY AND ELECTRICITY USE IN UNITED STATES INDUSTRY

Standard industry class. no.	Industry	Btu per $ value added	Million Btu per employee	kwhr per $ value added	kwhr per employee
2011	Meat-packing plants............	45,392	395	1.08	9,445
2013	Prepared meats................	24,661	222	0.85	7,653
2015	Poultry-dressing plants.........	25,852	130	1.07	5,355
2021	Creamery butter...............	158,435	1,370	1.88	16,235
2022	Natural cheese................	106,789	895	1.49	12,462
2023	Condensed and evaporated milk..	126,453	1,975	1.23	19,231
2024	Ice cream and frozen desserts....	17,950	196	1.31	14,657
2025	Special dairy products..........			1.38	8,250
2026	Fluid milk....................	37,519	354	0.99	9,379
2031	Canned and cured seafoods......	14,650	98	0.41	2,733
2032	Canned specialties.............	38,768	551	0.52	7,417
2033	Canned fruits and vegetables....	42,079	340	0.47	3,780
2034	Dehydrated fruits and vegetables.	15,395	146	0.64	6,125
2035	Pickles and sauces.............	17,424	144	0.58	4,800
2036	Fresh or frozen packaged fish....	9,756	47	0.78	3,765
2037	Frozen fruits and vegetables.....	40,648	329	1.53	12,425
2041	Flour and meal................	14,198	199	2.61	36,679
2042	Prepared animal feeds..........	22,979	322	1.28	17,965
2043	Cereal preparations............	19,012	420	0.77	17,000
2044	Rice milling..................	3,774	50	1.26	16,750
2045	Blended and prepared flour......	8,305	196	0.54	12,800
2046	Wet corn milling..............	141,647	2,519	3.23	57,429
2051	Bread and related products......	39,560	325	0.48	3,965
2052	Biscuit and crackers...........	23,410	278	0.45	5,364
2061	Raw cane sugar................	196,364	1,440	0.91	6,667
2062	Cane sugar refining............	131,676	1,624	1.64	20,200
2063	Beet sugar....................	309,308	4,021	2.35	30,600
2071	Confectionery products.........	20,391	158	0.74	5,758
2072	Chocolate and cocoa products....	33,111	559	1.42	24,000
2073	Chewing gum.................	6,520	133	0.36	7,400
2082	Malt liquors..................	31,336	492	0.75	11,732
2083	Malt.........................	121,455	3,340	3,16	87,000
2084	Wines and brandy..............	10,439	198	0.81	15,333
2085	Distilled liquor, except brandy...	13,596	288	0.59	12,476
2086	Bottles and canned soft drinks...	22,698	200	0.39	3,469

Standard industry class. no.	Industry	Btu per $ value added	Million Btu per employee	kwhr per $ value added	kwhr per employee
2087	Flavorings......................	4,809	140	0.21	6,222
2091	Cottonseed oil mills.............	61,094	489	8.61	68,875
2092	Soybean oil mills...............	148,286	2,595	4.12	72,125
2093	Vegetable oil mills (n.e.c.)*.....	77,976	1,638	2.95	62,000
2094	Grease and tallow..............	106,929	1,132	1.56	16,500
2095	Animal oils (n.e.c.).............	78,542	943	1.17	14,000
2096	Shortening and cooking oils......	87,432	1,618	1.45	26,833
2097	Manufactured ice..............	9,722	70	7.69	55,400
2098	Macaroni and spaghetti........	10,746	103	1.09	10,429
2099	Food preparations (n.e.c.)......	20,994	329	0.45	7,059
2111	Cigarettes.....................	5,137	160	0.28	8,676
2121	Cigars........................	5,246	33	0.34	2,172
2131	Chewing and smoking tobacco...	19,070	273	0.28	4,000
2141	Tobacco stemming and redrying..	31,570	181	0.88	5,067
2211	Weaving mills, cotton..........	34,291	152	5.17	22,921
2221	Weaving mills, synthetics.......	22,751	129	2.94	16,829
2231	Weaving, finishing mills, wool....	57,626	347	1.94	11,679
2241	Narrow fabrics mills...........	9,930	57	0.87	4,960
2251	Full-fashioned hosiery mills......	9,942	51	1.27	6,441
2252	Seamless hosiery mills..........	9,347	39	0.75	3,145
2253	Knit outerwear mills...........	11,000	61	0.39	2,197
2254	Knit underwear mills..........	19,449	94	0.61	2,964
2256	Knit fabric mills..............	38,913	} 291	1.18	9,611
2259	Knitting mills (n.e.c.)..........			0.33	1,667
2261	Finishing plants, cotton........	141,869	837	2.34	13,816
2262	Finishing plants, synthetics......	140,000	1,006	1.57	11,250
2260	Finishing plants (n.e.c.)........	87,115	566	4.87	31,025
2271	Woven carpets and rugs........	57,344	408	1.16	8,278
2272	Tufted carpets and rugs........	25,229	229	0.79	7,167
2279	Carpets and rugs (n.e.c.).......	4,783	28	0.83	4,750
2281	Yarn mills, except wool........	17,432	75	4.82	20,691
2282	Throwing and winding mills.....	29,950	169	3.21	18,167
2283	Wool yarn mills................	26,099	148	1.81	10,313
2284	Thread mills...................	2282	2282	3.11	17,818
2291	Felt goods (n.e.c.).............	20,455	180	1.16	10,200
2292	Lace goods....................	15,294	74	0.71	3,429
2293	Padding and upholstery filling....	15,263	124	1.19	9,714
2294	Processed textile waste.........	15,161	94	1.23	7,600
2295	Coated fabric, not rubberized....	46,600	466	1.00	10,000
2296	Tire cord and fabric...........	13,429	78	5.67	33,083

Standard industry class. no.	Industry	Btu per $ value added	Million Btu per employee	kwhr per $ value added	kwhr per employee
2297	Scouring and combing plants.....	81,389	488	1.86	11,167
2298	Cordage and twine............	8,000	52	1.43	9,300
2299	Textile goods (n.e.c.)...........	32,459	248	1.31	10,000
2311	Men's and boys' suits and coats..	3,079	16	0.22	1,148
2321	Men's dress shirts and nightwear..	2,749	11	0.28	1,125
2322	Men's and boys' underwear......	2,500	10	1.58	6,308
2323	Men's and boys' neckwear.......	1,429	9	0.24	1,500
2327	Separate trousers..............	3,541	14	0.29	1,173
2328	Work clothing.................	2,902	11	0.27	1,062
2329	Men's and boys' clothing (n.e.c.).	2,400	11	0.25	1,156
2331	Blouses......................	1,550	7	0.23	957
2335	Dresses......................	1,504	8	0.26	1,357
2337	Women's suits, coats, and skirts..	2,117	13	0.28	1,714
2339	Women's outerwear (n.e.c.)......	1,930	10	0.24	1,227
2341	Women's and children's underwear	2,213	10	0.27	1,284
2342	Corsets and allied garments......	1,365	9	0.21	1,395
2351	Millinery.....................	2,936	18	0.38	2,278
2352	Hats and caps.................	9,890	90	0.40	2,000
2361	Children's dresses.............	1,856	9	0.25	1,167
2363	Children's coats...............	1,912	10	0.28	1,462
2369	Children's outerwear (n.e.c.)....	1,712	8	0.25	1,156
2371	Fur goods....................	2,947	31	0.39	4,111
2381	Fabric dress and work gloves....	4,259	16	0.29	1,076
2384	Robes and dressing gowns.......	2,142	11	0.25	1,318
2385	Waterproof outergarments.......	2,603	15	0.29	1,596
2386	Leather and sheep-lined clothing..	2,143	13	0.22	1,297
2387	Apparel belts.................	2,408	13	0.34	1,773
2389	Apparel (n.e.c.)...............	2,439	13	0.34	1,860
2391	Curtains and draperies..........	2,011	11	0.19	1,039
2392	House furnishings (n.e.c.)........	4,908	29	0.46	2,720
2393	Textile bags..................	5,000	29	0.43	2,414
2394	Canvas products..............	6,038	32	0.34	1,823
2397	Schiffli machine embroideries.....	3,409	26	0.41	3,136
2398	Trimmings and stitching........	2,640	14	0.53	2,880
2399	Textile products (n.e.c.)........	4,184	23	0.36	1,952
2411	Logging camps and contractors...	49,548	268	0.15	825
2421	Sawmills and planing mills......	27,337	133	2.07	10,045
2426	Hardwood dimension and flooring.	7,909	35	1.90	8,313
2429	Special-product sawmills (n.e.c.)..	10,833	54	0.94	4,738
2431	Millwork plants...............	5,340	36	0.78	5,197

Standard industry class. no.	Industry	Btu per $ value added	Million Btu per employee	kwhr per $ value added	kwhr per employee
2432	Veneer and plywood plants......	9,026	59	1.82	11,981
2433	Prefabricated wood products.....	3,033	27	0.49	4,428
2441	Nailed wooden boxes and shooks.	8,039	39	1.07	5,211
2442	Wire-bound boxes and crates.....	3,140	14	0.95	4,378
2443	Veneer and plywood containers...	4,444	15	0.60	2,031
2445	Cooperage.....................	7,750	40	1.16	5,942
2491	Wood preserving..............	122,083	804	0.70	4,665
2499	Wood products (n.e.c.)..........	8,727	50	1.00	5,729
2511	Wood furniture, not upholstered..	10,952	62	0.85	4,764
2512	Wood furniture, upholstered.....	9,872	63	0.41	2,602
2514	Metal household furniture.......	19,635	140	0.77	5,504
2515	Mattresses and bedsprings.......	7,097	56	0.40	3,154
2519	Household furniture (n.e.c.).....	3,750	27	0.37	2,721
2521	Wood office furniture..........	6,842	45	0.60	3,951
2522	Metal office furniture..........	7,816	78	0.53	5,266
2531	Public building furniture.......	6,814	48	0.67	4,764
2541	Partitions and fixtures..........	6,412	51	0.51	4,133
2591	Venetian blinds and shades......	6,627	49	0.55	4,106
2599	Furniture and fixtures (n.e.c.)....	9,000	68	0.53	4,005
2611	Pulp mills....................	145,408	2,001	9.11	125,961
2621	Paper mills, except building.....	160,934	1,893	9.97	117,015
2631	Paperboard mills..............	233,095	3,430	9.67	142,277
2661	Building paper and board mills...	157,907	1,643	8.19	85,245
2641	Paper coating and glazing.......	44,000	507	1.17	13,492
2642	Envelopes....................	6,159	48	0.46	3,604
2643	Bags, except textile bags........	10,356	82	0.64	5,097
2644	Wallpaper....................	54,800	546	0.65	4,990
2645	Die-cut paper and board........	6,550	60	0.49	4,500
2646	Pressed and molded pulp goods...	2644	2644	3.51	39,150
2649	Paper and board products (n.e.c.).	14,547	144	0.61	6,056
2651	Folding paperboard boxes.......	12,455	106	0.59	5,043
2652	Set-up paper boxes............	10,240	53	0.42	2,208
2653	Corrugated shipping containers...	28,358	238	0.69	5,803
2654	Sanitary food containers........ } 11,722	} 113 {	0.96	10,241
2655	Fiber cans, tubes, drums, etc.....			1.21	8,818
2711	Newspapers...................	2,137	18	0.40	3,395
2721	Periodicals...................	1,168	17	0.22	2,191
2731	Books, publishing and printing...	877	14	0.13	2,000
2732	Book printing.................	3,833	30	0.53	4,138
2741	Miscellaneous publishing........	1,401	15	0.19	2,000

Standard industry class. no.	Industry	Btu per $ value added	Million Btu per employee	kwhr per $ value added	kwhr per employee
2751	Printing, letterpress...........	4,970	39	0.53	4,185
2752	Printing, lithographic..........	3,476	31	0.48	4,211
2753	Engraving and plate printing....	4,375	31	0.38	2,667
2761	Manifold business forms........	2,449	25	0.36	3,667
2771	Greeting cards.................	2,793	23	0.28	2,273
2782	Blankbooks, loose-leaf binders....	2,857	21	0.28	2,056
2789	Bookbinding and related work...	3,158	19	0.33	2,000
2791	Typesetting...................	2,065	18	0.34	2,944
2793	Photoengraving................	2,267	23	0.33	3,294
2794	Electrotyping and stereotyping...	5,873	53	0.71	6,429
2812	Alkalies and chlorine..........	325,163	4,975	24.16	369,650
2813	Industrial gases..............	33,046	523	11.08	175,273
2814	Cyclic (coal-tar) crudes........	115,000	1,725	1.63	24,500
2815	Intermediate coal-tar products...	227,668	3,266	3.17	45,423
2816	Inorganic pigments............	137,966	2,960	2.25	48,182
2818	Organic chemicals (n.e.c.)......	167,943	3,647	5.22	113,455
2819	Inorganic chemicals (n.e.c.).....	146,018	2,383	49.36	814,820
2821	Plastic materials..............	87,271	1,492	2.28	38,941
2822	Synthetic rubber..............	60,031	1,368	3.06	65,500
2823	Cellulosic man-made fibers......	176,000	1,610	5.00	45,700
2824	Organic fibers, noncellulosic......	2822	2822	1.67	39,250
2831	Biological products............	13,205	129	0.51	5,000
2833	Medicinals and botanicals.......	67,102	1,181	1.86	32,700
2834	Pharmaceutical preparations.....	9,527	219	0.34	7,780
2841	Soap and other detergents.......	24,534	702	0.37	10,667
2842	Polishes and sanitation goods....	} 15,259	} 266 {	0.34	6,250
2843	Surface-active agents..........			0.79	13,667
2844	Toilet preparations............	2,013	48	0.13	3,034
2851	Paints and varnishes..........	14,732	202	0.46	6,386
2852	Putty and calking compounds....	4,792	58	0.33	4,000
2861	Gum and wood chemicals.......	25,765	313	2.39	29,000
2871	Fertilizers...................	} 30,658	} 301	1.97	19,300
2872	Fertilizers, mixing only........				
2873	Agricultural pesticides..........	} 7,973	} 111	0.84	11,625
2879	Agricultural chemicals (n.e.c.)...				
2891	Glue and gelatin..............	122,000	1,548	1.06	14,000
2892	Explosives...................	30,947	272	1.35	11,867
2893	Printing ink..................	6,193	84	0.89	12,125
2894	Fatty acids...................	2891	2891	2.57	27,000
2895	Carbon black.................	977,808	23,793	3.62	88,000

284

Standard industry class. no.	Industry	Btu per $ value added	Million Btu per employee	kwhr per $ value added	kwhr per employee
2899	Chemical preparations (n.e.c.)....	60,714	884	0.90	13,080
2911	Petroleum refining.............			6.09	88,459
2951	Paving mixtures and blocks......	90,708	1,281	1.27	18,000
2952	Asphalt felts and coatings.......	100,449	979	1.13	11,063
2992	Lubricating oils and greases......	29,806	384	0.38	4,875
2999	Petroleum and coal products (n.e.c.).....................	47,407	640	1.41	19,000
3011	Tires and inner tubes..........	35,797	475	1.97	26,146
3021	Rubber footwear..............	} 25,600	} 199	0.75	5,650
3031	Reclaimed rubber.............			8.48	89,000
3069	Fabricated rubber products (n.e.c).....................	39,077	325	1.51	12,525
3079	Plastics products (n.e.c)........	17,696	142	1.44	11,543
3111	Leather tanning and finishing....	73,696	550	1.57	11,730
3121	Industrial leather belting........	5,556	50	0.42	3,750
3131	Footwear cut stock............	5,714	31	0.56	3,056
3141	Footwear, except rubber........	2,431	12	0.28	1,437
3142	House slippers................	2,250	11	0.28	1,417
3151	Leather gloves................	5,000	22	0.23	1,000
3161	Luggage.....................	2,680	16	0.36	2,188
3171	Handbags and purses.........	1,532	8	0.24	1,227
3172	Small leather goods...........	4,211	23	0.42	2,286
3199	Leather goods (n.e.c.).........	3,548	22	0.29	1,800
3211	Flat glass....................	128,745	1,612	3.06	38,381
3221	Glass containers..............	140,545	1,359	2.49	24,091
3229	Pressed and blown glass (n.e.c.)..	107,019	902	1.81	15,270
3231	Products of purchased glass......	22,551	228	0.73	7,417
3241	Cement, hydraulic.............	510,897	9,034	9.53	168,537
3251	Brick and structural tile........	390,609	2,482	2.41	15,290
3253	Ceramic wall and floor tile......	68,602	491	1.02	7,308
3255	Clay refractories..............	184,619	1,615	1.56	13,667
3259	Structural clay products (n.e.c.)..	346,771	2,378	1.33	9,143
3261	Vitreous plumbing fixtures.......	43,908	382	1.02	8,900
3262	Vitreous china food utensils.....	32,143	169	0.88	4,625
3263	Earthenware food utensils.......	35,882	136	1.03	3,889
3264	Porcelain electrical supplies......	27,424	201	1.18	8,667
3269	Pottery products (n.e.c.)........	30,370	182	0.93	5,556

Standard industry class. no.	Industry	Btu per $ value added	Million Btu per employee	kwhr per $ value added	kwhr per employee
3271	Concrete block and brick........	37,947	313	0.89	7,391
3272	Concrete products..............	23,513	199	0.50	4,217
3273	Ready-mixed concrete...........	34,763	379	0.48	5,258
3274	Lime..........................	644,324	6,811	4.12	43,571
3275	Gypsum products..............	110,046	1,999	2.18	39,667
3281	Cut stone and stone products....	14,612	94	1.26	8,150
3291	Abrasive products..............	26,259	304	1.91	22,083
3292	Asbestos products..............	40,872	457	1.60	17,905
3293	Gaskets and insulations........	36,524	295	0.91	7,385
3295	Minerals, ground or treated......	92,072	1,278	1.94	26,875
3296	Mineral wool..................	169,964	1,955	2.63	30,250
3297	Nonclay refractories...........	101,863	1,299	1.75	22,250
3299	Nonmetallic minerals (n.e.c.).....	39,688	318	0.88	7,000
3312	Blast furnaces and steel mills....			4.04	47,928
3313	Electrometallurgical products....	30,168	415	41.68	574,000
3315	Steel-wire drawing..............	41,633	429	1.73	17,842
3316	Cold finishing of steel shapes.....	53,451	690	1.82	23,545
3317	Steel pipe and tubes...........	36,514	432	1.40	16,625
3321	Gray-iron foundries............	61,837	444	1.37	9,850
3322	Malleable-iron foundries.........	122,500	784	2.45	15,700
3323	Steel foundries.................	47,188	370	3.26	25,571
3331	Primary copper................	232,595	2,450	6.08	64,000
3332	Primary lead..................	309,444	2,785	4.06	36,500
3333	Primary zinc..................	404,861	3,239	25.47	203,778
3334	Primary aluminum.............	...	...	65.46	1,478,706
3339	Primary nonferrous metals (n.e.c.)	16,900	282	13.40	223,333
3341	Secondary nonferrous metals.....	81,837	859	1.29	13,500
3351	Copper rolling and drawing......	48,112	535	2.74	30,500
3352	Aluminum rolling and drawing...	58,054	663	3.74	42,766
3356	Rolling and drawing (n.e.c.).....	38,686	398	2.41	24,824
3357	Nonferrous wire drawing, etc.....	25,641	261	1.67	17,000
3361	Aluminum castings............	41,925	316	1.49	11,233
3362	Brass, bronze, copper castings....	44,091	323	0.87	6,400
3369	Nonferrous castings (n.e.c.)......	28,667	228	1.32	10,471
3391	Iron and steel forgings..........	124,645	1,073	1.50	12,944
3392	Nonferrous forgings............	63,902	437	3.83	26,167
3399	Primary metal industries (n.e.c.)..	59,670	543	1.35	12,300
3411	Metal cans....................	18,625	231	0.81	10,037
3421	Cutlery.......................	4,841	51	0.54	5,667
3423	Edge tools....................	8,109	72	0.71	6,300

Standard industry class. no.	Industry	Btu per $ value added	Million Btu per employee	kwhr per $ value added	kwhr per employee
3425	Hand saws and saw blades.......	11,389	103	0.91	8,167
3429	Hardware (n.e.c.)..............	17,033	146	0.75	6,466
3431	Plumbing fixtures.............	50,000	496	1.30	12,917
3432	Plumbing fittings, brass goods....	15,537	125	0.79	6,333
3433	Nonelectric heating equipment...	14,249	137	0.60	5,778
3441	Fabricated structural steel.......	11,594	105	0.59	5,352
3442	Metal doors, sash, and trim......	10,107	82	0.57	4,603
3443	Boiler-shop products...........	19,219	159	0.99	8,220
3444	Sheet metal work..............	11,298	99	0.45	3,915
3449	Miscellaneous metal work (n.e.c.)	11,870	113	0.48	4,571
3451	Screw machine products.........	13,920	109	0.66	5,156
3452	Bolts, nuts, washers, and rivets...	21,168	202	0.82	7,774
3461	Metal stampings..............	21,830	182	0.90	7,492
3471	Plating and polishing..........	21,239	148	2.04	14,176
3479	Metal coating, engraving, etc.....	24,174	167	1.31	9,056
3481	Fabricated wire products (n.e.c.).	7,978	63	0.67	5,300
3491	Metal barrels, drums, and pails...	26,230	257	1.03	10,062
3492	Safes and vaults..............	4,300	49	0.43	4,864
3493	Steel springs..................	29,186	234	1.16	9,322
3494	Valves and pipe fittings........	17,904	171	0.69	6,547
3496	Collapsible tubes..............	9,502	63	1.27	8,340
3497	Metal foil and leaf............	7,103	78	0.91	10,016
3498	Fabricated pipe and fittings......	7,390	76	0.71	7,296
3499	Fabricated metal products (n.e.c.)	7,106	63	0.64	5,693
3511	Steam engines and turbines......	15,546	195	0.49	6,197
3519	Internal-combustion engines.....	15,841	157	0.68	6,809
3522	Farm machinery and equipment..	22,650	227	0.72	7,174
3531	Construction machinery........	20,278	218	0.80	8,573
3532	Mining machinery and equipment	14,533	135	0.66	6,177
3533	Oil-field machines and equipment.	5,405	57	0.91	9,662
3534	Elevators and moving stairways..	3,405	45	0.32	4,259
3535	Conveyors....................	6,273	58	0.44	4,041
3536	Hoists, cranes, and monorails....	6,253	61	0.53	5,147
3537	Industrial trucks and tractors....	5,617	45	0.64	5,072
3541	Metal-cutting machine tools.....	6,889	55	0.72	5,770
3542	Metal-forming machine tools.....	7,272	57	0.66	5,155
3544	Special dies and tools..........	5,422	51	0.43	1,005
3545	Machine-tool accessories........	6,053	51	0.78	6,575
3548	Metalworking machinery (n.e.c.)..	8,454	84	0.60	6,001
3551	Food-products machinery........	4,765	46	0.41	4,005

Standard industry class. no.	Industry	Btu per $ value added	Million Btu per employee	kwhr per $ value added	kwhr per employee
3552	Textile machinery.............	9,524	59	0.76	4,750
3553	Woodworking machinery........	7,172	38	0.80	4,241
3554	Paper-industries machinery......	9,454	74	0.74	5,855
3555	Printing-trades machinery.......	5,136	45	0.43	3,776
3559	Special-industry machinery (n.e.c.)	7,446	63	0.71	6,018
3561	Pumps and compressors........	18,836	170	0.65	5,846
3562	Ball and roller bearings........	9,908	87	1.06	9,346
3564	Blowers and fans..............	9,755	89	0.46	4,139
3565	Industrial patterns............	5,121	45	0.33	2,931
3566	Power-transmission equipment...	8,742	80	0.72	6,582
3567	Industrial furnaces and ovens....	4,977	47	0.38	3,596
3569	General-industry machinery (n.e.c.).....................	1,866	19	0.61	6,104
3571	Computing and related machines.	2,884	21	0.65	4,675
3572	Typewriters..................	5,921	51	0.44	3,741
3576	Scales and balances............	8,142	75	0.37	3,366
3579	Office machines (n.e.c.).........	3,171	35	0.40	4,416
3581	Automatic vending machines.....	8,811	72	0.54	4,434
3582	Commercial laundry equipment..	5,185	52	0.44	4,421
3584	Vacuum cleaners, industrial......	5,874	58	0.24	2,315
3585	Refrigeration machinery........	15,334	135	0.80	7,059
3586	Measuring and dispensing pumps.	5,720	60	0.39	4,032
3589	Service-industry machines (n.e.c.)	4,880	52	0.41	4,442
3599	Machine shops................	1,126	9	0.63	5,237
3611	Electric measuring instruments...	2,482	22	0.45	4,021
3612	Transformers.................	18,681	194	1.08	11,200
3613	Switchgear and switchboards.....	3,937	41	0.40	4,189
3621	Motors and generators.........	10,185	88	0.93	8,064
3622	Industrial controls.............	5,603	59	0.56	5,889
3623	Welding apparatus.............	7,345	83	0.65	7,300
3624	Carbon and graphite products....	29,216	331	8.45	95,778
3629	Electric industrial goods (n.e.c.)..	6,014	49	1.01	8,235
3631	Household cooking equipment....	25,138	253	1.06	10,667
3632	Household refrigerators.........	33,256	351	1.32	13,976
3633	Household laundry equipment....	8,765	114	0.84	10,840
3634	Electric housewares and fans.....	5,615	58	0.54	5,655
3635	Household vacuum cleaners......	3,690	62	0.44	7,400
3636	Sewing machines..............	9,677	60	0.77	4,800
3639	Household appliances (n.e.c.)...	16,564	180	0.78	8,467
3641	Electric lamps................	5,704	73	0.74	9,476
3642	Lighting fixtures..............	7,909	67	0.74	6,213

Standard industry class. no.	Industry	Btu per $ value added	Million Btu per employee	kwhr per $ value added	kwhr per employee
3643	Current carrying devices........	4,354	37	0.43	3,600
3644	Non-current-carrying devices....	10,791	116	0.66	7,050
3651	Radios and TV receiving sets....	5,968	53	0.39	3,463
3652	Phonograph records...........	7,957	106	0.55	7,286
3661	Telephone, telegraph apparatus..	8,340	72	0.56	4,860
3662	Radio, TV communication equipment.................	4,299	43	0.38	3,808
3671	Electron tubes, receiving.......	6,364	49	0.70	5,432
3672	Cathode-ray picture tubes.......	14,030	104	2.13	15,889
3673	Electron tubes, transmitting.....	9,217	77	1.21	10,050
3679	Electronic components (n.e.c.)...	7,049	49	0.67	4,667
3691	Storage batteries..............	12,933	129	2.31	23,133
3692	Primary batteries, dry and wet...	6,400	60	0.49	4,625
3693	X-ray and therapeutic apparatus.	2,586	30	0.48	5,600
3694	Engine electrical equipment......	4,071	37	0.63	5,800
3699	Electrical products (n.e.c.).......	5,676	42	0.65	4,800
3713	Truck and bus bodies...........	12,089	88	0.65	4,750
3715	Truck trailers.................	12,405	102	0.64	5,250
3717	Motor vehicles and parts........	10,216	122	1.08	12,921
3721	Aircraft......................	3,995	36	0.62	5,565
3722	Aircraft engines and parts.......	13,020	132	0.97	9,811
3723	Aircraft propellers and parts.....	6,339	44	1.24	8,688
3729	Aircraft equipment (n.e.c.).....	7,234	61	0.69	5,762
3731	Shipbuilding and repairing.......	15,755	121	0.90	6,941
3732	Boat building and repairing.....	11,115	70	0.72	4,520
3741	Locomotives and parts..........	18,421	187	1.14	11,533
3742	Railroad and streetcars........	29,762	208	1.23	8,625
3751	Motorcycles, bicycles, and parts..	10,962	71	0.87	5,625
3791	Trailer coaches................	8,125	55	0.39	2,632
3799	Transportation equipment (n.e.c.)	6,711	51	0.58	4,400
3811	Scientific instruments..........	2,523	23	0.43	3,910
3821	Mechanical measuring devices....	3,325	30	0.38	3,500
3822	Automatic temperature controls..	3,282	33	0.46	4,615
3831	Optical instruments and lenses...	4,802	40	0.36	3,143
3841	Surgical and medical instruments.	4,815	40	0.39	3,300
3842	Surgical appliances and supplies..	4,774	51	0.41	4,375
3843	Dental equipment and supplies...	4,052	40	0.36	3,714
3851	Ophthalmic goods..............	4,820	36	0.58	4,389
3861	Photographic equipment........	11,068	145	0.70	9,167
3871	Watches and clocks............	3,996	28	0.34	2,333
3872	Watchcases...................	4,077	28	0.49	3,000

Standard industry class. no.	Industry	Btu per $ value added	Million Btu per employee	kwhr per $ value added	kwhr per employee
3911	Jewelry, precious metal.........	2,537	20	0.27	2,143
3912	Jewelers' findings and materials...	7,477	49	0.82	5,400
3913	Lapidary work..................	2,739	21	0.13	1,000
3914	Silverware and plated ware......	7,017	56	0.74	5,786
3931	Musical instruments and parts...	5,998	45	0.42	3,294
3941	Games and toys (n.e.c.).........	5,227	35	0.60	4,047
3942	Dolls.....................	4,213	23	0.49	2,714
3943	Children's vehicles.............	8,825	59	0.53	3,400
3949	Sporting and athletic goods (n.e.c.)	4,967	42	0.46	3,865
3951	Pens and mechanical pencils.....	2,550	21	0.46	3,727
3952	Lead pencils and art goods......	8,975	64	0.60	4,143
3953	Marking devices...............	4,006	29	0.35	2,800
3955	Carbon paper and inked ribbons..	5,428	55	0.41	4,000
3961	Costume jewelry...............	3,695	20	0.41	2,240
3962	Artificial flowers..............	6,926	35	0.34	1,714
3963	Buttons.....................	6,848	40	0.84	5,333
3964	Needles, pins, and fasteners......	5,326	38	0.54	3,833
3981	Brooms and brushes............	4,364	35	0.42	3,353
3982	Hard-surface floor coverings.....	40,582	473	1.56	18,125
3983	Matches.....................	5,146	42	0.74	6,200
3984	Candles......................	14,150	99	0.22	1,333
3987	Lamp shades..................	3,499	17	0.37	1,750
3988	Morticians' goods..............	6,518	48	0.41	3,118
3992	Furs, dressed and dyed.........	3,733	33	0.25	2,000
3993	Signs and advertising displays....	6,046	47	0.40	3,111
3995	Umbrellas, parasols, and canes....	4,518	26	0.29	1,667
3999	Miscellaneous products (n.e.c.)...	7,228	51	0.49	3,481
1911	Guns, howitzers, and mortars....	25,493	299	1.33	15,936
1921	Artillery ammunition...........	101,451	675	1.56	10,500
1922	Ammunition loading and assembling..................	...	...	0.33	3,000
1925	Complete guided missiles........	16,756	178	0.56	6,009
1929	Ammunition (n.e.c.)............	2,538	21	0.80	6,833
1931	Tanks and tank components.....	9,731	88	0.95	8,714
1941	Sighting and fire-control equipment...................	2,185	22	0.42	4,217
1951	Small arms, 30-mm and under....	162,337	1,034	0.88	5,625
1961	Small-arms ammunition.........	16,801	154	0.94	8,667
1999	Ordnance and accessories........	3,206	34	0.48	5,200

* n.e.c. signifies "not elsewhere classified."

SOURCE: *1958 United States Census of Manufactures.*

Appendix 3

SELECTED PRODUCTS SUBJECT TO MODERATE TARIFFS IF EXPORTED TO THE UNITED STATES

Product*	Tariff, %†
Cotton garments:	
Gloves and mittens made from woven fabric	25
Hose and half hose made from knit fabric	
(hose not made on knitting machine)	15
Knit headwear	25
Men's and boys' knit coats	25
Men's and boys' knit pajamas	25
Men's and boys' knit playsuits, etc.	25
Men's and boys' knit shirts, sweaters	25
Men's and boys' knit trousers and shorts	25
Men's and boys' knit ties	25
Women's, girls', and infants' knit blouses	25
Women's, girls', and infants' knit coats	25
Women's, girls', and infants' knit dresses, gowns, robes, housecoats	25
Women's, girls', and infants' knit pajamas	25
Women's, girls', and infants' knit playsuits, etc.	25
Women's, girls', and infants' knit shirts	25
Women's, girls', and infants' knit skirts	25
Women's, girls', and infants' knit sweaters	25
Women's, girls', and infants' knit slacks, shorts	25
Men's and boys' knit underwear valued over $4 per lb	18
Women's, girls', and infants' knit underwear	18
Shirts made from woven fabric	25
Men's and boys' raincoats valued at $4 or more each	10
Men's and boys' jackets	10
Women's, girls', and infants' raincoats valued at $4 or more each	10
Women's, girls', and infants' other coats valued at $4 or more	10
Men's and boys' dressing gowns valued at $2.50 or more	10
Women's, girls', and infants' dressing gowns, robes, housecoats, valued at $2.50 or more	10
Men's and boys' pajamas valued at $1.50 or more	10
Women's, girls', and infants' pajamas valued at $1.50 or more	10
Men's and boys' underwear valued at 75¢ or more each	10
Women's, girls', and infants' underwear	10
Headwear from woven cloth	20
Men's and boys' outer coats valued under $4 each	20
Men's and boys' dressing gowns, valued under $2.50	20
Men's and boys' pajamas valued under $1.50	20
Men's and boys' playsuits	20
Men's and boys' trousers, slacks, shorts	20
Men's and boys' neckties	20
Men's and boys' underwear valued under 75¢ each	20
Women's, girls', and infants' blouses	20

Product	Tariff, %
Cotton garments (*Continued*):	
Women's, girls', and infants' coats valued under $4	20
Women's, girls', and infants' dresses including uniforms	20
Women's, girls', and infants' dressing growns, etc.	20
Women's, girls', and infants' pajamas valued under $1.50	20
Women's, girls', and infants' playsuits, etc.	20
Women's, girls', and infants' skirts	20
Women's, girls', and infants' slacks, shorts	20
Women's, girls', and infants' underwear valued under 75¢	20
Foundation garments:	
Brassieres, etc., made partly from elastic fabric	23
Other cotton products:	
Chenille rugs	18
Shoelaces	15
Cut-pile carpets, not including orientals	15½
Labels for garments	12½
Pillowcases and sheets	12½
Hand-hooked rugs	17½
Footwear:	
Leather shoes with molded soles laced to uppers	10
Leather shoes, welt process, valued under $2 per pair	17
Leather shoes, welt process, valued between $2 and $6.80 per pair	34¢ per pr.
Shoes, including ski boots, valued over $6.80 per pair	5
Moccasins of Indian handcraft type	10
Slippers for housewear	10
Rubber boots, shoes, sandals	12½
Men's and boys' boots, shoes, McKay process	20
Footwear with leather soles, cloth uppers	20
Other leather goods:	
Belts and buckles	17½
Cowhide or horsehide gloves	15
Small items such as wallets, purses, etc.	18
Rubber goods:	
Rubber gloves	10½
Packing, gaskets, and valves	11
Small rubber goods including soles and heels, golf-ball cores, druggists' sundries	12½
Motor-vehicle tires	8½
Bicycle tires	10
Metal products:	
Typewriters	Free
Adding machines with motors	12½
Calculating machines with motors	10½
Electric motors, 0.1–1 hp	9½
Electric motors, under 0.1 hp	12½
Television receiving sets	10
Christmas tree lighting sets and portable electric lamps	13¾
Loudspeakers for radios, etc.	13¾
Radios and phonograph combinations	13¾
Electric shavers	13¾
Scale-model railroad equipment	13¾
Dictating and transcribing machines, tape	12½

Selected Products Subject to Moderate Tariffs if Exported to the United States (*Continued*)

Product	Tariff, %
Metal products (*Continued*):	
Dictating and transcribing machines, nontape	15
Photographic flash units	12½
Office photocopying machines	12½
Electronic sound apparatus	12½
Electric or electronic testing, recording, checking, analyzing, or control instruments	12½
Microphones	15
Radar equipment	15
Radios	12½
Telephones	17½
Hearing aids	13½
Rifles under $10	22½
Rifles over $50	14
Shotguns over $50	18
Parts for motor vehicles	9½
Parts for aircraft	11
Cash registers and parts	11
Accounting machines	11
Photographic exposure meters	10½
Sewing machines	10
Wood products:	
Chairs	17
Furniture, other	10½
Small mahogany products such as forks, spoons, bowls, trays, bookends	14
Picture and mirror frames	12½
Doors	15
Sporting goods:	
Tennis and badminton rackets and frames valued at $1.75 or more each, hockey sticks, etc. (mainly wood)	10
Tennis and badminton rackets and frames, valued under $1.75 each	14
Croquet mallets, field-hockey sticks, table-tennis bats, tennis nets, etc.	9
Tennis rackets	17½
Badminton nets	15
Baseball gloves and boxing gloves	15
Footballs and other nonrubber balls	10
Baseballs	15
Golf balls	12½
Lawn-tennis balls	11
Table-tennis balls	18
Roller skates	10
Miscellaneous:	
Toys—stuffed animal figures without spring mechanism, high-priced	20
Precious and semiprecious stones, cut not set	9
Candles	20
Umbrellas, parasols, and sunshades	20

* The abbreviated product descriptions given do not take into account many qualifications, restrictions, and limitations in regard to some items. For details consult the current edition of *United States Import Duties Annotated*, obtainable from the U.S. Government Printing Office, Washington. Dollar figures shown in this appendix are all United States dollars.

† Note that the tariff on individual products changes from time to time.

Appendix 4

MAJOR PUERTO RICAN MANUFACTURING INDUSTRIES

Industry	Total employment	No. of plants
Brassieres and accessories..............................	6,279	43
Tobacco manufactures...............................	3,638	6
Women's and children's underwear and nightwear.......	2,553	21
Children's shoes and other footwear (except rubber)......	2,119	13
Sweater-knitting mills...............................	2,325	15
Miscellaneous fabricated plastic products...............	1,961	31
Other stone, clay, and glass products..................	1,413	9
Household appliances................................	1,280	8
Leather billfolds, wallets, etc........................	1,187	12
Canning and preserving of fruit, vegetables, and seafood..	1,170	8
Watches, clocks, light meters........................	1,157	4
Petroleum refining and related industries..............	1,136	7
Baseballs, softballs and other leather sport goods........	1,096	7
Professional, scientific, and control instruments..........	1,031	14
Work shirts and pants...............................	864	9
Electrical transmission and distribution equipment.......	989	7
Dress and work gloves (except knit and all leather)......	965	9
Other leather goods, including belts, gloves.............	898	14
Other women's outerwear............................	895	9
Girdles and corsets.................................	762	7
Electric components and accessories...................	754	15
Children's and infants' outerwear.....................	745	10
Men's and boys' underwear..........................	573	4
Industrial chemicals................................	593	5
Embroideries......................................	534	12
Men's and boys' shirts, nightwear and miscellaneous apparel.............................	548	7
Other knitting mills................................	546	7
Costume jewelry and novelties.......................	453	5
Rubber footwear and other rubber products.............	425	7
Broad-woven-fabric mills, man-made fiber and silk.......	425	3
Miscellaneous paper products........................	411	5
Grain mill products................................	411	5
Electric lighting and wiring equipment.................	392	8
Wood household furniture............................	372	9
Women's blouses and skirts..........................	347	5
Storage batteries and other electrical machinery and equipment.....................................	342	6
Miscellaneous fabricated textile products...............	329	11
Women's dresses...................................	327	5
Miscellaneous fabricated metal products...............	305	14

SOURCE: Puerto Rico, Economic Development Administration, *Annual Statistical Report of EDA Manufacturing Plants*, 1961-1962 edition.

Appendix 5

PRODUCTS MANUFACTURED IN PUERTO RICO FOR EXPORT FROM IMPORTED MATERIALS BY SUBSIDIARIES OF UNITED STATES AND FOREIGN COMPANIES

Canned tuna fish
Canned pet food
Full-fashioned ladies' hosiery
Seamless ladies' hosiery
Sweaters, ladies', men's, cut and sewn
Knitted men's and boys' underwear and polo shirts
Knitted gloves, hairnets, mufflers, shawls, mittens
Hand-hooked woolen rugs and carpets
Machine-tufted woolen rugs
Wool and jute yarns
Men's and boys' pajamas, shirts, sport shirts, shorts
Men's and boys' underwear, T shirts, athletic shirts
Men's and boys' pants, slacks
Work pants, shirts, and coveralls
Men's and boys' swimwear, athletic uniforms
Ladies' and girls' blouses
Ladies' and girls' dresses
Ladies' and girls' skirts
Ladies' swimwear, sportswear, nurses' uniforms
Ladies' nightgowns, housecoats, slips, panties, petticoats, pajamas, brassieres, girdles, corsets, garter belts
Crocheted ladies' hats
Navy hats
Girls' dresses, infants' dresses, sunsuits, jumpers
Children's coats
Children's sportswear, snowsuits, bathrobes
Ladies' dress gloves, fabric, leather, hand- and machine-sewn
Leather, plastic and elastic belts
Men's and ladies' handkerchiefs
Canvas tents
Embroidery on laces, underwear, blouses, insignias, lingerie
Flags, auto seat covers
Rubber and canvas shoes
Electroplated plastic novelties, plastic shoe heels
Leather splitting, tanning, and finishing fine leathers
Leather moccasins, children's shoes
Crocheted and other ladies' slippers
Leather work gloves, women's and men's dress gloves
Flight bags, cases
Ladies' handbags
Wallets, billfolds
Artificial abrasives, grinding wheels
Metal trophies, flower vases, lamps

Products Manufactured in Puerto Rico for Export from Imported Materials by Subsidiaries of United States and Foreign Companies (*Continued*)

Small arms, shotguns
Power tools, saws, drills, sanders
Panel instruments, exposure meters, galvanometers
Circuit breakers, switches
Fractional horsepower motors
Relays
Soldering guns
Electric solenoids, capacitators
Electrical flat irons, shavers, hair dryers
Electric lamps
Electrical contacts, terminals, connectors
Microphones, pick-ups
Phonograph records
Telephone type relays
TV guns for cathode-ray tubes
Chokes, filters, resistors, attenuators, coils, transformers, transducers
Ignition coils
Christmas lighting sets
Drafting devices
Medical thermometers, accelerometers, transducers
Hypodermics, surgical instruments
Sanitary belts
Ophthalmic lenses
Electrical measuring devices, exposure meters
Assembly of watches
Diamond cutting and polishing, diamond points for phonograph needles
Cutlery, hollow ware
Toy telephones, plastic cameras, binoculars, airplanes
Doll dresses
Baseballs, softballs, gloves, mitts, fishing tackle, boxing gloves
Expansion bracelets, artificial pearl necklaces, costume jewelry
Plastic artificial flowers, feather ornaments
Zippers, hair curlers, bobby pins
Paint brushes, artists' brushes, plastic atomizers, cigarette holders

Appendix 6

SELECTED PRODUCTS MADE IN JAMAICA FOR EXPORT

Aluminum furniture
Baseball gloves and mitts
Baseballs and softballs
Blankets, woolen
Brassieres
Cigarettes
Cigars
Coffee liqueur
Confectionery and jellies
Containers, paper
Cosmetics and toilet preparations
Cotton yarn and cloth
Drinking straws
Dyeing extracts
Embroidered articles
Essential oils
Footwear
Handicrafts
Jams and jellies
Knitted goods
Leather

Leather wallets and purses
Lighting fixtures
Metal awnings
Metal containers
Paints and pigments
Perfume
Pharmaceuticals
Preserved fruit
Phonograph records
Rum
Shirts and pajamas
Soap and cleaning preparations
Spices
Straw goods
Textile printing rollers
Undergarment accessories
Underwear
Vegetables, preserved and dried
Work trousers
Zippers

Selected Bibliography
of Recent Books

Barlow, E. R., and Ira T. Wender: *Foreign Investment and Taxation,* Harvard University Press, Cambridge, Mass., 1955. A study resulting from the Harvard Law School International Program in Taxation. Analyzes foreign investment by American companies, summarizes previous studies in the field, and evaluates motives for overseas investment as well as obstacles that deter it. Also lists American manufacturing companies with foreign operations. Important material for anyone concerned with incentives to attract foreign investment.

Brannen, T. R., and F. X. Hodgson: *Overseas Management,* McGraw-Hill Book Company, New York, 1965. A practical guide for managers on how to adjust modern industrial management concepts to the environment of developing countries.

Bryce, Murray D.: *Industrial Development: A Guide for Accelerating Economic Growth,* McGraw-Hill Book Company, New York, 1960. (Spanish edition, *Desarrollo Industrial,* McGraw-Hill Book Company, New York, 1961.) A practical manual on the preparation, analysis, and appraisal of industrial projects. Also deals with criteria for judging the value of projects to the economy, the pros and cons of state industries, and the technical and financial feasibility of industrial projects.

Eicher, Carl K., and Lawrence W. Witt: *Agriculture in Economic Development,* McGraw-Hill Book Company, New York, 1964. A collection of significant articles that are useful background material for anyone concerned with economic development, even if his work is mainly in the industrial sector.

Friedmann, Wolfgang G., and George Kalmanoff (eds.): *Joint International Business Ventures,* Columbia University Press, New York, 1961. The comprehensive study of joint ventures—their positive and negative aspects, operations, and legal features—based on a four-year survey of joint ventures in twelve countries. Contains thirty-six detailed case studies.

Fryer, D. W.: *World Economic Development,* McGraw-Hill Book Company, New York, 1965. An introductory text in economic geography which blends economics and geography in a comprehensive analysis of world economic development and problems. Useful in examining the international situation in regard to industrial possibilities in a developing country.

Harbison, Frederick, and Charles A. Myers: *Education, Manpower and Economic Growth: Strategies of Human Resource Development.* McGraw-Hill Book Company, New York, 1964. An excellent exposition of the problems of developing people. Contains practical guidelines for use in improving human capabilities in developing countries.

Harbison, Frederick, and Charles A. Myers: *Manpower and Education*, McGraw-Hill Book Company, New York, 1965. A valuable collection of essays on education for development in eleven developing countries. The authors of the essays are education and training specialists who worked in the countries.

Heller, Jack, and Kenneth M. Kauffman: *Tax Incentives for Industry in Less Developed Countries*, Law School of Harvard University, Cambridge, Mass., 1963. A comprehensive analysis of tax incentive laws, especially income tax exemption laws, and an evaluation of their utility for developing countries. While generally critical of tax incentives, important reading for anyone concerned with devising industrial incentives.

Johnson, Harry G.: *The Canadian Quandary*, McGraw-Hill Book Company, New York, 1963. A collection of essays and addresses by a Canadian economist whose perceptive analysis of such problems as nationalism and protectionism have relevance for policy makers in countries now facing development questions that have been controversial issues in Canada for many years.

Kindleberger, Charles P.: *Foreign Trade and the National Economy*, Yale University Press, New Haven, Conn., 1962. A basic and readable introduction to the economics of international trade. Important for an understanding of the relationship of trade to industrial development.

Meier, Gerald M.: *Leading Issues in Development Economics*, Oxford University Press, New York, 1964. A distillation of important writings on nine of the key issues in development economics. These include: inflation; relative emphasis on industrialization and agricultural development; international trade; the scope of development planning; and criteria for allocating investments.

Powelson, John P.: *Latin America, Today's Economic and Social Revolution*, McGraw-Hill Book Company, New York, 1964. A book about such basic and controversial questions as planning, inflation, foreign investment, land reform, the role of government, and the policies of developed countries which affect developing countries everywhere. Most attractively written in the form of commentaries on discussions with Latin American students whose views on development questions and on American policies are sympathetically and competently analyzed.

Singer, H. W.: *International Development: Growth and Change*, McGraw-Hill Book Company, New York, 1964. A valuable collection of articles, written by a leading United Nations expert on economic development, ranging from an evaluation of development prospects, through development theory, to practical examples of how to carry out various development projects.

Taylor, Milton C.: *Industrial Tax-exemption in Puerto Rico: A Case Study in the Use of Tax Subsidies for Industrializing Underdeveloped Areas*, The University of Wisconsin Press, Madison, Wis., 1957. Contains a good analysis of Puerto Rico's experience in tax exemption, including its administration. Also evaluates the relative importance of factors influencing the selection of Puerto Rico as an industrial location. A valuable guide for countries developing industrial tax incentives.

Thoman, Richard S.: *Geography of Economic Activity*, McGraw-Hill Book Company, New York, 1962. A broad and readable survey of world material and energy sources and their use in manufacturing. Gives descriptions of processes and basic data on the economics of the major materials-based industries. A valuable introduction to industrial economics.

United States Papers Prepared for the United Nations Conference on the Application of Science and Technology for the Benefit of the Less Developed Areas, 1962. Twelve vols. Vol. IV, *Industrial Development,* and Vol. VIII, *Organization, Planning, and Programming for Economic Development,* contain many papers of special interest to those engaged in industrial development work.

Walinsky, Louis J.: *The Planning and Execution of Economic Development: A Nontechnical Guide for Policy Makers and Administrators,* McGraw-Hill Book Company, New York, 1963. A concise and refreshingly frank exposition of how to make and implement an economic development plan and how to avoid the pitfalls. A practical and readable book which should be read by everyone in the industrial development field.

Young, John H.: *Canadian Commercial Policy: A Study for the Royal Commission on Canada's Economic Prospects,* The Queen's Printer, Ottawa, Ontario, 1958. More than a history and analysis of Canada's protectionist tariff policy, it is a case study of value to other developing countries. Also a good restatement of the case for and against protection. Contains an important evaluation of the real cost of a tariff to a developing country and shows how the cost can be measured.

Index